The Relevance of Thomas Merton's Spirituality for the Consecrated Life in India

JDV Philosophy Series - 8

The Relevance of Thomas Merton's Spirituality for the Consecrated Life in India

Refueling to Confront the Social Evils in the Interreligious Context

Fabian Jose, UMI

Jnana-Deepa Vidyapeeth

&

Christian World Imprints

First Published in 2019 by

Jnana-Deepa Vidyapeeth
Ramwadi, Nagar Road, **Pune-411014**
jdvoffice@jdv.edu.in
www.jdv.edu.in
Phone: +91 20 41036111

&

Christian World Imprints
Christian Publishing & Books from India
Shop No. 14, Ground Floor
C-3, Wazirpur Industrial Area
Delhi-110052
cwidelhi2017@gmail.com, info@christianworldimprints.com
www.ChristianWorldImprints.com

ISBN: 978-93-5148-362-5

Published with the help of the Institute of Missiology – Germany

Printed in India.

DEDICATION

My Mother, Annamma Kaviyil (1933-2016)

Who inspired me by her authentic contemplative-prophetic life

As a married woman, she lived her daily life in deep prayer, gained wisdom from the word of God, expressed devotion to Mother Mary, trusted in God amidst the thick and thin of life, loved her children and husband (my father, Sebastian) with a magnanimous heart, expressed deep concern for the wellbeing of others, particularly the poor, and worked hard. She was a quiet, unassuming woman who lived her Christian life in fullness.

CONTENTS

JDV PHILOSOPHY SERIES - 8

Since 1893 Jnana-Deepa Vidyapeeth has been pioneering philosophy discussion and debate inspired by prominent personalities like Richard De Smet, Jean de Marneffe, Salvino Azzopardi, Cyril Desbruslais, Noel Sheth, John Vattanky, etc. It has been in the forefront of promoting Indian philosophy and making philosophical thinking relevant for contemporary times. In its effort to reach out to like-minded scholars, JDV Philosophy Series has been visualized as a catalyst for interdisciplinary thinking and contemporary exploration on social issues fostering holistic liberation, integral development and creative engagement.

JDV Philosophy Series (Books published so far)

1. Salvino Azzopardi: **Epistemology and Phenomenology of Religions** (2018)
2. Kuruvilla Pandikattu & Thomas Karimundackal (eds): **Melodies from the Flute** (2018)
3. Kurien Kunnumpuram: **Freedom and Joy** (2018)
4. Cyril Desbruslais SJ: **Postmodernity: An Indian Christian Philosophical Appraisal** (2019)
5. Cyril Desbruslais SJ: **Metaphysics Philosophy of Be-ing for Today** (2019)

ABSTRACT

Consecrated life in the Catholic Church is a vital and healing presence in Indian society. Religious men and women make an integral contribution to the society through their institutions in the fields of education, spirituality, medical care, social services, and other charitable activities. In the present context of India, however, consecrated men and women can experience challenges of relevance and identity in their vocations. These concerns have their basis in the fundamental need for a renewal of religious life itself in India, one which is imbued with a Christ-centered spirituality and reflects the prophetic charism that marks apostolic religious life.

Indian religious life upholds three values: contemplation, prophecy, and community. Given these values, I find a deep affinity between the ideals of Indian consecrated life and Thomas Merton's contemplative-prophetic spirituality. This study proposes therefore, that the spirituality of Thomas Merton can serve as a vital resource for the relevance of the consecrated life in India.

Thomas Merton was a 20th century Christian spiritual leader in the United States, a priest and a Cistercian monk who sought to find a balance between contemplation and social action. He believed that contemplation and action had to go hand-in-hand, making him a forerunner of the modern-day emphasis on the intersection of faith and social justice. Though he often experienced deep insecurity, spiritual darkness, confusion, and restlessness, his spirituality remained Christ-centered. While he lived his life in deep interiority and contemplation, Merton went beyond the confines of his monastic life and engaged prophetically in the world through his involvement in interfaith dialogue and his powerful writings, many of which denounced injustices such as violence and war, economic disparity, the breakdown of community, the nuclear arms race, racism, and ecological degradation.

Today, Indian consecrated men and women are called to deepen their spirituality in order to fuel a renewal of the structures of the Indian Church, to confront the social evils of our time, and to seek out new forms of interreligious dialogue in our pluralistic and multi-religious context. Through my exploration of Thomas Merton's writings, I consider how his contemplative-prophetic spirituality can serve as a valuable resource for a renewal of consecrated life in India, one that is immersed in the concrete realities of the society, the Church, and the post-modern world. Though my study makes a contribution to the existing field of contextual analysis of consecrated life and mission in India, it is unique in that it brings Merton's contemplative-prophetic spirituality into dialogue with the Indian context, proposing renewed forms of spirituality that are characterized by a deep integration of contemplation and action, solitude and engagement with the world.

Regarding methodology, the study employs Sandra Schneiders' hermeneutical approach, which consists of three steps: description, critical analysis, and interpretation. In the *descriptive* phase, I explore the life and spiritual journey of Thomas Merton. Corresponding to the *critical analysis* phase, I consider the contemplative and prophetic dimensions of Merton's spirituality as well as salient points from sociological studies of religious life in India. In the *interpretative phase,* Iconsider how the contemplative-prophetic spirituality of Thomas Merton may vitalize consecrated life in India today.

Fabian Jose UMI
JDV, PUNE
March, 2019

PREFACE

The knowledge and wisdom reflected in this book *The Relevance of Thomas Merton Spirituality for the Consecrated Life in India* by Fabian Jose UMI, is a significant contribution to the renewal of consecrated life in India to awaken consecrated men and women from their stagnation and follow the path of Christ the liberator. The Lord has called men and women to continue His earthly mission through the consecrated life, by surrendering their whole being to God, and by committing to serve the humanity in compassion and love. Today, if we consider the life of the consecrated people they are encountering various dark forces in India and around the world. Their human limitations are projected in an exaggerated manner through public accusations in the social Medias and in other communication means locally and globally. In the present context, the consecrated person's integrity and identity is being questioned and confronted by the secular world.

In the current milieu the consecrated people are invited to introspect and find solution to these existing problems in their relationship to the person of Christ. Unless the consecrated build a solid contemplative spirituality it would be rather tough to live an authentic life worthy of their call in this challenging world. They need to spend quality time with the Lord in silence, solitude, and contemplative prayer. The author has attempted to focus and acme the various trials Thomas Merton the Catholic priest and monk of the United States encountered. He was unafraid to confront the darkness of his time. He addressed each destructive forces through his contemplative prayer and solitary life which navigated him to act prophetically for the transformation of the world, universal church and the American society. He was a man of dialogue, promoter of peace between people and religions. As Paul Pearson, the former president of the International Thomas Merton's Society observes in his foreword to the text, *Thomas Merton: Twentieth Century Wisdom for Twenty First Century Living* that, "In facing the darkness of the bomb, our ecological degradation of the planet, our unbridled, rampant technology, the breakdown of community and ultimately of communion between people . . . " In *New Seeds of Contemplation* Merton affirms that "The world was made as a temple, a paradise, into which God Himself would descend to dwell familiarly with the spirits He had placed there to tend it for Him." Therefore, *"Our vocation is not simply to be, but to work together with God in the creation of our own life, our own identity, our own destiny. . . To work out our identity in God."* It is a tender invitation to renew our religious identity and commitment with great joy and zeal in collaboration with God's grace.

Fabian Jose's this noteworthy book offers to the twenty first century consecrated men and women in particular to the Ursuline sisters, to imbibe the true spirituality of Thomas Merton, a spirit filled monk, a mystic, and a thinker who confronted the certitudes of his time and opened a new possibility for souls and for the universal church. Today, the consecrated people are called to integrate contemplation and prophetic actions into their daily lives, as true Disciples of Christ in promptness and generosity. Pope Francis through his Apostolic Exhortation *Gaudete Et Exsultate* encourages us saying, "Let us ask the Lord for the grace not to hesitate when the Spirit calls us to take a step forward. Let us ask for the apostolic courage to share the Gospel with others . . . In every situation, may the Holy Spirit cause us to contemplate history in the light of the risen Jesus." May the Spirit of the Risen Lord guide us through this wild and stormy world, to bear witness to Him as true contemplatives, mystics and prophets like Thomas Merton, and thus live the dynamism of reconciliation in the peripheries of the fractured world.

Sr. Elvira Mattappally, UMI (Superior General)
Roma, Italy
March, 2019

FOREWORD

Thomas Merton (1915-1968) is one of the most prolific and best-known spiritual writers of the twentieth century. He published over 70 books as well as numerous essays, reviews, and poems. His journals and his letters have, in separate projects, been collected into several volumes. Analyses of and commentaries on his works have become almost a cottage industry, with numerous published studies.

Merton's writings, however, are best known in places like the United States, Canada, Western Europe, and Australia. In this groundbreaking study, whose audience is principally women and men in consecrated life, Sr. Fabian Jose, UMI, places Merton in dialogue with the Indian context. While acknowledging that consecrated persons in India must draw on the spiritual sources of India's rich and varied cultures, she argues that Merton can be an exemplar in bringing together a deep commitment to contemplative prayer with an equally deep commitment to social justice.

Sr. Fabian's study unfolds in four stages:

As a first stage, Sr. Fabian begins her study with an overview of Merton's life. His childhood was unusual and, in many ways, tragic. His parents were artists living in France and during World War I. Thomas was born there, but for safety the family relocated to New York City. His mother died when Thomas was six years old, and after that Merton moved between living with his maternal grandparents and with his father, a painter, who traveled a great deal. His father died when Thomas was sixteen, leaving him an orphan in England and very much at sea in finding a direction in is life. The scars of his unusual childhood would mark Merton throughout his life.

Eventually, as a young adult, Merton decided to enter the Trappist monastery of Gethsemani in Kentucky. Here he wrote his best-selling autobiography, *The Seven Storey Mountain*. This book established him as a famous Catholic author, and he began to turn out books, essays, and poems. As a writer, he also carried on a wide correspondence with the hundreds of people who wrote to him. As he matured as a monk, he was given greater responsibility within the monastery, eventually serving as Director of Novices. After concluding his term, he was given permission to move into a hermitage on the monastery grounds, thus fulfilling a long-standing desire of his to seek greater solitude.

After providing an overview of Merton's life, Sr. Fabian next looks at his development as a contemplative. As a young monk he was enamored of the monastic life he found at Gethsemani, and he looked upon life in "the world" as inferior. Yet even in his early years as a monk, he felt the need for greater solitude than was usually accorded in communal life. His Abbot recognized this need and over the years allowed Merton to use various places for refuge: a storeroom for books, an abandoned tool shed, and eventually a small building outside of the enclosure; this building would eventually be the hermitage. Sr. Fabian traces Merton's deepening contemplative life by examining his devotion to both solitude and silence. He became increasingly concerned that the monastery (which was growing in numbers due largely to the popularity of his writing) was becoming too busy and too noisy.

Sr. Fabian's third stage explores Merton's development as a prophetic figure. As he grew and matured in his understanding of his vocation, Merton made two bold moves. The first was to begin commenting on social issues from his viewpoint as a contemplative. He rightly understood that issues of justice involved a spiritual dimension. He began to publish articles condemning the nuclear arms race, the prevalence of racism in the United States (and his support for the civil rights movement), and he argued strongly for a position of Christian nonviolence. The second move was to open himself to interreligious dialogue. He carried on correspondence with scholars and religious leaders from Hinduism, Buddhism, Judaism, and Islam. In this regard he was in many ways a trailblazer among Christian writers. In fact, at the end of his life he was engaged in a journey through Southeast Asia, where he met the Dalai Lama. He died tragically while attending a meeting near Bangkok.

The final stage of Sr. Fabian's study is an invitation to consecrated persons in India to dialogue with Merton from the Indian context. From his profound commitment to contemplative prayer, Merton engaged some of the justice issues of his historical context: the nuclear arms race, the struggle for civil rights, and the prevalence of violence in U.S. society. Yet Merton did not live in India. Sr. Fabian points out some of the unique challenges of the Indian context calling for a response from contemplative persons: the multiplicity of religions, the dire situation of gender injustice and its threat to women, caste discrimination, and the resurgence of Hindu fundamentalism. How might consecrated persons respond to these issues from a contemplative stance?

So this book is a double invitation: first, to become better acquainted with Thomas Merton as a contemplative and prophet, and second to explore how Merton's spirituality might serve as a model for contemporary consecrated life. Enjoy a fruitful read!

Dr. Bruce H. Lescher, Ph.D., Director
Jesuit School of Theology of Santa Clara University
Berkeley, California
March, 2019

GRATITUDES

I am deeply grateful to God for providing me the opportunity to pursue my doctoral studies at the Jesuit School of Theology (JST) of Santa Clara University, in Berkeley. My study of the contemplative-prophetic spirituality of Thomas Merton has revitalized my commitment to consecrated life. It is my hope that the insights gained from my research will enrich the life of other consecrated men and women in India and in some way help them to bear witness to Christ amidst the current challenges facing the Indian Church and society.

This endeavor was actualized through the help and support of many generous, loving, and compassionate people who accompanied me academically, spiritually, and financially. Thanks to everyone whom I have encountered during my research, for their kindness, consideration, and generosity. I owe a special debt of gratitude to Dr. Bruce H. Lescher, who, as a Merton scholar, guided and encouraged me with his wisdom, knowledge, compassion, commitment, timely help, and challenging questions, enabling me to gain deeper knowledge of my subject. I am immensely grateful to Dr. Paul G. Crowley, SJ, Dr. Mary E. McGann, RSCJ, and Dr. Alison M. Benders, for their keen interest, conscientiously going through my work and offering valuable recommendations and enriching contributions.

I am indebted to Dr. Julia Prinz, VDMF, the Director of the Women of Wisdom and Action Initiative, and the sisters of the *Verbum Dei Missionary Fraternity* for the opportunities, support and help they have rendered through the financial contribution of the Luce and Hilton Foundations, to accomplish this endeavor. I am thankful to the sisters at Sophia House for our dynamic community life, which enabled me to live my consecrated life meaningfully and joyfully in their companionship.

I am indebted to the faculty, staff, and students of the JST for their constant encouragement, help, and prayerful support. I am grateful to the Jesuit Community at Berkeley for providing everything necessary for studies. I am especially grateful to the Rector, John P. McGarry, SJ, for accompanying me spiritually through his prayerful support, listening heart, and understanding mind. I cannot forget the friendship, generosity, help and support of my Indian friends at the JST, who reached out to me whenever I was in need of any help, particularly Shantharaj Thomas, S.J, and Louis Leveil, S.J, for their generosity and availability in formatting my final draft and providing computer support. I cannot fail to acknowledge with gratitude the librarians of the Graduate Theological Union, and in particular Marie Hempen and Elizabeth Kumar, for their generosity and kindness in providing the resources which were essential to my research.

I honor my writing coach, Dr. Andrea Giovannoni, for her genuine love, vast knowledge, critical thinking, writing skills, sacrifice, generous help, and thorough copyediting of my dissertation.

I thank Dr. Paul Pearson, the Secretary of the Thomas Merton Center at Bellarmine University, Louisville, Kentucky, for his generosity in responding to my many email requests for clarification, accommodating me at the center for three days in June 2017, and providing helpful resources for this project.

Thanks to Rev. Ivan Tou, CSP, pastor of Newman Hall Holy Spirit Parish, and the parishioners, for reaching out to me in times of need. I acknowledge gratefully the Catholic Workers, JC Orton and team, for helping me to contextualize my studies through the ministry of caring for our homeless brothers and sisters at People's Park and Peace Park in Berkeley.

I am thankful to Rev. Dr. George Pattery, SJ, the Jesuit Provincial of South Asia, Rev. Dr. Selva Rathinam, SJ, the President of Jnana-Deepa Vidyapeeth (JDV), and the professors at JDV Pune, for providing this great opportunity to pursue my doctorate at the Jesuit School of Theology. I am thankful to my Congregation, the Ursulines of Mary Immaculate: the Superior General, Sr. Elvira Mattappally and her team; the Provincial Superior, Sr. Kusum Panthalanickal; and all my Ursuline sisters, for their constant, prayerful support, love, and care.

I fondly remember with gratitude and love my late parents, Sebastian Kaviyil and Annamma Kaviyil, and my brother James Kaviyil, whose heavenly intercession I have continually sought, and whose hidden, powerful presence I have experienced throughout my research. Thanks to my other family members and friends in India, whose constant prayers, love and encouragement contributed to the success of my research.

I am obliged to Rev. Dr. Kuruvilla Pandikattu SJ, for guiding me through the process of publication and providing help and support of the Christian World Imprints. Thanks to Bro. Arnold Mathias SDB, and Bro. Alex Carvalho SDB, for their generosity and availability in designing the cover page creatively and meaningfully. May God continue the good work in us, to witness Christ amidst the contradictions and challenges of the world.

Fabian Jose, UMI
JDV, Pune
March, 2019

PROLOGUE

Consecrated life in the Catholic Church is a vital and healing presence in Indian society. Though Catholics overall constitute only 2.3 percent of the total population of India, consecrated men and women make an integral contribution to Indian society through their spirituality, institutions in the fields of education, medical care, social services, and other charitable activities. In the present context of India, however, consecrated men and women can experience challenges of relevance and identity in their vocations.[1] These issues have their basis in the fundamental need for a renewal of religious life itself. Some of the challenges include the loss of a vital spirituality and a dimming of the prophetic charism that marks apostolic religious life.

Indian religious life upholds three values: contemplation, prophecy, and community. Given these values, I find a deep affinity

[1] My experience in religious life as well as my work in the initial and ongoing formation of the sisters in my congregation—the Ursulines of Mary Immaculate, engagement in the inter-congregational formators' meetings, participation in the Conference of Religious in India (CRI), and my reading and reflection on Indian consecrated life, enabled me to incorporate these realities into this study. For other references,see Joseph Mathias, "The Challenges To Consecrated Life in India Today," in his address to the religious of North-East India, Diphu, at the Conclusion of the Year of Consecrated Life (January 23 2016): 1-5; Inigo Joachim, "Spirituality for the Religious of Our Time," *Consecrated Life in the Third Millennium:Challenges and Prospects*, ed. Joe Eruppakkatt (Bandra, Mumbai: St. Pauls, 2004), 9-18; and Rekha M. Chennattu, "To be Rooted and Relevant a Call for a Paradigm Shift in the Life of Women Religious." This paper was presented at AMOR XV, October 13-21, 2009 at Bann Phuwaan, Nakhon Pathom, Thailand, 1-13.

between the ideals of Indian consecrated life and Thomas Merton's contemplative-prophetic spirituality. Through my exploration of Merton's spirituality, I consider how his prophetic mysticism can serve as a valuable resource for a renewal of consecrated life in India, one that is immersed in the concrete realities of the society, the Church, and the postmodern world.

As an Ursuline Sister from India studied the doctorate in the United States, I am glad to imbibe and share the spiritual treasures of this country. This opportunity has been made available to me through the study of the spirituality of Thomas Merton. My passion for the prophetic dimensions of mysticism, and my experience in religious life and the formation of young sisters, have motivated me to select this topic for research. In my own experience, the consecrated men and women in India must deepen their contemplative spirituality, which involves a fundamental intimacy with Christ and an apostolic zeal to find relevance and identity in the consecrated life. I am compelled by Merton's contemplative-prophetic spirituality.

Merton was a 20th century Christian spiritual leader, a priest and a monk who sought to find a balance between contemplation and social action. He believed that contemplation and action had to go hand-in-hand, making him a forerunner of the modern-day emphasis on the intersection of faith and social justice. Though he experienced deep insecurity, confusion, and restlessness throughout his life, his spirituality remained Christ-centered. While he lived his life in deep interiority and contemplation, Merton went beyond the confines of his monastic life and engaged prophetically in the life of the people. He shared his God-experience with the broken world through his involvement in interfaith dialogue and his powerful writings, many of which denounced the injustices of violence and war, economic disparity, the breakdown of community, the nuclear arms race, racism, and ecological degradation.

As a contemplative prophet, Merton entered into the heart of social issues and read the signs of the times that remained obscure to most. He wrote, "You do not need to know precisely what is happening, or exactly where it is all going. What you need is to recognize the possibilities and challenges offered by the present moment, and to embrace them with courage, faith and hope."[2] Today, consecrated men and women of India who strive to discover the true relevance and purpose of our mission can draw encouragemnt from Merton to respond to the signs of the times with passion for the Lord and compassion for God's people. Consecrated life will be most meaningful and fruitful when it is rooted in a form of mysticism that arises from the concrete historical realities of its time. In Merton, we have an example of a prophetic mysticism which I believe finds deep resonance in the Indian context given that India is known to be a land of mystics, prophets, and reformers.

With regard to the historical realities of India, enormous wealth is concentrated in the hands of a few while the majority of our people live in abysmal poverty. The rich are becoming richer while the poor are being further impoverished. What is worse, the State seems to be working more and more for the interests of the affluent. In addition, women are subject to multiple forms of oppression and discrimination in the church and in the Indian society. There is a multiplicity of religions, castes, languages, and ethnic identities, and a predominance of religious fundamentalism. Consecrated people have a mission to actualize the possibilities for interreligious dialogue and ecumenical meetings, and to confront the social evils of economic disparity and gender injustice in order to collaborate in the building of a more just and humane Indian society. I suggest that Merton's prophetic mysticism might offer relevance for the consecrated men and women of India as they strive to follow Christ and to respond effectively to the signs of the times.

The contemplative-prophetic spirituality of Thomas Merton can serve as a vital resource for the relevance of consecrated life in India today. This is located within the broader context of the academic discipline of Christian spirituality, specifically the study of the prophetic dimensions of mysticism and contemplation. In addition, it makes a contribution to the existing field of contextual

[2] Thomas Merton, *Conjectures of a Guilty Bystander* (Garden City, New York: Image Books, 1968), 208. (Hereafter cited as CGB).

analysis of consecrated life and mission in India through its examination of the contemporary challenges to consecrated life. It is unique, however, in that it brings Merton's contemplative prophetic spirituality into dialogue with the Indian context, proposing renewed forms of spirituality that are characterized by a deep integration of contemplation and action, solitude and engagement with the world.

My attempt seeks to make a unique contribution to the academic discipline of Christian Spirituality for the Indian context. It proposes that the contemplative-prophetic spirituality of Thomas Merton can serve as resource for the relevance of the consecrated life in India. As already noted, Merton, who was deeply grounded in a contemplative spirituality, addressed the social injustices in U.S. society, the Church, and the world, and engaged in fruitful dialogue with other religious traditions. Likewise, Indian consecrated men and women are called to cultivate an integrated spirituality in order to fuel a renewal of the structures of the Indian Church, to confront the social evils of our time, and to seek out new forms of inter-religious dialogue in our deeply pluralistic and multi-religious context.

To my knowledge, no one has yet placed Merton's contemplative-prophetic spirituality in dialogue with the Indian context. My work makes a unique contribution in this regard, suggesting that Merton's thought can challenge Indian consecrated men and women to cultivate a spirituality characterized by a profound integration of contemplation and action, solitude and engagement with the world, not seeking to escape from its struggles and pain. At the same time, we must note that there are aspects of the Indian context that would stretch Merton into new territory such as gender injustice, deep-seated caste discrimination, and the difficulties of interreligious dialogue in the face of radical Hindu fundamentalism, which rejects any form of rapprochement with other religions. Nevertheless, Merton's integrative spirituality invites Indian consecrated men and women to a life of ongoing conversion which recognizes the need to move beyond traditional practices of piety and penance, the security of life inside one's own religious order, and the preservation of the status quo of our religious institutions, and to enter into the concrete struggles of the suffering world in our own context.

The first chapter defines some of the key concepts used in this project such as spirituality as an academic discipline, contemplation, mysticism, Christian mysticism, prophecy, and prophetic mysticism. *The second chapter* examines the life of Thomas Merton, considering the social, historical, cultural, educational, and spiritual forces that shaped him. *The third chapter* explores the contemplative dimensions of Merton's spirituality, considering his immersion into silence and solitude and his journey to God through prayer and contemplation. *The fourth chapter* traces Merton's gradual awakening to the prophetic dimensions of the contemplative life, exploring his response to the "signs of the times" through his writings on violence, poverty, the nuclear arms race, and the Vietnam War. *The fifth chapter* highlights the sociological studies of religious life in India, exploring the challenges of identity, relevance, and mission currently faced by consecrated men and women. And the relevance of the contemplative and prophetic dimensions of Merton's spirituality to the context of Indian consecrated life.

Fabian Jose, UMI
JDV, Pune
March, 2019

Chapter 1

Defining Key Concepts

In this chapter I define key concepts such as contemplation, mysticism, Christian mysticism, the prophetic and prophetic mysticism as they will be used in this book Thomas Merton's *The Contemplative-Prophetic Spirituality*. Before proceeding, however, I offer a brief consideration of Christian spirituality as a contemporary academic discipline.

1. Christian Spirituality as an Academic Discipline

Before considering Christian spirituality as an academic discipline, it is necessary to establish a basic working definition of the concept of "spirituality" itself and then to consider what it is that makes spirituality specifically "Christian." David Perrin considers working definitions helpful with regard to spirituality because there is no universally accepted understanding of spirituality, or of what constitutes spiritual progress. This is true even for Christian spirituality.[3]

Working Definition of Spirituality

According to Sandra Schneiders, "spirituality as lived experience can be defined as conscious involvement in the project of life integration through self-transcendence toward the ultimate value one

[3] David B. Perrin, *Studying Christian Spirituality* (New York and London: Routledge, Taylor and Francis Group, 2007), 16.

perceives."[4] This broad definition seems adequate to describe most forms of spirituality, whether Christian, non-Christian, or secular. Rather than merely a set of particular practices, rules, or doctrines, spirituality is an ongoing and dynamic process whose "ultimate purpose is life integration." Schneiders' argues that spirituality is a "process of self-transcendence," in which one transcends one's own narcissistic tendency to self-absorption, even regarding perfection in the spiritual path. As a "life project," spirituality is oriented toward some "ultimate value," what Paul Tillich would call an "ultimate concern," whether this is God, transcendence more generally, human or planetary wellbeing, or some other all-encompassing value.[5]

Professor of Christian Spirituality David Perrin considers Schneiders' definition of spirituality useful when considering both those spiritualities that do not include any explicit belief in God and those which do. In the latter, the "ultimate value" could be God. This ultimate value links the spiritual person to the whole of reality and provides the ground from which to wrestle with the deep questions of life and death, innocent suffering, and human destiny.

---

[4] Sandra M. Schneiders, "The Study of Christian Spirituality: Contours and Dynamics of a Discipline," in *Minding the Sprit: The Study of Christian Spirituality,* ed. Elizabeth A. Dreyer and Mark S. Burrows (Baltimore and London: The John Hopkins University Press, 2005), 6. In this definition, Schneiders' is drawing on a previous article by Walter Principe, "Toward Defining Spirituality," *Sciences Religieuses/Studies in Religion* 12 (Spring 1983): 123-141. Principe distinguishes three different, though related, levels of spirituality. The first, *the real or the existential* level, "is the quality—the lived quality—of a person. It is the way some person understood and lived, within his or her historical context, a chosen religious ideal in sensitivity to the realm of the spirit or the transcendent." The second level is the *formulation of a teaching about the lived reality*, often articulated by a moral exemplar or spiritual guide. The formulations or patterns of life of such exemplars have in turn given rise to many different spiritual traditions and schools of spirituality. The third level of spirituality entails the scholarly *study* of the first and second levels of spirituality, employing the resources and methods of other academic disciplines. See 135-7.

[5] Sandra Schneiders, "Christian Spirituality: Definition, Methods and Types," in *The New Westminster Dictionary of Christian Spirituality,* ed. Philip Sheldrake (Louisville, Kentucky: Westminster John Knox, 2005), 1.

In relation to Schneiders' definition, Perrin characterizes spirituality as a fundamental human capacity for self-transcendence inherent within human experience prior to identification with any particular religious affiliation or ethical system. This fundamental orientation entails the capacity for involvement in and commitment to the world outside of oneself. For Perrin, all human life unfolds between "two inescapable points of reference: life and death."[6] Spirituality helps one to integrate and find meaning in the disparate elements of life that lie between these two poles and to commit oneself to a cause greater than individual self-preservation and wellbeing.

In similar terms, theologians Elizabeth Dreyer and Mark Burrows identify some essential characteristics of spirituality, adding to the general definition (noted above) the communal nature of spirituality and the quest for an authentic existence. They define spirituality as

> the daily lived aspect of one's faith commitment in terms of values and behaviors; how one appreciates beliefs about God and the world; the process of conscious integration and transformation of one's life; the journey of self-transcendence; the depth dimension of all human existence; a dialectic that moves one from the inauthentic to the authentic and from the individual to the communal; the quest for ultimate value and meaning.[7]

These definitions may include explicitly religious elements such as prayer, sacraments, spiritual practices, or reading of sacred texts. In sum, a working definition of "spirituality" may broadly be conceived as a state in which one is oriented toward some ultimate, all-encompassing value that links one to the whole of reality. It is a process which leads to life integration, self-transcendence, and commitment to a cause greater than the individual self and moves the spiritual seeker toward authenticity and self-transparency.

---

[6] Perrin, 20.

[7] Elizabeth A. Dreyer and Mark S. Burrows "Preface," in *Minding the Sprit: The Study of Christian Spirituality*, ed. Elizabeth A. Dreyer and Mark S. Burrows (Baltimore and London: The John Hopkins University Press, 2005), xv.

2. What Makes Spirituality "Christian"?

Christian spirituality involves what Dryer and Burrows describe as "conscious discipleship," the opening of the self to the love and grace of God the Creator and to Jesus Christ, in the power of the Holy Spirit.[8] According to theologian of spirituality Peter Feldmeier, the English word "spirituality" derives from the Latin *spiritualitas*, a translation which is influenced by the Greek noun *pneuma* (spirit). In the New Testament, "*pneuma*" indicates the Holy Spirit as well as the "life of God working within" the follower of Jesus Christ, that which "makes someone *pneumatikos* (spiritual)."[9] In the Gospel of John, Jesus announces a "rebirth in the Spirit and in truth" (Jn 3:2-8: rebirth; 4:23: spirit and truth), and in both Luke's Gospel and the Acts of the Apostles, the Spirit forms the community of believers (Lk 4:14; Acts 2:32-33). For Paul, the Spirit is so essential to the presence of the risen Lord that he identifies Christ with the Spirit: "Now the Lord is Spirit, and where the spirit of the Lord is, there is freedom" (2 Cor. 3:17). Being "Christian" means to enter the realm of the Spirit (1 Cor 6:17), and through God's "indwelling presence" to become "a spiritual person" (1 Cor 2: 14-15).[10]

For theologian of spirituality Philip Sheldrake, "spirituality," in Christian terms, "refers to the way our fundamental values, life styles, and spiritual practices reflect particular understandings of God, human identity, and the material world as the context for human transformation." He emphasizes the rootedness of all Christian spirituality in the Hebrew and Christian scriptures, particularly in Jesus' life and teaching. In brief, Christian spirituality is concerned with "following the way of Jesus Christ."[11]

---

[8] Ibid.

[9] Peter Feldmeier, *Christian Spirituality: Lived Expressions in the Life of the Church* (Winona, Minnesota: Anselm Academic, 2015), 11-12.

[10] Ibid. Feldmeier is using the *New American Bible*, revised edition, 2010, 1991, 1986, and 1970 by the Confraternity of Christian Doctrine, Inc., Washington, D.C.

[11] Philip Sheldrake, *Spirituality: A Brief History*, 2nd edition (Chichester, UK: Wiley-Blackwell, 2013), 7.

Feldmeier likewise stresses that the ideas, themes, and images of Christian spirituality have their basis in the biblical witness as it is interpreted and mediated through the tradition. "The Bible," he says, "is the foundational and indispensable text for Christianity." Ultimately, though the various denominations may differ in their understandings of the role of tradition in the life of the community, "Christians believe that Jesus is the absolute revelation of God, that the Bible is the written authoritative witness to that revelation, and that the tradition is the context through which the church understands both the Bible and its own existence." The Bible is hence the ground of Christian theology and spirituality, and itself contains a rich pluralism of spiritualities reflecting the contexts from which they emerge.[12] Feldmeier lists several characteristics and core values of an authentic Christian spirituality, all of which are rooted in the witness of scripture and its life in the Christian communities.[13]

1) *A Life of Grace and Faith*

Christians believe that they cannot attain salvation through their own efforts but only by the grace of God, to which the proper human response is faith—fully entrusting oneself to God. Faith leads one to experience the fullness of freedom, a freedom which enables the Christian to serve others without compulsion and to live the Christian life in its fullness.

2) *A Life in the Spirit*

For Paul, being spiritual means living in the Holy Spirit, the divine person who influences and directs one's life. The Spirit-directed life will reflect the fruits of "love, joy, peace, patience, kindness, generosity, faithfulness, gentleness, [and] self-control" (Gal 5: 22-23). Above all, the Christian who is guided by the Spirit will be disposed to love of God and neighbor.

---

[12] Feldmeier, 42, 55.

[13] Feldmeier uses the *New American Bible* (see note 9) throughout the following list of themes, 14-19.

3) *Christocentric*

The essential dimension of Christian spirituality is the ever-deepening "intimacy with Jesus Christ," which Paul describes as being "baptized into Christ" (Rm 16:3). This involves the incorporation of the fundamental mysteries of Christ into the life of the believer: the Incarnation, in which humanity is united with God and participates in the divine life itself; the cross, which entails a daily dying to self; and the resurrection, which empowers the believer to live a new life in the here and now.

4) *Trinitarian*

Christian spirituality is a participation in the Trinitarian love among the three divine persons, which "reflects the communal dynamism of the one God." Spirituality is thus a "manifestation of life in the Spirit." The Spirit is the bond between the Father and the Son, and the way in which the risen Christ is made known in the world. The Spirit infuses believers with the love of the Trinitarian God.

5) *Communal*

Paul imagines the diverse members of the community as the one Body of Christ, whose head is Christ himself (Rom 12:5; 1 Cor 12: 12-13). The Body of Christ metaphor describes the very nature of Christian identity, as the call to holiness is not merely individual but communal. Thus the community of believers prays together and supports one another in faith as together they seek to discern God's presence and action among them.

6) *Just*

The Judeo-Christian tradition emphasizes justice as one of the most important themes of Christian spirituality. Therefore, spirituality cannot limit its scope to the relationship between God and the individual self, but needs to be deeply connected to the community and the world, particularly concerning matters of justice and right relationship. The letter of James declares: "If a brother or sister has nothing to wear and has no food for the day, and one of you says to them, 'Go in peace, keep warm, and eat well,' but you do not give them the necessities of the body, what good is it?" (2:15-16). Feldmeier asserts that Christian faith that does not concern itself with human suffering and injustice is "seriously deficient."

7) *Prayerful*

Prayer is the foundation of Christian spirituality, the indispensable dimension through which a Christian cultivates a deep intimacy with God and sensitivity to the Spirit's movements in the soul. Such prayer is expressed in various ways: through praise and worship, petition, meditation, scriptural reflection, and contemplation.

8) *Divinizing*

Ultimately, the *telos*, or "ultimate horizon," of the Christian life is "divinization," or *theosis,* which literally means "becoming God." However, though this process seeks complete union with the divine, it does not involve an actual, ontological change from human to divine nature, but indicates a participation in God's very life as it is lived by God—a living in and through the Divine. For Paul, Christian discipleship entailed the bearing of Christ's likeness, and growth into the very holiness of God. In this way, all of creation moves toward the ultimate goal, wherein God becomes "all in all" (1 Cor 15: 28).

Considered collectively, these characteristics represent a "robust" expression of Christian spirituality. Feldmeier notes, however, that the absence of any one of these elements in a lived spirituality constitutes the basis for a rigorous critique of such spirituality with regard to its adequacy and authenticity.

3. Spirituality as a Contemporary Academic Discipline: Antecedents

The existing academic discipline of spirituality has a long and multifaceted history. In the patristic and early medieval periods, theology and spirituality were all of a piece. Spirituality was considered the "living and lived faith," and served as the foundation for all study, whether sacred or profane. In this period, "Theology was [articulated] spirituality and spirituality was lived theology. Scripture was the source and norm of all knowledge."

During the high Middle Ages, theology moved from the monastery to the universities, thus fragmenting the integrated approach to knowledge which characterized the previous period. Consequently, in the universities, philosophy became the "handmaid of theology," and within the context of modernity, theology slowly came to understand itself more as a "scientific" than a spiritual endeavor. Mystical theology—the wisdom gained through prayer and meditation on the Scriptures—became the purview of the monastery. Entering the Enlightenment period, theology was increasingly marked by the ideals of rationalism, and became a predominantly scholastic, university discipline while spirituality became a non-academic enterprise consisting of devotional practices and the "cultivation of mystical prayer."[14]

The more recent antecedents of the contemporary academic discipline of spirituality lie in the field of "spiritual theology," a sub-discipline of theology in the nineteenth and early twentieth centuries. It emerged in the seminaries to train future clergy in guiding the faithful to spiritual perfection and treated the areas of mystical and ascetical theology.

In the United States, theologians Sandra Schneiders and Michael Buckley developed the first comprehensive doctoral program in spirituality. Their approaches emphasize religious experience as a key aspect of spirituality and situate this experience within a framework of theological beliefs and commitments. Feldmeier notes that their approaches express the significance of "profound encounters with God, ways of engaging God and the world, and the dynamics of inner transformation." Further, both theologians hold that spirituality deals with religious practices and their transformative potential. Finally, according to them, all religious experience must be interpreted.[15]

Today, though it is useful to consider the contemporary discipline of spirituality in relation to the non-religious disciplines employed to interpret spiritual experience, spirituality as a discipline nevertheless now has a broader application. Christian spirituality is

---

[14] Schneiders, "Christian Spirituality: Definition, Methods and Types," 2.

[15] Feldmeier, 9-10.

no longer merely a subset of systematic theology or historical studies as it was in the past. In the current cultural milieu, it is becoming an important means to express more broadly how people understand and engage transcendence.[16] As an academic discipline, Christian spirituality concerns the "ultimate value" of union with God and the capacity of that union to bring freedom and truth to the follower of Christ (Jn. 8:31-33).

Describing the development of spirituality as an academic discipline in its own right, Schneiders observes that it arose out of a felt need by students for a new discipline, one that investigated something which did not yet have a specific designation, but whose antecedents, as noted above, lie in the field of "spiritual theology."[17] Scholars in the field of spirituality bring to this discourse their respective disciplines, which may include biblical studies, history, theology, pastoral counseling, religious psychology, or literary criticism. Their contributions to the field of spirituality through their reflections, discussions, writings, and teaching, helped it to emerge and grow as an academic discipline.[18] Schneiders and other scholars have attempted to maintain the study of spirituality as an academic discipline through a rigorous, systematic exposition of the interdisciplinary nature of spirituality.

Having reviewed the field of spirituality, this study, in accord with Schneiders, construes the academic discipline of spirituality as the study of lived religious experience and its transformative potential for both the spiritual subject and the world. As an academic discipline it employs a multiplicity of methodologies and resources, both the non-theological university disciplines and the fields of biblical studies and theology while situating religious experience within the framework of religious belief and faith commitments. In the

---

[16] Dreyer and Burrows, "Introduction," xxiii.

[17] Schneiders, "The Study of Christian Spirituality: Contours and Dynamics of a Discipline," 5, 22; Schneiders, "Christian Spirituality: Definition, Methods and Types," 2.

[18] Schneiders, "The Study of Christian Spirituality: Contours and Dynamics of a Discipline," 5.

study of Merton's lived religious experience, this study brings both religious and non-religious disciplines to bear on the interpretation of that experience. Regarding the latter, literary and socio-political analyses will constitute two of the primary disciplines. Through its exploration of the forces which shaped Merton as a contemplative-prophetic mystic, the study considers the transformative potential of Merton's spirituality for consecrated life in India today.

4. Method of Spirituality

Spirituality may be studied through human events, human psychology, and various art forms and sacred texts, among other media. As an academic discipline, it is analyzed through interdisciplinary methods.[19] According to Schneiders, Christian spirituality seeks to understand the experience of faith itself, "as it actually occurs, as it actually transforms its subject toward fullness of life in Christ, that is, toward self-transcending life integration within the Christian community of faith."[20]

Spirituality as an academic discipline is essentially interdisciplinary because of the multi-faceted nature of the object it studies—transformative Christian experience. In an essay from 2005, Schneiders identifies three approaches to the study of spirituality as an interdisciplinary academic discipline: "the historical, the theological, and the anthropological or hermeneutical."

The *historical* approach uses modern historical methodology for the study of Christian religious experience as it is transmitted through texts and other products of culture. Because its primary focus is the lived experience of the faith itself rather than ecclesiastical life or the systematization of theology, it is different from church history or historical theology. This approach easily finds a home in university settings, where historical studies are already clearly defined and established, are related more directly to the predecessors of the

[19] Perrin, 20.

[20] Schneiders, "The Study of Christian Spirituality: Contours and Dynamics of a Discipline," 6-7.

field of spirituality, and provide foundational data for all other forms of research in this area.

The second approach, the *theological,* is situated within the context of denominational seminaries. This approach conceives spirituality as one area of theological study along with others such as "systematic theology, moral theology or biblical studies." It uses theological categories to analyze the Christian experience of faith and is understood as a form of practical theology. This approach is more holistic, integrated, and less dogmatic and prescriptive than its predecessor, "spiritual theology," referenced above. It is much more concerned with contributing to the formation of the churches than in academic research as such.

Schneiders designates the third approach the "anthropological" or "hermeneutical," noting that it is newer than the other approaches. It sees spirituality not as a particular subject matter or dimension of theological studies, but as part of the much broader scope of human spirituality. This approach locates Christian spirituality within the universal human capacity for the "spiritual quest" that belongs to and is realized in some way in all religious traditions. This approach is more open, engaging, praxis-oriented, interdisciplinary, and interreligious. It is particularly appropriate for the graduate theological setting or the field of religious studies. While remaining centered in its own Christian commitments, it is primarily concerned with research into the experience of the Christian search for God in its concrete and experiential reality and in the constructive work of reinterpreting that experience in and for the contemporary context.

The three methodological approaches are mutually enlightening, and scholars engaging in these approaches recognize their shared disciplinary concerns. Interdisciplinarity raises the yet unresolved question of how to relate Christian resources from the fields of scripture, theology, or history to the various non-theological disciplines such as "psychology, sociology, aesthetics, and science" in order to analyze religious experience as such in its concrete particularity.[21]

---

[21] Schneiders, "Christian Spirituality; Definition, Methods and Types," 4.

Ultimately, then, the reason for an interdisciplinary approach to the academic study of spirituality is twofold: on the one hand, as Schneiders notes, it was to counter a reduction of spirituality to the domain of the human sciences, and on the other, to avoid subsuming spirituality into one of the sacred sciences (namely theology or biblical studies). Rather, because of its complex and singular nature, Christian spirituality as an academic discipline strives to be "maximally inclusive" of all these disciplines—both the human and sacred sciences—in order to comprehensively engage its object, which Schneiders describes as "the experience itself of living the paschal mystery of Jesus Christ in all its ramifications, under the formal object of experience." She explains that ultimately,

> Christian spirituality as an academic discipline is an attempt to realize, by bringing serious and personally transforming study to bear on the ultimate human value of union with God, what is arguably the most cited text in the Christian canon, Jesus' promise, "If you remain in my word you will become my disciples and you will know the truth and the truth will set you free" (Jn. 8:31-33).[22]

In exploring Thomas Merton's contemplative-prophetic spirituality, I will utilize Schneiders' *hermeneutical* approach, which involves the interpretation of the "phenomena of the Christian spiritual life as experience." The hermeneutical method consists of three steps: description, critical analysis, and interpretation.

Description takes account of the experience itself, considering the historical facts, the textual witness to the experience, the theological and ecclesiastical setting, the psychological conflicts faced by the person, and the transformative dimensions of the experience. I will employ this *descriptive* phase of Schneiders' model to explore Merton's life and spiritual journey.

Critical analysis considers the social, economic, political, and religious influences on the person's experience and will be used in this case to explore the contemplative and prophetic dimensions

---

[22] Schneiders, "The Study of Christian Spirituality: Contours and Dynamics of a Discipline," 22.

of Merton's spirituality. *Constructive interpretation* entails the transformative appropriation of the phenomenon for the subject. In this it leads to "enlightenment of the current situation, a contribution to the understanding of the spiritual life today."[23] In this step, I will consider how the prophetic spirituality of Thomas Merton may enliven the current context of consecrated life in India today.

5. The Definition and Meaning of Contemplation

Contemplation comes from the Latin word *contemplari*, which describes acts of looking for God's will within a sacred enclosure called the *templum*. It is related to the Greek word *theoria*, which means "to look towards God," and to the Sanskrit word *Samadhi*, which describes an "act of concentrated thought." Therefore, contemplation might be defined, at least in part, as "looking towards God and thinking deeply about Him."[24]

However, this is not a purely intellectual form of "thinking," but an encounter of the whole person with the divine. In this vein, spiritual writer Brian Taylor places the concept of contemplation within the broader context of human knowing, contrasting it to the purely rational mode of thinking characterized by Descartes—"I think, therefore I am." Taylor proposes breaking out of the "tomb" of a purely cerebral form of knowledge into a broader, more comprehensive way of knowing, one which "Christians might call the 'mind of Christ,' and others might call enlightenment."[25] For Thomas Aquinas, contemplation is the "simple enjoyment of the truth."[26] For Aquinas, harking back to Gregory the Great, this pertains not only

---

[23] Schneiders, "A Hermeneutical Approach to the Study of Christian Spirituality," 56-57.

[24] Herbert Slade, *Exploration into Contemplative Prayer* (Great Britain, London: Darton, Longman and Todd, 1975), 26.

[25] Brian C. Taylor, *Becoming Christ: Transformation through Contemplation* (Cambridge, Massachusetts: Cowley Publications, 2002), ix.

[26] Laurence Freeman, *Journey to the Heart: Christian Contemplation through the Centuries- an Illustrated Guide*, ed. Kim Nataraj (Maryknoll, New York: Orbis Books, 2012), 9.

to the intellect but to the affections, notably love, desire, and delight in God's presence.

For Merton, contemplation is "a sudden gift of awareness, an awakening to the Real within all that is real." The "real" is God, "Who is pure Reality and the source of all that is real!"[27] Such encounter with the real draws one into the kind of "unknowing" that characterizes the Christian apophatic tradition, leading "beyond our knowledge, beyond our own light, beyond systems, beyond explanations, beyond discourse, beyond dialogue, beyond our own self."[28] It leads to the anguished place of existential darkness wherein one "*no longer knows what God is.*" Here one encounters the I Am in whose light one finds the true self, and utters "I Am."[29]

For contemporary spiritual writer Laurence Freeman, "Contemplation is a path, an experience, a lifelong practice, an expansion and deepening of consciousness. It is about being in the present moment. . . .Above all, it leads to self-knowledge." Such self-knowledge is a "necessary prelude" to knowing God.[30] Though the precise meaning of contemplation may differ from one spiritual tradition to another, the focus is the experience of the Divine and a superseding of the normal modes of human knowing.

Christian theological tradition, with its emphasis upon grace, considers contemplative experience as "a gift from God," one not achieved through human effort. Through the activity of silent prayer, guided by the Spirit, a person is "led into a loving and life-changing relationship with God." In the human/divine relationship, God seeks to awaken one in joy to the divine life within and to make possible the response to God's presence with love, compassion, and self-transparency. In contemplation, one's being rests in God and trusts God's hidden presence, which is invisible to the human eye.

---

[27] Thomas Merton, *New Seeds of Contemplation* (New York: New Directions, 1961), 3. (Hereafter cited as *NSC*).

[28] Merton, *NSC,* 2; see also Bruce H. Lescher, "*Thomas Merton* (1915-68) *New Seeds of Contemplation,*" in *Christian Spirituality the Classics,* ed. Arthur Holder (London and New York: Routledge, 2010), 357.

[29] Merton, *NSC,* 13 (emphasis in original).

[30] Freeman, 8-9.

Contemplation thus seeks to bring all the dimensions of the human—spirit, mind and body—into an integrated whole within the experience.[31] The ancient prayer from the Sarum Rite beautifully captures the integrative nature of contemplation:

> God be in my head and in my understanding;
> God be in my eyes and in my looking;
> God be in my mouth and in my speaking;
> God be in my heart and in my thinking;
> God be at my end and at my departing.[32]

This contemplative posture is intrinsic (in some form) to Eastern and Western Christian as well as non-Christian traditions.

The basis of Christian contemplation is the intimate union between Jesus and his Father, which led him to declare that "the glory that you have given me I have given them, so that they may be one, as we are one, I in them and you in me " (Jn 17: 22-23). The Christian contemplative experiences the same unity and glory by abiding in Christ. Thus, through the intimacy of his indwelling, Jesus takes us with him into the presence of God.

In this regard, Taylor observes that the Christian contemplative must focus on the relationship with Jesus that lies at the core of one's being. This relationship is not chiefly based on particular doctrinal formulations or a strict imitation of Jesus' behavior, but upon a direct experience of his indwelling spirit. Jesus promised that He will be with us to the end of the age. Remaining in him, he says, human persons remain in God.

It is crucial to note that contemplation is not an end in itself, but is intrinsically linked to action in the world. Christian contemplatives are called to enter into Jesus' human consciousness in order to feel, think and act as Jesus acts. It is not enough that they study, reflect upon, and look *at* Jesus, but must learn to look *through* Jesus, even as they give to him their eyes, ears, bodily senses, and minds. As Jesus looks through them, they become one with him through this

[31] Taylor, 4, 60, 79.

[32] Slade, 6, 61.

"interpenetration of minds and hearts," unifying their faculties, linking Jesus' objectives with theirs, and purifying their vision. Indeed, they "try to be him as he looks on Peter or a leper or a sinner . . . but with love." Through this intimate union in contemplation, contemplatives experience the personal and creative love of Jesus. By participating in the very life of Christ, they are enabled to share this love with others in such a way that their entire lives becomean act of love for God and all creatures.[33]

6. Definition of Mysticism

In broad, theistic terms, the mystic may be defined as one who is intimately bound in dynamic union and reciprocal relationship with the deity. A mystic "experiences to an extraordinary degree, the profoundly personal encounter with the energy of divine life," writes Ursula King.[34] The word "mystic" comes from the Latin word *mysticus* and the Greek word *mystikos,* meaning "the mystical."[35] In ancient Greece, one who has been initiated into the mysteries of existence and the esoteric knowledge of the realities of life and death was known as *mystes* (mystic). They were the ones who were initiated into a superior wisdom and whose eyes of sensation and reason were closed for a while in order to perceive everything through the eyes of faith.[36] King characterizes mystics as those who perceive the presence of God in the whole of creation and in all sentient beings, "leading to a transfiguration of the ordinary all around them." The touch of God, however, "is most strongly felt deep within their own hearts."[37]

---

[33] James M. Somerville, *The Mystical Sense of the Gospels: A Handbook for the Contemplatives* (Lexington Avenue, New York: The Crossroad Publishing Company, 1997), 16.

[34] Ursula King, *Christian Mystics: Their Lives and Legacies throughout the Ages* (Mahwah, New Jersey: Hidden Spring, 2001), 3.

[35] V.F. Vineeth, "Mysticism," in *A Concise Encyclopedia of Christianity in India*, ed. Errol D' Lima and Anthony De Silva (Pune, Mumbai: Jnana–Deepa Vidyapeeth and St. Paul's Publications, 2014), 611.

[36] Sheila Kannath, *A Journey into Mysticism* (Palakkad: Mercy College, 1993), 1.

[37] King, 3.

The spiritual vision of the mystic is characterized by the manner of looking at all that is visible and material as housing the divine. Therefore, the more deeply the mystic experiences union with God, the more profoundly she is united with God's creation.

Going back to the roots of "mysticism" will disclose the rich treasures of its wisdom and knowledge. The word "mysticism" implies "mystery," and is derived from the Greek verb *muw*, meaning to close the lips, eyes and ears, and to shut the doors of fleeting senses and passions. Withdrawing from everything external and sinking within oneself allows a person to receive inner, divine illuminations.[38] The *Oxford English Dictionary* gives the meaning of mysticism as "the belief that knowledge of God and of real truth can be found through prayer and meditation rather than through reason and the senses."[39] Evelyn Underhill's definition of mysticism may be applied to all religions:

> Mysticism is the expression of the innate yearning of the human spirit towards total harmony with the transcendental order, whatever may be the theological formula in which this order is expressed. This yearning with the great mystics gradually takes possession of the whole field of consciousness; it dominates their whole life, attains its climax in that experience called mystic union, whether it is with the God of Christianity, the World soul of pantheism or the Absolute of philosophy. This desire for union and straining towards it, in as much as they are vital and real, constitute the real subject of mysticism. Through this, human consciousness reaches its further and richest development.[40]

From this perspective, then, mysticism may thus be construed as an inherent longing for complete harmony and union with the

---

[38] Harvey Egan, *Christian Mysticism: The Future of a Tradition* (New York: Pueblo Publishing Company, 1984), 1.

[39] A.S. Hornby, ed., *Oxford English Dictionary,* New 8th ed. (New York: Oxford University Press, 2010), 1012.

[40] Evelyn Underhill, *The School of Charity and the Mystery of Sacrifice* (New York: Green and Co., 1965), 235.

transcendent order, a longing which increasingly takes full possession of the entire scope of human consciousness and desire.

According to the Christian tradition, God has placed a deep longing in the human being for self-transcendence. Humans are endowed with a spiritual sense that opens up inwardly just as the physical sense opens up outwardly. Augustine of Hippo speaks of the "eye" of the soul and the "ear" of the mind, and others refer to the "eyes of faith," which open up to higher spiritual realities.[41] Thus, the mystical dimension opens the inner eye to experience the divine intimately.

The mystical sphere is not restricted to Christianity. The first letter of St. John declares that, "everyone who loves is begotten of God, and knows God" (1 Jn. 4:7). Every great religion has at its core a mystical dimension. These religions have fashioned great spiritual leaders and teachers, men and women who have encountered God and experienced deep personal transformation. That which is common to the mystical and contemplative dimensions of all the religions is the experience of awe.[42] As a result of this wonder, the mystic finds the transcendent everywhere, in all things, and above all, in every person. A beautiful passage from the *Svetasvatara Upanishad* reflects this sense of the all-pervasive presence of the divine at the heart of everything, which constitutes the essence of mysticism:

---

[41] Augustine of Hippo, Sermons on Selected Lessons of the New Testament, Sermon on the Words of the Gospel, Mt. 10: 28, 'be not afraid of them that kill the body,' "Delivered on a Festival of Martyrs," accessed December 5, 2015, http://kingsgarden.org/English/Organizations/LCC.GB/LCIS/Scriptures/Fathers/Doctors/AugustinOfHippo/Sermons/Sermon15.html.

[42] Somerville, 170-173; Somerville explains that "there is a mystical element at the core of all the great religions: in Buddhism, Hinduism, Islam, Judaism, and Christianity. . . The constellation of the world's religions constitutes an organism of beliefs and practices for which the mystical spirit is the common thread sustaining them all. It unites them according to what is least contingent, relative, and culture bound. Mystics and contemplatives the world over have similar experiences." The "awe" experience as each one come in contact with the center of the soul is common to all, though their outward expressions may differ.

All heads are Your Head, all faces Your Face,
You dwell in the cave of the heart and all hidden places.
Through the whole universe, You have extended Yourself.
You are Shiva, the auspicious, the ever-present Lord.
With hands and feet everywhere, eyes and ears
Everywhere, heads and mouths everywhere,
You have filled up every corner of space.
Smaller than the smallest and larger than largest.[43]

In the Christian tradition, this mystical sense finds expression in the basic insight that all people, from the least to the greatest, bear the image of God and are thereby accorded intrinsic value as extensions of God's very self.

7. Meaning of Christian Mysticism

Christians participate in the divine life through communion with God. "The story of the Christian mystics is one of an all-consuming, passionate love affair between human beings and God," writes King.[44] Christian mysticism adds a very clear personal dimension to the experience of the Divine. Christian life and faith are based on a profound desire to seek and find God by following Jesus' teaching and his "way" as described in the Gospels. Christian mysticism encounters the visible presence of the invisible God through the person of Jesus Christ. At its heart is Jesus' own experience, expressed in the words "I and Father are one" (Jn 10:30), the message of utter divine unity. Christian mystical experience entails self-transformation into "another Christ," or as St. Paul would acclaim, "It is no longer I who live, but it is Christ who lives in me" (Gal 2:20). In Christ, the Christian mystic is purified, illuminated, and ultimately united with God, who is love.

This complete union of the soul with God is the culmination of the spiritual journey, which, according to a widely-held understanding within the Christian tradition, is marked by three stages: purgation, illumination, and union. The stage of *purgation*,

[43] Ibid.

[44] King, 4.

a time of great suffering, entails the purification of the soul through the relinquishment of the passions, the false self, the self-will, and of life's lesser goods in favor of the greatest good, in order to be united with God. The *illuminative* stage entails a greater degree of self-knowledge as the spiritual seeker begins to see his/her imperfections and limitations in the light of God's perfect goodness and infinitude. This stage also affords "knowledge of the cosmic order, the angelic hierarchy, and the structure of Being." In the *unitive* stage, the self-will, having been dissolved completely, is now transformed by God's grace, and the seeker desires only God's will. In this disposition of complete surrender, the soul at last achieves its goal of union with God, which amounts to the anticipation of the Beatific Vision.[45]

Rooted in Christ, the mystic seeks only God's will and desires to serve God fully. This means that an authentic mysticism will always have a praxical or political dimension. Thus, filled with the love of God, the true mystic will become socially and politically active, reaching out to the poor and marginalized members of the society because they see in their suffering brothers and sisters the image of God.[46]

8. Description of Prophet

In the Bible, the Hebrew word for prophet is "nabi," which means "one who speaks for the divine." Thus, the prophets are mediators sent by God with a "primordial relationship to the word of God."[47] Prophets are people who speak "by divine inspiration or as the interpreter through whom the will of God is expressed."[48] In the

[45] Ibid. Wayne Teasdale, *Essays in Mysticism: Explorations into Contemplative Experience* (Lake Worth, Florida: Sunday Publications, Inc., 1982), xiii-xiv.

[46] Vineeth, 613; There are also mystics who are cloistered monastic's not directly engaged in the social activities of the world but they sanctify the world in remaining united with the world through prayer and contemplation.

[47] Rui de Menezes, *Voices from Beyond: Theology of the Prophetical Book* (Mumbai: St Pauls, 2003), 20.

[48] Rui de Menezes, "Prophet," in *A Concise Encyclopedia of Christianity in India* (Pune, Mumbai: Jnana–Deepa Vidyapeeth and St. Paul's Publications, 2014), 676.

scriptures, they were "men and women moved by the Holy Spirit, [who] spoke from God" (2 Peter 1:21). In short, they echo the voice of God to humanity.

In the Hebrew Scriptures, the prophets were men and women called by God from various walks of life: poets, preachers, patriots, statesmen, social critics and moralists. They stood in the "presence of God" (Jer 15:19) and "in the council of the Lord" (Jer. 23:18). They sought only God's will and communicated the will of God to the people. They were moved by God to confront the leaders and kings of their day for their extravagant lifestyle and excess of wealth, and for the injustice done to the poor, widows, orphans, strangers, and other vulnerable members of the society.

Thus, the prophetic voice is not irenic but acerbic and denunciatory in the face of evil and the indifference of society to injustice. The prophet seeks to awaken the conscience of a society that attempts to close its eyes to suffering and injustice, to obliterate the memories, to calm the nerves, and to silence our conscience. According to Abraham Heschel,

> The prophet is a man who feels fiercely. God has thrust a burden upon his soul, and he is bowed and stunned at man's fierce greed. Frightful is the agony of man; no human voice can convey its full terror. Prophecy is the voice that God has lent to the silent agony, a voice to the plundered poor, to the profaned riches of the world. It is a form of living, a crossing point of God and man. God is raging in the prophet's word.[49]

Most important, the prophet speaks with an eye toward a transformed future, in which God's will of *shalom* for all of creation is realized.

In this regard, according to Pope Francis, prophets are the ones who have learned to read the signs of the times in light of the future. In a homily given in the Vatican's Casa Santa Marta on December 16, 2013, Pope Francis elucidated the task of the true prophet:

---

[49] Abraham J. Heschel, *The Prophets* (New York and Evanston: Harper and Row Publishers, 1962), xiv, 3-8.

> A prophet is someone who listens to the words of God, who reads the spirit of the times, and who knows how to move forward towards the future. True prophets hold within themselves three different moments: past, present, and future. They keep the promise of God alive, they see the suffering of their people, and they bring us the strength to look ahead. God looks after his people by giving them prophets in the hardest times, in the midst of their worst suffering.[50]

Thus, the prophet bears the heavy burden laid on him/her by God to shape a future in accord with the will of God for the well-being of all creation through the enactment of justice and right relationship. Ultimately, the work of the prophet is aimed at the fostering of reconciliation and right relationship between God and humans and among human communities.

9. Prophetic Mysticism

The mystics are ordinary people who live their lives in an extraordinary way, after having been called or touched by the Lord. They love God passionately. At the same time, authentic mystics find themselves unable to keep this love to themselves but are compelled to transmit the message of God's mercy and justice to others. In order to do so, they inevitably encounter deep structures of injustice in the world that impede the will of God from being realized for all people, and find that this passion for God constrains them to confront such structures of oppression and domination for the sake of God's suffering children.[51] The prophet thus calls every member of the community to right relationship. In this way, mystics become *prophetic* mystics, those unable to separate God's love from God's justice.

The political theologian Johann Baptist Metz elucidates this form of mysticism, which he describes as a mysticism of "suffering unto God." He finds this mysticism expressed "particularly in Israel's

---

[50] Pope Francis, "Without Prophecy, Only Clericalism" (December 16, 2013); accessed, December 5, 2015, http://www.news.va/en/news/pope-francis-without-prophecy-`only-clericalism, Vatican Radio.

[51] Janet K. Ruffing, *Mysticism and Social Transformation*, with a forward by Robert J. Egan (Syracuse, New York: Syracuse University Press, 2001), ix.

prayer tradition," notably in the prophets. He writes, "the language of prayer is itself a language of suffering, a language of crisis, a language of affliction and of radical danger, a language of complaint and grievance, a language of crying out and, literally of the grumbling of the children of Israel."[52] The language of the prophetic mystic "is deeply rooted in the figure of night, in the experience of the soul's demise. It is less a song of the soul, more a loud crying out from the depths – and not a vague, undirected wailing, but a focused crying-out-to."[53] This "crying-out-to" would seem to presume a relationship, however fractured, one in which God hears and is moved by such cries.

Similarly, Heschel characterizes the prophetic voice in this way: "Instead of dealing with the timeless issues of being and becoming, of matter and form, of definitions and demonstrations," the prophet "is thrown into orations about widows and orphans, about the corruption of judges and affairs of the market place. Instead of showing us a way through the elegant mansions of the mind, the prophets takes us to the slums."[54] In Metz's view this form of mysticism constrains one to a willingness to remain alert to suffering, danger, and injustice rather than closing one's eyes to it. It calls the mystic to take on the burden of the situation and to assume responsibility for it. Metz calls this a "mysticism of open eyes," which attends to all suffering and injustice, and "takes responsibility for it, for the sake of a God who is a friend to human beings." This solidarity thus constitutes a witnessing to God, a God who cares much more about how we deal with the neighbor than what we "think" about God in Godself.[55] For the true prophet, the doing of justice to the weak and vulnerable takes priority over any correct way of worshipping or speaking of God, as eloquently stated by Jose Porfirio Miranda: "The question is not whether someone

---

[52] Johann Baptist Metz, *A Passion for God: The Mystical-Political Dimension of Christianity*, edited and translated with an introduction by J. Matthew Ashley (New York: Paulist Press, 1998), 66.

[53] Ibid., 67.

[54] Heschel, 3.

[55] Metz, 163.

is seeking God or not, but whether he is seeking him where God himself said that he is."[56] For the prophetic mystic, God is absent in the absence of justice and right relationship.

This form of witness is therefore "not allowed political innocence," Metz declares. Rather, it "is intimately involved, with eyes that see, in that history where people are crucified and tortured, hated and miserly loved; and no mythos far-removed from history, no world-blind gnosis, can give it back the innocence that is lost in such an historical trial."[57] In this regard, the mystical becomes the social in that whenever the prophet stands in solidarity with the defenseless against the structures of injustice, he/she unavoidably enters the realm of the political.

As a prophetic mystic, Thomas Merton sought to find a balance between contemplation and social action. He believed that contemplation and action for justice had to go hand-in-hand, making him a forerunner of the modern-day emphasis on the intersection of faith and social justice. While he lived his life in deep interiority and contemplation, Merton went beyond the confines of his monastic life and engaged prophetically in the life of the people. He shared his God-experience as a prophet with the broken world through his involvement in interfaith dialogue and his powerful writings, many of which denounced the injustices within society such as violence and war, economic disparity, the breakdown of community, the nuclear arms race, racism, and ecological degradation. The following chapter will consider the forces that shaped Merton as a contemplative-prophetic mystic with a unique capacity to integrate contemplation and social action.

---

[56] Jose Porfirio Miranda, *Marx and the Bible: A Philosophy of the Critique of Oppression,* trans. John Eagles (Maryknoll, NY: Orbis Books, 1974), 57.

[57] Metz, 163.

Chapter 2

The Pilgrim Journey of Thomas Merton the Contemplative-Prophet

Thomas Merton was called to be a contemplative prophet amid the socio-political and cultural turmoil of his time. His pilgrim journey began in France and ended with his untimely death in Asia at the age of fifty-three. This chapter examines Merton's life, considering how the historical, social, cultural, educational, and spiritual forces in his environment shaped him as a contemplative-prophetic mystic with a singular capacity to integrate contemplation and social action.

Part One explores his childhood and teenage years. Part Two considers the period of his young adulthood, focusing on his years at Cambridge and Columbia and the beginning of his vocational discernment. Part Three elucidates his journey through monastic life in four phases, including, in the last phase, the deeply-felt love affair with a young nurse which helped to shape him as a monk. These phases include: 1) the basics of Cistercianism (1941-1950), 2) discernment of vocation (1951-1955), 3) his role as novice master and turn to the world (1956-1965), 4) silence, solitude, deepening of prophetic mission, falling in love, and journey to Asia (1966-1968).

1. Childhood and Teenage Years

Parents: The Shaping of an Artistic Soul

Thomas Merton was born in Prades, France, on January 31, 1915, just a few hundred miles from the battlefields of World War I, and grew up under the tragic signs of international turmoil, family tragedy, and profound social upheaval.[58] Merton's parents, Ruth Jenkins (an American) and Owen Merton (a New Zealander), were artists. As artists, they were profoundly affected by the brokenness of this world, and felt the responsibility of lifting the world from its shadows.[59] Having two artistic parents stamped Merton as an essentially artistic person who remained interested in poetry, writing, painting, and all the other arts in which he was involved. This artistic legacy was foundational to the formation of his character and spirituality.

Merton recalls that his father Owen was a man of openness, optimism, and a deep faith rooted in the doctrines of the Anglican Church. He was energetic, responsible, and integrated. He painted landscapes in the manner of the French artist Cezanne. In *The Seven Storey Mountain*, Merton describes his father's artistic vision as "sane, full of balance, full of veneration for structure, for the relations of masses and for all the circumstances that impress an individual identity on each created thing." Noting that his father was a "very good artist," Merton characterizes his vision as "religious and clean," and his paintings, therefore, as "without decoration or superfluous comment, since a religious man respects the power of God's creation to bear witness for itself."[60] Owen was an independent person who had a great passion for painting. This passion often absorbed him

---

[58] Robert Inchausti, *Thomas Merton's American Prophecy* (New York: State University of New York Press, 1998), 7.

[59] Thomas Merton, *The Seven Storey Mountain* (New York: Harcourt Brace, 1948), 3; (Hereafter cited as *SSM*). For documentation I am using passages from *SSM* but I am aware that in this book Merton is writing from a perspective that reflects his own biases regarding his parents, his former life, and his monastic vocation.

[60] Ibid.

fully in terms of time and travel, though he worked as a landscaper and a church organist in order to support his family.

Merton had fond memories of his father, particularly with regard to his own foundational faith experiences. He recounts, "The only really valuable religious and moral training I ever got as a child came to me from my father, not systematically, but here and there and more or less spontaneously, in the course of ordinary conversations." Thus, Merton's awakening to faith unfolded naturally, within the context of casual, everyday conversations with his father, which became indelibly etched on his young imagination.[61]

His mother Ruth was deeply connected to her relatives and sought close ties with people.[62] Merton recalls a portrait of his mother which showed her "as a rather slight, thin, sober little person with a serious and somewhat anxious and very sensitive face. And this corresponds with my memory of her—worried, precise, quick, critical of me, her son." At the same time, others spoke of her as "gay and very light hearted." Merton remembers her as a person seemingly full of "insatiable dreams," and as a consummate perfectionist: "perfection in art, in interior decoration, in dancing, in housekeeping, in raising children." As a perfectionist, she was worried about her first born son's imperfections, as recounted in the diary she kept throughout his infancy and childhood. Merton notes that the diary "reflects some astonishment at the stubborn and seemingly spontaneous development of completely unpredictable features in my character, things she had never bargained for: for example, a deep and serious urge to adore the gas-light in the kitchen, with no little ritualistic veneration, when I was about four."[63]

Ruth was a Quaker, and as such, not overly concerned about formal religious observance. Merton writes: "Churches and formal

---

[61] Daniel P. Horan, *The Franciscan Heart of Thomas Merton: A New Look at the Spiritual Inspiration of His Life, Thought, and Writing* (Notre Dame, Indiana: Ave Maria Press, 2014), 36, 53.

[62] Antony T. Padovano, *The Human Journey Thomas Merton: Symbol of a Century* (Garden City, N.Y.: Doubleday and Company, 1982), 8.

[63] Merton, *SSM*, 5.

religion were things to which Mother attached not too much importance in the training of a modern child, and my guess is that she thought, if I were left to myself, I would grow up into a nice, quiet Deist of some sort, and never be perverted by superstition." He notes somewhat sardonically, "Father and Mother, who were concerned almost to the point of scrupulosity about keeping the minds of their sons uncontaminated by error and mediocrity and ugliness and sham, had not bothered to give us any formal religious training."[64]

Owen was "tolerant" while Ruth was "intense," as Anthony Padovano observes. Merton inherited qualities of openness, integrity, justice, and optimism from his father, and from his mother, her resourcefulness as well as some of her frustration with the messiness of the world. Padovano remarks that "the contradictions that characterized Merton's life was already present in his parents," and could be seen, for example in their conflicting views about the appropriateness of pacifism within the calamitous context of World War One. As a Quaker, Ruth espoused pacifism, while Owen, a New Zealander with ties to Britain, felt obliged to serve. From both parents he received the capacity for work, vision, enjoyment, and the power of expression.[65]

Despite his parents' deep differences of opinion and temperament and their lack of formal religious observance, Merton had been baptized when he was less than a year old, in Prades, at the initiative of his father. However, there was not "much power, in the waters of the baptism I got in Prades, to untwist the warpings of my essential freedom, or loose me from the devils that hung like vampires on my soul," he muses.[66] It would not be until his conversion to Catholicism in 1938, at age twenty-three, that he would begin to experience new birth in the waters of baptism.

[64] Ibid., 5-9.

[65] Padovano, 3-4, 8.

[66] Merton, *SSM,* 5.

Life in New York

A year after his birth, due to the upheaval of the war, the Merton family moved from France to Douglaston, on Long Island, in New York, to be closer to Ruth's parents, Samuel Jenkins (Pop) and Martha Jenkins (Bonnemaman).[67] Merton recalls that his grandparents were Protestants, though it was not evident what type of Protestant faith they practiced. Financially, they contributed to the Zion Church, as well as to the Salvation Army. They had sent Merton's uncle, and later, his younger brother, John Paul, to the choir school of the Cathedral of St. John the Divine and had even talked briefly about sending Merton to that school. Merton remembers that "It was not the religion that they patronized, but the school and the atmosphere . . . In practice, Bonnemaman used to read the little black books of Mary Baker Eddy, and I suppose that was the closest she got to religion."[68]

Merton grew up with a negative attitude toward Catholicism through the influence of his grandfather, who was deeply suspicious of the Catholic religion and considered it dishonest, crooked, and immoral. Merton recounts that

> [t]his was one of the few things I got from Pop that really took root in my mind, and became part of my mental attitude: this hatred and suspicion of Catholics . . . . It was simply the deep, almost subconscious aversion from the vague and evil thing, which I called Catholicism, which lived back in the dark corners of my mentality with the other spooks, like death and so on. I did not know precisely what the word meant. It only conveyed a kind of a cold and unpleasant feeling.[69]

Pop's capacity to shape Merton at such a profound level was due in part to Pop's expansive and headstrong nature. He describes his grandfather as, "a buoyant and excitable man who, on docks, boats, trains, in stations, in elevators, on buses, in hotels, in restaurants,

---

[67] Horan, 36.

[68] Merton, *SSM*, 25.

[69] Ibid., 26.

used to get keyed up and start ordering everybody around, and making new arrangements, and changing them on the spur of the moment." At the same time, Merton saw him as a generous and open man who shared his goodness freely with others. Bonnemaman, on the other hand, "was just the opposite, and her natural deliberateness and hesitancy and hatred of activity always seemed to increase in proportion to Pop's excesses in the opposite direction." The more generous, open, and boisterous Pop became, the more Bonnemaman objected to his behaviors.[70] In spite of their differences, however, Merton loved them deeply (and knew that they loved one another) and experienced their support in shaping his life.

In 1918, when Merton was three years old, his brother John Paul was born. Merton found him serene and happy, without the same volatility and excessive impulses as Merton. Because John Paul was an infant, Merton did not have a friend with whom to play and enjoy life, so he engaged with an imaginary friend—Jack, and his imaginary dog, Doolittle. Merton's mother recorded in her diary that Merton was sometimes anxious about losing this imaginary friend.[71]

Merton recounts his father's struggles to maintain the family while doing as much painting as time would allow him. During the war, he worked as a landscape gardener. Owen had a passion for gardening; he loved the plants and flowers and knew how to make things grow. Later on, he took on a new career as an organist at the Episcopal Church in Douglaston, but he was not content working there because he did not get along with the minister.[72] Merton, however, was happy to be there because he could participate in the Sunday liturgy.

Ruth's and Owen's lack of interest in formal religious practice, as well as Pop's aversion to Catholicism, discouraged the young Merton from embracing the Catholic faith. Merton recalls that even as a child he had an intense desire to go to church, but his parents did not encourage him in this direction. He recounts an incident which

---

[70] Ibid., 6-7.

[71] Ibid., 8.

[72] Ibid., 12.

possibly took place on Easter Sunday, 1920, in Bermuda, which brought this desire into sharp relief.

> From across the fields, and beyond the red farmhouse of our neighbor, I could see the spire of St. George's church, above the trees. The sound of the church bells came to us across the bright fields. I was playing in front of the house, and stopped to listen. Suddenly, all the birds began to sing in the trees above my head, and the sound of birds singing and church bells ringing lifted up my heart with joy.[73]

In this burst of joy, he exclaimed, "Father, all the birds are in their Church," and expressed his wish to be in the church that very moment. Owen told him it was too late by that time and that they would go some other Sunday.

On the other hand, even though they did not encourage him to grow in faith or formal religious practice, Merton's parents emphasized his education at home. Seeking to develop Merton's full intellectual capacity, Ruth introduced a progressive educational method she had found in a magazine. It consisted of books, charts, a desk and blackboard, and was designed to prepare a child to excel at a very early age. "The idea," Merton quips, "was that the smart modern child was to be turned loose amid this apparatus, and allowed to develop spontaneously into a midget university before reaching the age of ten."[74]

The only significant religious experience Merton could remember at this age was participating in Sunday liturgy at the Episcopal Church in Douglaston in 1921, where his father worked as a musician. Since at that time his mother had been admitted to the hospital, Merton made use of the chance to visit the church on Sundays. He recalls the details of the experience: the shape of the Old Zion church, the procession that came out of the sacristy, the choir members dressed in black and white, led by a cross, and the "stained glass windows up behind the altar."[75] He recalls the lectern, which had

---

[73] Ibid., 10.

[74] Ibid.

[75] Ibid., 13.

the shape of an eagle with outspread wings, on which rested a huge Bible. He describes the American flag near the lectern, the lighting of the candles on the altar, the taking up of the collection, the singing of hymns and the musical organ played by his father. Looking back on this time, Merton was profoundly grateful for receiving that much religious experience in his childhood. He would come to conclude that standing together with others to acknowledge a "common dependence upon God" was a fundamental law of human nature, inscribed in one's "very essence," and as much a part of one "as the desire to build houses and cultivate the land and marry and have children and read books and sing songs."[76]

Merton remembers fondly his paternal grandmother's visit from New Zealand. She taught him to pray the "Our Father," a prayer he never forgot though he went many years without using it. Learning this basic Christian prayer made a significant impact on Merton's spiritual life, sowing the seeds of Christian faith within him.[77]

An experience that profoundly shaped his life and spirituality was his mother's illness and death in 1921, when Merton was just six years old. Ruth prepared him to face her death through a letter she sent to him while she was in the hospital undergoing treatment. He recalls his deep sadness upon reading the letter: "It was not the grief of a child, with pangs of sorrow and many tears. It had something of the heavy perplexity and gloom of adult grief, and was therefore all the more of a burden because it was, to that extent, unnatural. I suppose one reason for this was that I had more or less had to arrive at the truth by induction." As a six-year-old child, Merton did not feel the urge to pray for her simply because did not know how to pray at that age. Twenty years would pass before Merton, having become a Catholic, would think to pray for his mother.[78] The loss of his mother haunted him throughout his life. As I will illustrate in Chapter Four, prior to his entry into the monastery, he had difficulties relating to

---

[76] Ibid.

[77] Ibid., 9.

[78] Ibid., 14-15.

women, perhaps reflecting his experience that his mother was distant from him.

After the death of his mother, Merton never really had a permanent home. As a wandering artist, Owen was away much of the time, or, taking Merton with him, moved frequently in pursuit of artistic opportunity and inspiration. Merton was constantly moving back and forth between his grandparents' home in Douglaston and the various places his father happened to settle for his work.[79] Though he enjoyed the freedom of traveling with his father, he was ultimately without the roots of a material home as well as spiritual grounding in his life. This constant movement created a sense of exclusion, exile, restlessness, and insecurity in Merton, leaving him with a simultaneous longing for home and a sense of strangeness and lack of belonging wherever he went.[80]

Life in France

Two years after the death of his mother, Merton had "more or less acclimatized," to living in Douglaston with Pop, Bonnemaman, and John Paul. In these two years, Merton was able to remain in one place, forming a stable pattern of activities and friendships. This engendered in him a sense of security which had been sorely lacking in his life to that point. Shannon comments that "stability (which would be one of the vows he would one day take as a monk) was something very attractive to him at this point in his life."[81]

When Owen, now a successful artist, returned from abroad and suddenly announced that he and Merton were to move to France, the ten-year-old Merton thus initially resisted the move with arguments and tears.[82] In spite of Merton's resistance, however, he and Owen departed for France on August 22, 1925, while John Paul remained behind with the grandparents in Douglaston. In his own way, Owen

[79] Inchausti, 8.

[80] Padovano, 9.

[81] William H. Shannon, *Silent Lamp*: *The Thomas Merton Storey* (New York, NY: Crossroad Publishing Company, 1992), 34. (Hereafter cited as *SL*).

[82] Merton, *SSM*, 29.

transmitted a solid sense of faith to his son. Merton observed that even in France, Owen never ceased to be a religious person, and reminded Merton "to pray, to ask God to help us, to help him paint, to help him have a successful exhibition, to find us a place to live."[83]

Though he had initially resisted his father's decision to settle in France, Merton would soon come to rejoice in the land of his birth: "France, I am glad I was born in your land, and I am glad God brought me back to you, for a time, before it was too late." He felt proud of being born in France, calling it "the fountain of the intellectual and spiritual life of the world."[84] They settled in St. Antonin, a city dominated by the church in the middle of the medieval town. Merton recalls: "Everywhere I went, I was forced by the disposition of everything around me, to be always at least virtually conscious of the church." For him, the centrality of the church, and the heavenward reach of its steeple, unified and imparted meaning to the entire landscape and seemed to draw all created things to their source in God. Reflecting back on his experience of St. Antonin two decades later, he declares, "Oh, what a thing it is, to live in a place that is so constructed that you are forced, in spite of yourself, to be at least a virtual contemplative! Where all day long your eyes must turn, again and again, to the House that hides the Sacramental Christ!"[85]

The move from New York to St. Antonin marked a significant milestone in Merton's life. Shannon speculates that it is here in St. Antonin that Merton's spiritual journey, which culminated in Gethsemani, truly began. Shannon writes, "He had come to a place where quiet, solitude, and a slower pace of life could begin to nurture in him the inner springs of a spirituality as yet unrecognized." Owen planned to settle in France with Merton. In 1925 he purchased a piece of land on the slopes of a large hill and started to build a beautiful little stone house with a medieval window and fireplace and

---

[83] Ibid., 33.

[84] Ibid., 30-31.

[85] Shannon, *SL* 36; Merton, *SSM*, 37.

a surrounding garden, though they never had a chance to inhabit the house, as they moved to England in the spring of 1928.[86]

In France, Merton's schooling was arranged with the Lycée Ingres at Montauban. In the beginning, he struggled to fit in with his schoolmates, and was bullied and beaten.[87] This was a dark period of his life. As he recounts, "I knew for the first time in my life the pangs of desolation and emptiness and abandonment."[88] Merton encountered many realities which frightened him at Montauban, as he describes in *My Argument with the Gestapo:* "I am afraid of the cold walls of the corridors in the Lycée . . . the gravel in the playgrounds . . . the sickly smell of the blossoming acacias in the spring . . . the sound of the harsh Church bells . . . [and] the rain that rained all winter . . . carrying away trees and dead cattle." Shannon remarks that, if "St. Antonin was called the place of virtual contemplation, of presence, Montauban and its Lycée are the place of abandonment, of absence, of darkness."[89]

While at the Lycée, he gained mastery of the French language. In addition, he became involved with a group of young intellectuals and began to write novels and essays. Nevertheless, the Lycée had represented a period of deep darkness and desolation for Merton. In 1928, Owen returned to St. Antonin from England after one of his exhibits in London, collected his son from the Lycée, and announced that they would be moving straightaway to England. In that moment, Merton felt the prison walls crumbling around him—he was finally freed from the hated Lycée. Feeling as though chains had been struck from his hands, he declared: "How the light sang on the brick walls of the prison whose gates had just burst open before me. . . .my escape from the Lycée was, I believe, providential." Though he

[86] Ibid., 59-60.

[87] Merton recalls that "they began to kick me, and to pull and twist my ears, and push me around, and shout various kinds of insults. I learned a great deal of obscenity and blasphemy in the first few days, simply by being the direct or indirect object of so much of it." Shannon, *SL*, 36, 49, 59-60.

[88] Merton, *SSM*, 49.

[89] Shannon, *SL*, 40; Thomas Merton, *My Argument with the Gestapo* (New York: New Directions, 1968), 205.

looked forward to England with great joy, he left France with a sense of sadness and regret that "we never lived in the house that Father built."[90]

Studies at Oakham School

Merton was enrolled in Oakham School in the autumn of 1929. During the three years of his studies there, he faced various experiences which indelibly shaped his life and spirituality, including his studies in the public school, the illness and the death of his father, the visit of the Jenkins family with John Paul, in which Merton's financial future was discussed, the guardianship of Dr. Tom Izod Bennett after Owen's death, and, after graduation from Oakham, his visit to Rome. Merton reflects on his development at Oakham:

> In this quiet back-water, under the trees full of rooks, I was to spend three and a half years getting ready for a career. Three and a half years were a short time: but when they were over, I was a very different person from the embarrassed and clumsy and more or less well-meaning, but interiorly unhappy fourteen-year-old who came there with a suitcase and a brown felt hat and a trunk and a plain wooden tuck-box.[91]

As Merton engaged in his studies, his teachers, especially the headmaster of the school, Frank C. Doherty, recognized his extraordinary gifts. Realizing Merton's potential, Doherty allowed him to take the modern language program according to his interest, while following the classics curriculum. His intellectual curiosity and capacity were incomparable. John Barber, a native of Oakham and a classmate of Merton, remarked that "he had a brain that was bigger than the curriculum."[92] Merton shared his ideas through articles, essays and novels.

In 1930, Pop and Bonnemaman, along with John Paul, came to England to visit Owen, who by this time was seriously ill. At this time, they discussed Merton's (and John Paul's) financial affairs and

---

[90] Merton, *SSM*, 52, 60; Shannon, *SL*, 42.

[91] Shannon, *SL* 49; Merton, *SSM*, 68.

[92] Shannon, *SL* 50.

the future of Merton's studies.[93] Merton realized that once again he would encounter tragedy in his life, as his father's health was deteriorating rapidly due to a malignant brain tumor. In 1931, Owen Merton died, leaving Merton and John Paul orphans. Merton recalls with great pain and deep affection the relationship he had with his father: "here was a man with a wonderful mind and a great talent and a great heart: and what was more, he was the man who had brought me into the world, and had nourished me and cared for me and had shaped my soul and to whom I was bound by every possible kind of bond of affection."[94]

After Owen died, Tom Bennett—Owen's long-time friend and physician, and Merton's godfather—was put in charge of Merton's finances and studies. Merton stayed with Bennett and his wife in London. Bennett treated Merton as a "grown-up," even though he was still a teenager, and profoundly influenced his intellectual and personal development during this period of his life.

The death of his father had left him with an unbearable sadness, and devoid of any sense of God. He was depressed and confused, without grounding or internal compass. As Shannon describes it, "There were no moorings to tie his ship to and no rudder to direct it, and he was on the open sea."[95] Reflecting back on this painful period of his life, Merton writes,

> It was in this year . . . that the hard crust of my dry soul finally squeezed out all the last traces of religion that had ever been in it. There was no room for God in that empty temple of dust and rubbish . . . And so I became the complete twentieth-century man . . . a true citizen of my own disgusting century: the century of poison gas and atomic bombs... a man with veins full of poison, living in death.[96]

Without guidance, direction, faith, or stability, his life was in a downward spiral. Nevertheless, his rediscovery of a favorite childhood

---

[93] Ibid., 51.

[94] Merton, *SSM*, 84.

[95] Ibid.

[96] Shannon, *SL*, 54; Merton, *SSM*, 85.

poet, William Blake, would prove to be a stabilizing influence for him, and key to his development as an artist and a visionary. Blake's artistic vision was a conduit of grace and hope for Merton, stirring in him the awakenings of faith.

In 1932, he completed the higher certificate examination in French, German and Latin. The final semester was spent in preparation for a scholarship to Cambridge. At the end of his studies at Oakham, Merton experienced a sense of freedom, feeling that he could "stretch out his hands," and achieve what he wanted in life. He realized that he was becoming an adult.[97]

Merton looked back on his experience at Oakham with profound affection for and gratitude to the institution. He appreciated the simplicity, the sincerity, and the genuineness of his teachers and schoolmates. Though there were moments he felt loneliness, he was able to convert those times into solitude. Merton gradually began to enjoy silence, solitude, peace and quiet—with himself and with nature.

2. Young Adulthood and the Stirrings of Vocation

Rome

Merton won the scholarship to Cambridge for which he had applied in his last semester at Oakham. In the fall of 1933, at age 18, he entered Clare College, Cambridge. Before beginning Cambridge, however, he traveled to Italy. In Rome, Merton began to encounter the Christian past in the great churches, with their impressive frescos and mosaics. He was deeply attracted to the Byzantine mosaics and began to frequent the churches and chapels where they were housed. He was suddenly struck by the reality that the Church represented Christ: the "Christ of the Apocalypse, the Christ of the Martyrs, the Christ of the Fathers . . . the Christ of St. John, and of St. Paul, and of St. Augustine and St. Jerome and all the Fathers—and of the Desert Fathers. It is Christ God, Christ King. . . "[98] Merton recounts

---

[97] Shannon, *SL*, 60.

[98] Edward Rice, *The Man in the Sycamore Tree: The Good Times and Hard Life of Thomas Merton* (Garden City, New York: Doubleday & Company, Inc.

that it was in Rome, in gazing upon the ancient frescoes and mosaics, that his conception of Christ was formed. "It was there," he writes, that "I first saw Him, Whom I now serve as my God and my King, and Who owns and rules my life."[99]

He recalls a significant incident which took place in Rome. While he was in his room in the pension at night, Merton felt the presence of his late father, communicating to him the perilous state of his soul. He recounts:

> I was overwhelmed with a sudden and profound insight into the misery and corruption of my own soul, and I was pierced deeply with a light that made me realize something of the condition I was in, and I was filled with horror at what I saw, and my whole being rose up in revolt against what was within me, and my soul desired escape and liberation and freedom from all this with an intensity and an urgency unlike anything I had ever known before. And now I think for the first time in my whole being I really began to pray—praying not with my lips and my intellect and my imagination, but praying out of the very roots of my life and my being, and praying to God, the God that I had never known, to reach down towards me out of his darkness and to help me to get free of the thousand terrible things that held my will in their slavery.[100]

However this experience may be interpreted, either by Merton himself or his readers, one thing was quite certain to Merton as he looked back upon the event thirteen years later: "this was really a grace, and a great grace." Shannon speculates that the monk writing his autobiography may have been "projecting onto the young man [in Rome] the moral lapses that would occur later that year at Clare College, Cambridge."[101] Whatever the significance of the event, one thing was certain: Merton was driven to prayer and surrender to God in a way he had never experienced before, though this initial

---

1970), 18-19.

[99] Merton, *SSM*, 100.

[100] Ibid., 111.

[101] Shannon, *SL*, 70.

awakening to faith would subside for a time, and give way to a life of debauchery, as he "swept into the dark, sinister atmosphere of Cambridge."[102]

Cambridge

After his unforgettable voyage to Rome in October 1933, Merton proceeded to New York for summer vacation, and returned to England for his freshman year at Clare College, Cambridge. Though Clare was considered one of the most beautiful colleges at Cambridge, for Merton, it was a very dark period in his life. Merton's study there was short-lived: after one year, he left the college in disgrace and despair.

During his time there, he lacked concentration and commitment to his studies. He fathered a child illegitimately, participated in a mock crucifixion at a drunken fraternity party, and lost his academic scholarship.[103] Shannon sums up Merton's disastrous year at Cambridge:

> It was as if the lack of any real guidance in his youth and the loneliness that had set him apart almost from his childhood caught up with him. . . he was frightened at what seemed to be a life without meaning or purpose. He knew he was drifting. He could choose either to turn his life about or to squeeze out of life all the pleasures he could get. . . he spent more time at the Lion Inn and the Red Cow Bar than he did his studies. He read Freud and decided that sexual repression was unhealthy. Drinking and womanizing aptly describe all too much of his time at Clare. His sexual drives, unaccompanied by any sense of their true human meaning, led to disaster, not just for him but for the unmarried woman who bore his child.[104]

---

[102] Merton, *SSM*, 118.

[103] Inchausti, 10. It is important to note here that both the mother and the child were killed in the London bombings. During this period, the fraternity parties and so forth were not as significant as was the paternity issue, which was ultimately a large part of the reason for the loss of his scholarship at Cambridge.

[104] Shannon, *SL*, 73.

He was emotionally crushed, hopeless and guilt-ridden. He had reached the nadir of his existence, and at this point, he had "touched bottom," morally, spiritually, and academically.[105]

In 1965, Merton, reflecting back on his time at Cambridge, writes, "There were whole seasons of insecurity, largely when I was under twenty-one and followed friends who were not really my own kind." He speaks of a deep regret at "my lack of love, my selfishness, and glibness which covered a profound shyness and an urgent need for love. My glibness with girls who after all did love me, I think, for a time. My fault was my inability to believe it and my efforts to get complete assurance and perfect fulfillment."[106]

The news of Merton's loose living at Clare College reached his guardian, who confronted Merton and asked for an account of his shameful comportment. With his scholarship to Cambridge cancelled, Merton left England for New York, advised in no uncertain terms by Bennett not to return. He was shattered and acutely aware of his brokenness. Moreover, he was not clear where he was headed. The Europe he left behind in November 1934 "was a sad and unquiet continent, full of forebodings." When Merton got back to the United States, though freed from his entanglements at Cambridge, he was spiritually and morally adrift.

Columbia

Merton entered Columbia University in January 1935. With the help of many inspiring people, he flourished at Columbia. "The lights seemed to go on in his life," writes Shannon.[107] Some of the factors which played a vital role in Merton's intellectual, moral, personal, and spiritual growth at Columbia included the building of good relationships with friends and faculty, the death of his grandparents,

---

[105] Ibid., 75. Despite the darkness of Cambridge, Merton notes one grace—his encounter with the greatest of Catholic poets—Dante Alighieri. Merton, *SSM*, 122-123; See also Shannon, *TME,* 424.

[106] Thomas Merton, *Vow of Conversation,* edited and with a Preface by Naomi Stone (New York: Farrar, Straus and Giroux, 1988), 140-194; cited in Shannon, *SL*, 76.

[107] Shannon, *SL,* 84.

his conversion to Catholicism, his encounter with Brahmachari, and his devotion to Mary.

During his time at Columbia, he forged lasting friendships with several prominent thinkers, including Robert Lax, Daniel Walsh, Edward Rice, and Mark Van Doren, among others. In his book *Love and Living*, penned in 1965, he reflects on his time at Columbia:

> The thing I always liked best about Columbia was the sense that the university was on the whole glad to turn me loose in its library, its classrooms, and among its distinguished faculty, and let me make what I liked out of it all. I did. And I ended up being turned on like a pinball machine by Blake, Thomas Aquinas, Augustine, Eckhart, Coomaraswamy, Traherne, Hopkins, Maritain, and the sacraments of the Catholic Church.[108]

One of the faculty members who had a profound influence on Merton at Columbia was his English literature professor Mark Van Doren. Van Doren's pedagogy made a great impact on students, teaching them to think critically in response to his thought-provoking questions. His classes were educational in the truest sense of the word in that he did not impose his ideas on the students, but in communicating to them his own vital interest in things, equipped the students to form their own thoughts and draw their own conclusions. Van Doren persuaded Merton that "by age eighteen or nineteen, one finally has had enough experiences to read literature profitably."[109] Deeply inspired by Van Doren, and more broadly, life at Columbia, Merton blossomed, throwing "himself into his writing and into his studies—becoming the editor of the yearbook, a member of all the literary clubs, an athlete on the track team, and a brother of the Alpha Delta Phi fraternity."

During this time of literary fecundity and personal growth, however, Merton faced yet another great loss in his life. In 1936,

---

[108] Thomas Merton, *Love and Living*, ed. Naomi Burton Stone and Patrick Hart (New York: Farrar, Straus and Giroux, 1979), 13; Shannon, "Columbia University," *TME*, 69.

[109] Inchausti, 12; See also Michael Mott, *The Seven Mountains of Thomas Merton* (Boston: Houghton Mifflin, 1984), 98.

his grandfather died. Pop had made a great impact on Merton's life. Merton's relationship with Pop was genuine, open and free. As Merton remained near the coffin of his grandfather, without any compulsion, he spontaneously knelt down and prayed for him. A year later, in 1937, Merton lost his grandmother. As he faced the death of Bonnemaman, who by now was seriously ill and suffering deeply, he uttered a prayer "for her to live, although in some sense it was obviously better that she should die. . . I was saying within myself: 'You Who made her, let her go on living.'" As it happened, she lived for several more weeks. Merton later expressed hope that during this time, God was imparting grace to her for the salvation of her soul. At this point, though he had not yet embraced an explicit Christian faith, he looked to the "supreme Principle of life" itself, as life was for him "the only good." He muses: "And now twice I had prayed, though I continued to think I believed in nothing."[110]

In February 1937, Merton was captured by Etienne Gilson's work *The Spirit of Medieval Philosophy,* which he had espied in the window of Scribner's Bookshop in Manhattan. Merton was attracted by the title of the book but was disappointed to discover that the book had the approval of the church authorities, as indicated in small print on the first page by the "Nihil Obstat . . . Imprimatur." He was immediately dismayed and disgusted, feeling he had been cheated, as he was not eager to read any book associated with the Catholic hierarchy. Though as an aesthete, he was naturally drawn to Catholic culture, he had always been afraid of the Catholic Church. Despite his repugnance, Merton read the book rather than disposing of it as he was tempted to do. Gilson's book enabled Merton to discover a new and palatable concept of God, that of *aseitas*: "God exists by reason of Himself . . . is Being itself," as the pure act of existence.[111]

Before reading this book, Merton had not possessed an adequate understanding of what Christians meant by the concept of "God." Prior to this time, he had always presumed the Christian God to be "a noisy and dramatic and passionate character, a vague, jealous,

[110] Merton, *SSM,* 160.

[111] Ibid., 171-172.

hidden being, the objectification of all [Christians'] own desires and strivings and subjective ideals." He pondered, "How could this fatuous, emotional thing be without beginning and without end, the creator of all?"[112]

However, as a result of reading Gilson and discovering this concept of God, Merton "at once acquired an immense respect for Catholic philosophy and for the Catholic Church." Most importantly, however, he "recognized that faith was something that had a very definite meaning and a most cogent necessity." He began to attend church services at the Zion Episcopal Church, where his father had once worked as an organist. Furthermore, though he was attracted by the Quakers, the tradition of his mother, he was drawn much more imperatively to the Catholic Church.[113] This interest in Catholicism would intensify over the course of the year.

After graduating from Columbia in January 1938, Merton continued on there in the Master's program in English, writing a thesis entitled "Nature and Art in William Blake: An Essay in Interpretation." The writing of the thesis helped him to finally reconcile the artistic and mystical dimensions of human experience in the encounter with nature. With Blake, the thesis repudiated a rationalistic, imitative, and merely sensible understanding of art, proposing an interpretive approach to nature and art through the lens of an imaginative and sacramental vision, one which understood art "as a natural analogue of mystical experience."[114]

While in the Master's program, Merton began to recognize the stirrings of God's call in his life, and specifically, his desire to embrace Catholicism. A Hindu friend, Mahanambrata Brahmachari, though aware of Merton's spiritual quest and interest in Eastern mysticism, encouraged Merton's journey into Catholicism. "There are many beautiful mystical books written by the Christians. You should read

---

[112] Ibid., 174.

[113] Ibid., 206; See also Susan Rakoczy, "The Dynamic of Discernment in the Life of Thomas Merton," in *The Merton Annual,* A Quarterly Review, Vol. 41, No. 4 (Winter 2016): 18.

[114] Merton, *SSM,* 202.

St. Augustine's *Confessions*, and *the Imitation of Christ*," he urged. And then he repeated, "Yes, you must read those books."[115] Merton was indeed eager to read and reflect on these books and was deepening his knowledge of and desire for the Catholic faith. Later he would come to realize the wisdom of Brahmachari's advice, recognizing that a person must be "firmly grounded in his or her own religious beliefs before he or she can achieve any meaningful understanding of other religious traditions."[116]

During this time, Merton began attending daily Mass. On the first day, as he entered the Corpus Christi Church, the churches of France and Italy "flooded his memories." He recalls that "the richness and fullness of the atmosphere of Catholicism that I had not been able to avoid apprehending and loving as a child, came back to me with a rush: but now I was to enter into it fully for the first time."[117] He participated enthusiastically in the liturgy and was inspired by the sermon, but he left at the consecration with the sense that he did not belong there. Participation in the liturgy was a transformative experience for Merton. Moving around in New York, he felt that he "walked in a new world."[118] Even the ugly buildings of Columbia were transformed by the sacramental grace and power of Christ.

Merton read the biography of Gerard Manley Hopkins, and the author's debate with himself about becoming a Catholic became Merton's own struggle. Prompted by the Spirit, and inspired by Hopkins' conversion experience, Merton sought out Father George Barry Ford at Corpus Christi Church in the fall of 1938 and expressed his desire to become a Catholic. The priest prepared him for the reception of the sacraments. On November 16, 1938, Merton received the sacraments of Baptism and First Holy Communion. Recalling the day of his baptism, he writes,

> I had entered into the everlasting movement of that gravitation which is the very life and spirit of God: God's own gravitation

[115] Ibid., 198.

[116] Shannon, *SL*, 90.

[117] Ibid., 92; Merton, *SSM,* 207.

[118] Merton, *SSM*, 211.

> towards the depths of His own infinite nature, His goodness without end. And God, that center who is everywhere, and whose circumference is nowhere, finding me, through incorporation with Christ, incorporated into this immense and tremendous gravitational movement which is love, which is the Holy Spirit, loved me. And he called out to me from His own immense depths.[119]

Through the sacrament of Baptism, he grasped that God would direct his path and that he would walk under the guidance of God. He reflects that, "It was for this that Christ had died on the Cross, and for this that I was now baptized, and had within me the living Christ, melting me into Himself in the fires of His love. This was the call that came to me with my Baptism." This call summoned him to an "appalling responsibility," one which he felt unable to heed with fidelity absent a "miracle of grace." Though Baptism had opened new paths of conversion in Merton, in this first year after his baptism, he was without direction, uncertain as how to proceed in the spiritual life.[120]

Gradually, Merton came to recognize the immense power of Mary in the Christian life. He realized that Christians do not truly understand her significance as the bearer of grace and succor. Through her, grace entered the world, because she participated in the salvation of humanity. Merton declares that, "She is the Mother of Christ still, His Mother in our souls. She is the Mother of the supernatural life in us. Sanctity comes to us through her intercession. God has willed that there be no other way." Mary is the font of the wisdom, poverty, and holiness of all the saints. To know her in her hidden sanctity is to find great wisdom. Merton would come to conclude that ultimately all our sanctity depends on her maternal love. This abiding devotion to Mary would anchor his soul throughout the rest of his life, and find its ultimate expression in his Cistercian spirituality. It was the solitude, sorrow of heart, and compassion of Mary for her suffering

---

[119] Ibid., 225.

[120] Ibid., 227-229.

and abandoned Son that would indelibly shape his contemplative spirituality.[121]

Though Merton had left Cambridge in 1934 in shame, rootlessness, and spiritual darkness, he finished his time at Columbia having walked into "a new world," now a baptized Catholic cognizant of the deep stirrings of desire for the consecrated life. In October of the same year, he would recognize explicitly his desire to be a priest.

Merton's Vocational Journey

Merton's lifelong journey toward monastic vocation was the outcome of his relentless search for God. Padovano suggests that Merton's religious vocation may have begun to take root when his father Owen was on his death bed and started to draw figures of the Byzantine saints, which he had never sketched before. When Merton had visited Rome in 1932, a year after his father's death, he was deeply attracted by the beauty of the city and haunted by the Byzantine mosaics in the churches that housed them, recalling his father's artistic inspiration on his deathbed. Merton had prayed in the Church of Santa Sabina in Rome. At the Trappist monastery there, for the first time, he recognized the desire to be a Trappist monk, though he was not yet a Catholic nor even attracted to Catholicism at that point.[122] The conversion experience and call to vocation which had been awakened in Rome continued to unfold throughout his life, from St. Bonaventure to Gethsemani.

Discernment of Vocation to the Priesthood

In late 1939, Merton was living in Greenwich Village and working on the novel to which he would give the name *The Labyrinth*. By this time, his desire to be a priest had become explicit. Merton went to the Jesuit Church of St. Francis Xavier on Sixteenth Street in New York City to spend time in prayer. While he was participating in the

---

[121] Merton, *NSC*, 168-173; Thomas Merton, *The Hidden Ground of Love: The Letters of Thomas Merton on Religious Experience and Social Concerns,* ed. William H. Shannon (New York: Farrar, Straus and Giroux, 1985), 47. (Hereafter cited as *HGL*).

[122] Padovano, 15-16.

Eucharistic benediction, he felt confusion and interior probing, as well as inexplicable joy. As he gazed upon the Host on the altar, the Lord confronted him with a simple though profound question, "Do you really want to be a priest?" In that moment, Merton expressed his heart's longing: "Yes I want to be a priest, with all my heart I want it. If it is Your will, make me a priest—make me a priest." When he uttered those words, he recognized the power of the union that had been sealed between himself and God.[123]

With great anticipation, he approached Fr. Ford, the priest at Corpus Christi Church, and expressed his deep desire to be a priest in any of the religious orders. Fr. Ford advised him to become a secular priest, but Merton was not happy with this proposal. The Gospel injunction to "Give up everything to the poor and follow me!" encouraged Merton to remain firm in his resolve to embrace a religious life.[124]

Merton therefore decided to meet Daniel Walsh, whose course on Aquinas he had taken at Columbia, and with his help discerned joining the Franciscan. Walsh directed him to meet Fr. Edmund Murphy, a Franciscan priest. Murphy inquired about Merton's childhood, family, vocation, Church, sacraments, material needs, and studies, and then accepted him into the Franciscan order as a friar, with the understanding that he would enter the novitiate in the summer of 1940.[125]

Early in 1940, while he was awaiting his entry into the novitiate and teaching at the extension school at Columbia, Merton sought to grow in mental prayer by contemplating the mysteries of the life of Christ in the *Spiritual Exercises of St. Ignatius of Loyola*. Through the "composition of place," in which he sat before Jesus, Mary and Joseph in the house at Nazareth and listened to their dialogue, he recognized the dimension of venial sin. Shannon comments that "the ugliness of venial sin led him to reflect on the importance of mortification in the Christian life and brought him once again to the theme of giving up

---

[123] Merton, *SSM*, 255; Shannon, *SL*, 104.

[124] Shannon, *SL,* 105-106.

[125] Merton, *SSM,* 105, 265.

everything." Merton had never before thought about the existence of venial sin in his life.[126] His resolve to renounce everything and take up the cross and follow Jesus Christ took on new urgency at this time in his life.

In the summer of 1940, as he eagerly anticipated his entry into the novitiate, Merton was suddenly struck with severe "scruples." He decided to return to New York City from Olean, where he was living on campus for the summer, and share with Fr. Murphy his past life at Cambridge.[127] After Merton shared the troubled moments of his history, the Franciscans refused to accept him into the novitiate. Merton recalls that with a broken heart, he prayed, "My God, please take me into the monastery. But anyway, whatever You want, Your will be done." Merton struggled to accept this experience as God's will and reflected painfully on his rejection by Fr. Murphy:

> He saw that I was only a recent convert, not yet two years in the Church. He saw that I had an unsettled life, and that my vocation was by no means sure, and that I was upset with doubts and misgivings. The novitiate was full, anyway. And when a novitiate is crammed with postulants year after year it is time for somebody to reflect about the quality of the vocations that are coming in. When there is such a crowd, you have to be careful that a few who are less desirable do not float in on the tide with the rest. . .[128]

Heartbroken at not being allowed to continue in the Franciscan way of life, Merton went to confession to share his struggles. However, the cold and unsympathetic confessor did not understand his brokenness and pain, and completely misunderstood Merton's plight. He "began to tell me in very strong terms that I certainly did not belong in the monastery, still less the priesthood and, in fact, gave me to understand that I was simply wasting his time and

---

[126] Thomas Merton, "Perry Street Journal," Unpublished manuscript (St. Bonaventure, N.Y.; St. Bonaventure University Library, 1940), 274-75; cited in Shannon, *SL*, 107.

[127] Horan, 69.

[128] Ibid., 297.

insulting the Sacrament of Penance by indulging my self-pity in his confessional." Merton recalls his utter devastation after the incident: "I was completely broken in pieces. I could not keep back the tears . . . so I prayed before the Tabernacle and the big stone crucified Christ above the altar." At this dark moment, Merton concluded, "I must no longer consider that I had a vocation to the cloister."[129] He resolved that if all the doors to the cloister were closed he would serve the Church in the capacity of a layman. Having surrendered to what he perceived as God's will, Merton moved to St. Bonaventure University in Olean to teach English.

From St. Bonaventure to Gethsemani

St. Bonaventure played a significant role in Merton's life though it was for a brief period, a time of transition and discerning of vocation. He recalls that this was one of the "happiest periods" of his life. God had a plan for him and was leading him on a necessary path to realizing that plan.[130] He was deepening his spiritual life through devotion to the Blessed Sacrament, spiritual readings, the Stations of the Cross, the Divine Office, daily liturgy, and meditation. Though he was engaged in teaching English Literature, he was living a semi-monastic life during this time. He gave up all comforts and pleasure-seeking, including drinking, smoking, gambling, and movies, and rejected all the books he considered detrimental to his moral and spiritual well-being. In so doing, he began to enjoy a deep sense of peace, freedom, and joy. As he recounts,

> My will was in order, my soul was in harmony with itself and with God, though not without battle, and without cost . . . there was in me the profound, sure certitude of liberty, the moral certitude of Grace, of union with God, which bred peace that could not be shattered or overshadowed by any necessity to stand armed and ready for conflict. And this peace was all-rewarding. It was worth everything. And every day it brought me back to Christ's

---

[129] Ibid., 298.

[130] Thomas Merton, *The Road to Joy: Letters to New and Old Friends,* ed. Robert E. Daggy (New York: Farrar, Straus and Giroux, 1990), 298; cited in Shannon, *SL*, 111.

> altars, and to my daily Bread, that infinitely holy and mighty and secret wholesomeness that was cleansing and strengthening my sick being through and through, and feeding with His infinite life, my poor shredded sinews of morality.[131]

During this period, itwas the teaching of the literature of the Middle Ages to ninety sophomores that brought him the deepest satisfaction and sense of wholeness with regard to his work.

During Holy Week of 1941, Merton visited the monastery at the abbey of Our Lady of Gethsemani, near Bardstown, Kentucky. He found in this place a profound peace and joy in the deep silence, austerity, and prayer with the monks. According to Shannon, "It was like a lover finding his beloved after years of futile searching . . . an emotional and spiritual high all the while he was there."[132]After the retreat, while preparing to leave the monastery, he was already longing to return: "I desire only one thing: to love God. Those who love Him, keep his commandments. I only desire to do one thing: to follow His will. I pray that I am at least beginning to know what that may mean. Could it ever possibly mean that I might someday become a monk in this monastery?"[133] Merton's life had been irrevocably transformed by this experience at Gethsemani.

On November 28, 1941, after much prayer and discernment with regard to the direction of his life, he met Fr. Philotheus and shared his strong desire to become a Trappist monk. Philotheus advised Merton to go to Gethsemani for the Christmas vacation and to share his whole story with the abbot. With gratitude and joy, Merton sang a "Te Deum of thanks and praise" and returned to his room. Unable to sleep, he lay pondering his future, which he fervently hoped would lie in Gethsemani, where time would for him essentially stop and life would move to the interior: "In four weeks, with God's grace, I may be sleeping on a board! And there will be no more future—not in the world, not in geography, not in travel, not in change, not in variety,

---

[131] Merton, *SSM*, 305.

[132] Shannon, *SL*, 112.

[133] Thomas Merton, *The Secular Journal of Thomas Merton* (New York: Farrar, Straus and Cudahy, 1959), 203.

conversations, new work, new problems in writing, new friends—none of that, but a far better progress, all interior and quiet!!!"[134]

At the beginning of December, he also received a letter from the draft board, advising him that his prior exemption from the draft would no longer be valid in the face of the escalating tensions of war. With a new sense of urgency, he decided to leave early for Gethsemani, and closed the chapter of his life at St. Bonaventure with great haste. On December 9, 1941, Merton took the evening train and began his journey toward Gethsemani, hoping fervently to begin a new life in the Trappist monastery as a monk. "Mile after mile," he reminisces, "my desire to be in the monastery increased beyond belief. I was all together absorbed in that one idea." On December 10, Brother Matthew opened the gate to him, asking, "This time have you come to stay?"[135]

3. Monastic Journey: Four Phases

Merton saw the monk as "a seeker of God," who has given up everything to possess God. He was inspired by the early Christian monks who withdrew from the world to the deserts of Egypt and Syria to seek deep communion with God. They considered "prayer, sacrifice and being alone" the best ways to seek God. Similarly, Merton considered the goal of monastic life to be "praise and love of God," in deep silence and solitude.[136]

Merton's monastic life may be divided into four phases. The first phase extends from his entrance into the Abbey of Gethsemani in December 1941 to 1949, when he took his final vows, published his autobiography, and was ordained a priest; the second from 1950-1955, as the master of the scholastics; the third phase 1955-1965 as novice master in the monastery; and the fourth phase from 1965-1968, which includes his life at the hermitage, his journey to Asia, and his death.

---

[134] Thomas Merton, "St. Bonaventure Journal," Unpublished Manuscript, St. Bonaventure University Library (St. Bonaventure: New York); Cited in Shannon, in *SL*, 117.

[135] Ibid., 371.

[136] Shannon, "Gethsemani: A Life of Praise," *TME*, 175.

3.1 A New Life at Gethsemani (1941-1949)

A new door was opened for Merton at Gethsemani in 1941 as he began his monastic life. Shannon describes Merton's arrival at Gethsemani:

> Merton arrived at Gethsemani on December 10, 1941. The first three days he spent in the monastery Guest House, while the decision was being made whether or not to accept him. Two days later, on December 13, the feast of St. Lucy, he and another postulant were summoned to Father Abbot's office. He told them that they would make the community better or worse. What they did would have an influence—for good or bad—on others. Admonishing them that the names of Jesus and Mary should always be on their lips, he extended his hand that they might kiss his ring, and then he blessed them. Now accepted at Gethsemani, they entered into the cloister.[137]

Father Abbot Dom Frederic Dunne officially welcomed him in an attitude of openness and generosity. This was a decisive moment in Merton's life. As he began the monastic journey, the thought of newness was very much in his mind, just as the experience of going to Mass for the first time at Corpus Christi Church had prompted him to say: "All I know is that I walked in a new world."[138] In keeping with the significance of monks leaving the world, a new name was given to Merton: Louis, which means "light." Merton reflects on the significance of entering the monastery in the time of Advent, the beginning of a new liturgical year, musing that one can hardly find a more propitious time to become a monk. At the beginning of the liturgical cycle, "everything that the Church gives you to sing, every prayer that you say in and with Christ in His Mystical body is a cry of ardent desire for grace, for help, for the coming of the Messiah, the Redeemer."[139]

He recalls his first experience of encountering his novice master: "Father Master was full of a most impressive simplicity and gentleness and kindness and we began to get along together very well from that

[137] Shannon, *SL,* 128.

[138] Merton, *SSM,* 221; Shannon, *SL,* 129.

[139] Ibid., 379.

hour." He asked Merton a few questions about his capacity to sing, his fluency in French, his reason for becoming a Cistercian, whether he had read the Life of St. Bernard, and about his baptism. After the interview, the father master showed Merton and the other postulant the way to the novitiate chapel and together they prayed before the Blessed Sacrament.[140] Merton experienced the goodness and kindness of the Lord through his Novice Master and felt welcomed and accepted as a new member of the monastery.

Merton came to the monastery occupied with the crucially important business of finding out God's will. He entered as a talented young man: a voracious reader, a poet, artist, musician, and especially, a gifted writer. As he relates, "I brought all the instincts of a writer with me into the monastery, and I knew that I was bringing them, too." However, he had entered thinking to "give up everything . . . for the love of God and use it in the service of God. Shannon speculates that this "everything" must have included writing.[141] However, his superiors encouraged him to continue writing. Merton's writing talents connected him with the world he had left behind. The monastic life provided Merton the context in which he produced some of the great spiritual literature of the twentieth century.

Moreover, it was in the process of writing itself that he grew into monkhood. Patrick Hart and Jonathan Montaldo explain the paradoxical nature of this process:

> Merton became a monk by writing about becoming a monk. He allowed the form of his particular monastic vocation to reveal itself to him in sequences of experience paradoxical to his readers but holding for him a dark clarity. He wrote about silence to become silent. He wrote about his being lost so that God would find him quickly. He hid himself from the world by fully disclosing himself to it.[142]

---

[140] Ibid., 373-379.

[141] Shannon, *SL*, 130.

[142] Patrick Hart and Jonathan Montaldo, ed., *The Intimate Merton: His Life from His Journals* (New York: Harper Collins Publishers, 1995), xii.

Merton wrote on contemplation because he lived the contemplative life. In an attitude of contemplation, he accepted the challenges and blessings of seeking God, which laid the foundation for his monastic life.

Learning the Cistercian Way of Life

Merton lived as a monk in the Abbey of Our Lady of Gethsemani from December 10, 1941, until his death near Bangkok on December 10, 1968. During the first phase of his monastic life, he was prepared for the priesthood and was ordained on May 26, 1949. When he entered the monastery, he had a limited knowledge of the monastic life. His mind was centered only on the Trappist motto, "God Alone," which was painted over the door of the entrance to the old guest quarters in Gethsemani.[143] He was drawn by the simplicity and austerity of the Cistercian way of life. In a letter to his closest friends composed two weeks after he entered, he writes, "This is the one place where everything makes sense. . . . Everything that was good when I was a kid, when I was in England, when I was anywhere, has been brought back to life here." He noted that the things failing to promote human growth, such as "pride, vanity, arguments, selfishness, ambition, showing off," are not welcomed in the monastery. In a letter to Lax, Merton speaks of the sweetness of his life at Gethsemani: "It is very good and sweet to be occupied with God only, and to sit simply in His presence and shut up and be healed by the mere fact God likes to be in your soul." At the same time, this immersion into God's healing love and presence has relational implications in that love of God and neighbor cannot be separated. Thus, one begins to love others to the greatest extent possible through one's own actions, and to desire their salvation.[144]

In preparation to be a monk, Merton was introduced into a lifestyle that is commonly called "life under rule" (*vita regularis*). One day, Father Abbot explained to Merton that a monk in Gethsemani should expect "the Cross, sickness, contradictions, troubles, sorrows,

---

[143] Rice, 54.

[144] Ibid., 55-62.

humiliations, fasts, sufferings, and, in general, everything that human nature hates."[145] Merton accepted the rules and guidance of the monastery without any complaints. And he observed that one of the charitable acts which can be practiced in the monastery is that of "keeping the Rule as perfectly as one can, even when it seems silly, because it is the fact of everybody doing things according to the Rule that stops arguments and opposition and fights and leads people to go about quiet and happy."[146] As an aspirant, he was accompanied and instructed by a master on the basics of monastic thought, the rule of life, the cycle of prayer, and the culture of monasticism, until he was admitted to the novitiate. Merton accepted the instructions of the master with an attitude of openness and generosity.[147]

Merton recognized that at this stage, the goal of the monastic life is for the monk to grow in deep union with the Lord. In the aspirancy and novitiate, Merton was gradually growing in contemplative prayer. He recalls:

> I was hidden in the secrecy of His protection. He was surrounding me constantly with the work of His love, His wisdom and His mercy . . . sometimes I would be preoccupied with problems that seemed to be difficult and seemed to be great, and yet when it was all over the answers that I worked out did not seem to matter much anyway. . . He had worked the solution into the very tissue of my own life and substance and existence by the wise incomprehensible weaving of His providence.[148]

Merton experienced total dependency upon, and trust in the Lord amidst the realities of the monastery. A primary concern of this period in his life was to recover the "authentically contemplative character of Cistercianism." During this formative stage, he therefore engaged in an intense study of St. Bernard and other Cistercian

---

[145] Merton, *SSM,* 387.

[146] Rice, 62.

[147] Lawrence Cunningham, *Thomas Merton and the Monastic Vision* (Grand Rapids, Michigan: William B. Eerdmans Publishing Company, 1999), 25.

[148] Merton, *SSM,* 385.

fathers.[149] Merton recorded his personal experience every day of his monastic life. Hart and Montaldo explain that, "Writing a journal was Merton's way of doing a poet's 'heart work,' a scholar's 'inner work,' a monk's 'work of the cell.'" Merton desired only one thing: "solitude—to disappear into God, to be submerged in His peace, to be lost in the secret of His Face."[150] He longed for the contemplative silence that would deepen his union with God. However, at Gethsemani, "Doing things, suffering things, thinking things, making tangible and concrete sacrifices for the love of God—that is what contemplation seems to mean." He took issue with the notion of active contemplation, questioning if this was indeed a legitimate form of true contemplation.[151]

After completing the novitiate, Merton took the temporary vows and pursued his theological studies to the priesthood. Since the monks were not sent out for studies, he was tutored under a priest in the monastery "in the scholastic treatises of dogmatic and moral theology, as well as an introduction to a smattering of canon law and the other courses needed by a priest."[152] During this stage of spiritual formation, he was deepening his knowledge of the teachings of the church.

After eight years of study, inner struggles, and conflicts, Merton was ordained on May 26, 1949. In his priestly ordination, he felt he had found his true identity and destiny: "at last, I have found the place in the universe that has been destined for me by the mercy of God."[153] As a priest, he believed that Christ in the Eucharist is a visible, tangible sign of God's love. The priesthood emerged for him as the integration of his life and the sacramental expression of God's life. The power of grace in the Mass evoked in him the sense of the unity of "God's love, solitude, and society." Merton believed that

---

149 O'Connell, "Monasticism," *TME*, 300.

150 Ibid., xi, 47.

151 Merton, *SSM,* 389.

152 Cunningham, 28.

153 Merton, *The Road to Joy,* 193.

through the gift of his priesthood, he, along with every priest, shared the solitude of Christ.[154]

3.2 The Discernment of Vocation (1950-1955)

Merton's whole life consisted of growth in discernment and a continuous seeking of God's will through personal prayer, meditation, and contemplation on his spiritual, religious and psychological experience.[155] During the second phase of his monastic life, which ran from the end of 1951 to the end of 1955, Merton went through an intense process of self-reflection. The desire to seek God in deep silence, solitude, and simplicity motivated him to consider other religious orders such as the Carthusians or the Camaldolese, which afforded more solitude.

The Crisis in Vocation

During this second phase of his monastic life, Merton experienced intense restlessness. The Carthusian charism had been in his mind even before he joined Gethsemani, while he made the Holy Week retreat and read the Carthusian way of living the solitary life. Reading of this form of life, which he says pierced him "to the heart like a knife," he imagined, "What wonderful happiness there was, then, in the world! There were still men on this miserable, noisy, cruel earth, who tasted the marvelous joy of silence and solitude, who dwelt in forgotten mountain cells, in secluded monasteries, where the news and desires and appetites and conflicts of the world no longer reached them."[156]

Merton struggled to live in the fullness of the blessings and challenges of the monastic life at Gethsemani. The desire to join the Carthusians asserted itself as the monastery at Gethsemani was becoming more crowded and the need to live a more solitary life

---

[154] John Antony Theodore Vazhakoottathil, *Thomas Merton's Mystical Quest for the Union with God*, Dissertationen Theologische Reihe, Band 63 (Zugal: EOS Verlag Erzabtei St. Ottilien, 1993), 280-281.

[280] 281.

[155] Rakoczy, 17.

[156] Merton, *SSM,* 316.

continued to grow in him. He writes; "all the time I was in the novitiate . . . I had no temptations to leave the monastery . . . if the thought of a transfer did come to me, as it did on occasion, it did not disturb my peace of mind or my belief that God wanted me to be at Gethsemani. I did not come here for myself, but for God . . . He has put me in this place because He wants me in this place."[157] Thus, while thoughts of the Carthusians did not disturb him when he was in the novitiate, they surfaced later because of the overcrowding and busyness of Gethsemani. Shannon observes that, "the problem concerned not the reality of his monastic vocation but the place where God wanted him to live that vocation."[158]

Nevertheless, Merton was open to listening to his superiors and continued his life at Gethsemani as the master of the scholastics, guiding and accompanying the young monks "to become good Cistercians." He was committed to this responsibility to the scholastics for five years and then was appointed as the master of novices. During this time, Merton was facing the "tension between his public role and his private yearnings," while trying to keep a balance between the "vocations of writer and monk" and his longing for "solitude." His significant writings in this period include *The Sign of Jonas, The Silent Life,* and *Basic Principles of Monastic Spirituality.*[159]

Conflict with Dom James

When Merton entered the monastery at Gethsemani in 1941, Dom Frederic Dunne had been the abbot and Dom Robert the novice master. They accepted, encouraged and loved Merton and he enjoyed a good relationship with these two holy people of the monastery. Sadly, Abbot Dom Frederic died suddenly in 1948. Merton believed that Dom Frederic had helped to shape his whole monastic vocation.[160] In *The Sign of Jonas,* Merton reflects:

---

[157] Ibid., 149.

[158] Shannon, *SL,* 149.

[159] O'Connell, "Monasticism," *TME,* 301.

[160] Roger Lipsey, *Make Peace Before the Sun Goes Down* (Boston & London: Shambala, 2015), 31.

> It was he, together with my novice master, Dom Robert, who decided that I should write books. It was he who firmly and kindly encouraged me and indeed ordered me to continue, in spite of my own misgiving. . . I really think Dom Frederic was more interested in *The Seven Storey Mountain* than I was . . . He was glad that the book might find a way to convince men of the reality of God's love for us. . . He seemed to sense, in a way that I did not, something of the effect the book might have. . . I shall never forget the simplicity and affection with which he put the first copy of the book in my hand. He did not say anything. . . But I knew that he was happier about it than I could ever be. A few days later he was telling me to go on writing, to love God, to be a man of prayer and humility, a monk and a contemplative, and to help other men to penetrate the mystery of the love of God. It was the last time I ever spoke to him. . . His sympathy was deep and real. . . I don't know who was ever kinder to me.[161]

Since he had lost his own father at the age of sixteen, Merton certainly found in Dom Frederic a good-hearted, loving, understanding, and encouraging father figure. It was against this backdrop that Merton met Dom James Fox, who succeeded Dom Frederic in 1948.

In the initial stages of Merton's relationship with the new abbot, James Fox was kind and supportive. After some time, Merton began to share his struggles, pains, and self-doubts with Fox: "Dear Reverend Father, things are pretty dark. I feel as if had a hole burnt out of my heart. My soul is empty. . . Please pray for me and bless me."[162] Dom James misunderstood Merton and considered him to be a troubled person struggling to prove himself. The long-term struggle between them began with this experience.

According to Merton, there were deep-rooted problems in the monastery with Dom James Fox serving as abbot. He relates that the monastery was effectively becoming a commercial transaction

---

[161] Thomas Merton, *The Sign of Jonas* (New York: Harcourt, Brace and Company, 1953), 90-91; cited Lipsey, 31.

[162] Ibid., 32-33 (Thomas Merton, handwritten note to Dom James, June 1950).

center to increase the production of cheese, bacon, ham, and fruit cakes. It seemed that the true monastic life was being eclipsed by the commercial aspects of the enterprise. At the same time, a rigid and authoritarian imposition of the Rule affected the spiritual growth of the individuals. Edward Rice, a close friend of Merton, paints a picture of life in Gethsemani:

> The letter of the Rule was killing, and the large number of applicants and the high rate of their subsequent leaving shows the dichotomy: men were attracted by what Merton saw in monasticism and what he wrote about it, and turned away by the life as it was dictated by the abbot . . . Many novices left sooner or later, and leaving was a constant temptation for Merton himself, much as he tried to pretend it was not.[163]

In spite of Merton's conflict with Dom James, the abbot entrusted Merton with the responsibility of master of scholastics at Gethsemani in 1951. This enabled him to be the academic advisor and spiritual director for those preparing for the priesthood. As a spiritual guide to the scholastics, Merton continued to nurture their vocation even though he struggled to discern his own vocation—whether to leave or remain at Gethsemani. His writings, especially *The Sign of Jonas*, reflect wisdom and compassion for himself and the young scholastics for whom he was caring.[164] During this time his health was severely affected by the unhealthy food at the monastery (processed cheese and white bread, watery soup from leftovers, and so forth) as well as the irrational application of the Rules and the extra works. Moreover, the mystical quest to encounter the divine was causing him deep restlessness, and he experienced dryness spiritually, mentally, psychologically, and intellectually.

He longed to be a solitary monk in order to deepen his relationship with the Lord, and his interest in the Carthusian charterhouse never left him. In 1953, Merton wrote a petition which reached the Prefect of Religious in Rome, requesting to be transferred to the Carthusians,

---

[163] Rice, 77.

[164] Peter Kountz, *Thomas Merton as Writer and Monk: A Cultural Study,* 1915-1951(Brooklyn, New York: Carlson Publishing Inc., 1991), 173.

which was denied. He sometimes thought of going to Mount Athos to live a more solitary life—to be a hermit "among the colonies of Greek and Russian Orthodox monks."[165] Dom James and the Abbot General Gabriel Sortais strongly opposed Merton's transfer to another order. Therefore, in 1953, Dom James provided an unexpected opportunity for Merton to experience greater solitude. At Gethsemani, a tool shed was changed into a "hermitage" for Merton, which he named "St. Anne's." For Merton, St. Anne's "became a symbol of unity, where the whole world came together." His extended periods in complete solitude with himself, God, and the natural world were some of the most joyful and tranquil periods of his vocation, and would prove to be fertile ground for his reflections on silence and meditation.[166] "How rich for me has been the silence of this little house, which is nothing more than a toolshed," he muses.[167] It was here at St. Anne's that he penned *Thoughts in Solitude*, parts of *No Man is an Island*, and *Bread in the Wilderness.*

Recognizing the problems of the monastery, Merton wrote an essay entitled "Neurosis in Monastic Life," which unfolded the relationship between religion and the unconscious. This would lead Merton to a later conflict in 1956 with the Catholic psychoanalyst Gregory Zilboorg, who confronted Merton with the claim that, "his desire to write was evidence of an inability to commit himself to monasticism and charged him with personal inauthenticity. Merton was deeply insulted by these remarks, but agreed to undergo psychotherapy when he got back to Kentucky." The psychotherapist, James Wygal, found Merton to be an integrated person, and as a consequence of this diagnosis, Merton kept on writing with more courage and conviction than before.[168]

---

[165] Rice, 77-79.

[166] Jim Forest, *Living with Wisdom: A Life of Thomas Merton* (Maryknoll, New York: Orbis Books, 1991), 114.

[167] Thomas Merton, *A Search for Solitude: Pursuing the Monks True Life*, ed., Lawrence S. Cunningham (New York: Harper Collins Publishers, 1996), 181.

[168] Inchausti, 56.

In spite of his troubled relationship with Merton, Dom James chose him as his confessor. This would seem to suggest, as Roger Lipsey infers, a conflict in Dom James himself with regard to Merton. On the one hand, he considered Merton very discerning, insightful, and penetrating, and deemed him a good artist, poet, writer and thinker. On the other hand, he considered him emotionally out of balance, immature, impetuous, and unstable.[169] Through the difficult years with Dom James, Merton's quality of prayer life and spiritual insight deepened substantially.

Accepting God's Will

Merton was still in the process of discerning his vocation to leave Gethsemani and join another order for more solitude and silence. His desire to seek a transfer did not really subside until the fall of 1955. Dom James had consistently attempted to persuade Merton to continue his life as a monk at Gethsemani. In 1955, Merton contacted the Carthusians and the Camaldolese. He also kept in contact with Archbishop Montini (later Pope Paul VI) of Milan as well as with Monsignor Larraona, Secretary of the Sacred Congregation for Religious, regarding his desire to change orders.[170] However, unbeknownst to Merton, Dom James, realizing that Merton's departure would cause a scandal and reveal the negative side of the monastery, sought to undermine Merton's cause.[171] He considered Merton to be a "public figure" in the community of Gethsemani and "in the great world outside, both Catholic and non-Catholic." Furthermore, he was responsible for forty scholastics who respected him as a man of profound spiritual wealth. If Merton were to leave, James reasoned in a letter to Dom Jean Leclercq, "it would be a great source of scandal to our young professed and would betray them into the spirit of instability and change." In brief, from Dom James' perspective, Merton's leaving would reflect quite

[169] Lipsey, 204-205.

[170] Ibid., 156.

[171] Monica Furlong, *Merton: A Biography* (San Francisco: Harper and Row Publishers, 1980), 209.

"unfavorably" on Gethsemani, and give scandal because this famous monastic writer was leaving his monastery, one that he praised highly in *The Seven Storey Mountain*.[172] Ultimately, the decision was reached in a consensus among Montini, Larraona, Dom James, and Gabriel Sortais, discouraging Merton's request for a transfer. Montini kindly suggested that the way to know God's will for his life was through submission to his spiritual superiors.[173]

Merton formalized his submission in a letter of October 18, 1955, in which he consented to Abbot General Sortais' request to stay at Gethsemani. Merton writes that the abbot General's recommendations, joined with those of Monsignors Montini and Larraona,

> give me the most complete assurance that it would be most imprudent for me to leave Gethsemani or at least the Order and that there would not be much to gain. So I am quite sure I know God's will on this point, and I accept it willingly with the most complete peace and without regrets. This gives me the opportunity to sacrifice an appeal, a dream, an ideal, to embrace God's will in faith. Now it is over, and I promise you I will not worry you any more with this business.[174]

Merton's restlessness to leave the Cistercian order was settled when he surrendered to what he perceived to be God's will. In so doing, he came to understand that the restlessness he experienced was not directed toward joining a new the religious order but the desire to seek God in deeper solitude. The acceptance of God's will as mediated through his superiors enabled Merton to accept the new responsibility of accompanying the novices with generosity.

---

[172] Dom James Letter to Dom Jean, May 18, 1955, cited in Furlong, *Merton: A Biography*, 208.

[173] Furlong, 210-211.

[174] Thomas Merton, *School of Charity: The Letters of Thomas Merton on Religious Renewal and Spiritual Direction,* ed. Patrick Hart (New York: Farrar, Straus and Giroux, 1990), 92.

3.3 The Role of Novice Master and Turn to the World (1956-1965)

The third period of monastic life, extending from early 1956 through August 1965, corresponds to most of Merton's term as Gethsemani's novice master. It is also the time when he opened up to the world again and became involved in social and political issues. Merton's monastic writings during this period are marked by a concern with monastic reform, and enforced by the call for the renewal of religious life during the Second Vatican Council.[175]

Accompanying the novices

In 1955, Abbot James Fox appointed Merton as the master of novices at Gethsemani. Merton was always loyal to the novices as well as to the authorities. He was an inspiring novice master—intellectually, spiritually, and psychologically. He carried out this responsibility with passion and commitment.

Monica Furlong writes that his novices remembered Merton as being very human and loving in his dealings with them in the monastery. One of them recalls that "Everybody loved him. Some of the monks might think some of his ideas were wild, but he was much loved."[176] The feelings of mutual love and affection between the novices and the master were very strong. He was humorous and compelling during his lectures to the novitiate, which he often began with anecdotes about things going on in the world or in the monastery—perhaps an election, a point of social or political concern, the struggles in monastic life, or even secular examples of human love and sexuality. He related these realities to the particular subject matter he was teaching. Such subjects included contemplation, the mystical life, asceticism, the Blessed Virgin Mary, St. John's Gospel, martyrdom, the Early Fathers, Pseudo-Dionysius, St. Gregory of Nyssa, St. Maximus, St. Augustine, the Spanish mystics, the struggles

---

[175] Merton, *School of Charity*, 302.

[176] Furlong, 219.

in the spiritual direction of contemplatives, or modern psychology and how it affects the training and understanding of monasticism.[177]

Merton trained the novices according to his understanding of a true monastic spirituality. For him, the purpose of the monastic life is to abandon oneself completely to the Holy Spirit. It is a path to grow in "humility, obedience, solitude, silence, [and] prayer," in which the monk learns to renounce his own desires and will in order to live a life of freedom as a true child of God.[178]Amidst his responsibilities as a novice master, Merton was constantly seeking God through contemplation, which included contemplating the presence of God in nature, "in the hills, fields, flowers, birds and animals, the sky and the trees." In this way, Merton affirmed that in the monastic life, the monk's senses are "*educated* and elevated rather than destroyed."[179] He also encouraged the novices to continue seeking God in the movement toward chastity and wholeness. The first step on this path is the "total acceptance of one's whole being—body and soul, mind and instinct, emotions and will," in order to develop an integrated spirituality.

Merton helped the novices to discover their spiritual potentialities to be seekers of God. He had an integrated approach to life and insisted that "if our emotions really die in the desert, our humanity dies with them. We must return from the desert like Jesus or St. John, with our capacity for feeling expanded and deepened, strengthened against appeals of falsity, warned against temptation, great, noble and pure."[180] This *return from the desert* was to become one of Merton's central themes as a spiritual guide to the novices. The decision to join the Trappists was not about running away from the world but turning toward the true source of our being in God. Turning to God, a monk returns to his true self.

---

[177] Ibid., 219-220.

[178] Thomas Merton, *Basic Principles of Monastic Spirituality* (Bardstown, KY.: Abbey of Our Lady of Gethsemani, 1957), 10; cited Furlong, 230.

[179] Ibid.

[180] Thomas Merton, *Thoughts in Solitude* (New York: Farrar, Straus and Giroux, 1958), 14.

Return to the world

When Merton began his monastic life in Gethsemani in 1941, he never imagined he would return to the world. He had entered the monastery to seek God and leave the world behind. However, while remaining a monk, he would eventually return to the world he thought he had left behind forever, a world now "transfigured by his contemplative vision," bringing to it the compassion that grows out of true solitude. He saw a world influenced by a technological culture that controlled the interior freedom of human beings, and filled with men and women engulfed in delusion, not knowing themselves or what destiny awaited them.[181] As a contemplative, Merton looked at the world in compassion and love.

His re-engagement with the world was marked by a profound mystical experience which occurred in Louisville on an ordinary day in March of 1958 while he was running errands for the monastery. He recounts,

> Yesterday, in Louisville, at the corner of 4th and Walnut, suddenly I realized that I loved all the people and that none of them were, or, could be totally alien to me. As if waking from a dream—the dream of my separateness, of the 'special' vocation to be different. My vocation does not really make me different from the rest of men or put me in a special category except artificially, juridically. I am still a member of the human race—and what more glorious destiny is there for man, since the Word was made flesh and became, too, a member of the Human Race![182]

For Merton, this awakening was the catalyst for his becoming fully a man for others. It was a moment of revelation of the divine amidst the human. Merton became aware that the true meaning of being a "monk" lay in recognizing that he was merely "another member of the human race, like all the rest of them." In the mystical

---

181 Shannon, *SL,* 178.

182 Merton, *Search for Solitude,* 181-182.

insight of his oneness with the rest of humanity, he recognized his "shared responsibility for the future of human kind."[183]

On November 10, 1958, a few months after his awakening in Louisville, Merton wrote a letter to Pope John XXIII, in which he congratulated him for taking up his new responsibility as the "Vicar of Christ Our Lord," and expressed his desire to become a contemplative monk in the world in order to serve humanity in a more radical way.[184] He writes,

> It seems to me that, as a contemplative, I do not need to lock myself into solitude and lose all contact with the rest of the world; rather this poor world has a right to a place in my solitude. It is not enough for me to think of the apostolic value of prayer and penance; I also have to think in terms of a contemplative grasp of the political, intellectual, artistic and social movements in this world—by which I mean a sympathy for the honest aspirations of so many intellectuals everywhere in the world and the terrible problems they have to face. I have had the experience of seeing that this kind of understanding and friendly sympathy, on the part of a monk who really understands them, has produced striking effects among artists, writers, publishers, poets, etc., who have become my friends without my having to leave the cloister.[185]

In this letter, Merton expressed to the Holy Father his wish to form a "monastic foundation," or apostolic friendship group, which would be supported by monks and contemplatives and would include "special groups, such as writers, intellectuals, etc., into [the] house for retreats and discussions."[186] In great humility, trust and complete commitment, Merton presented this request to the Holy Father for the "salvation of souls and to the growth of the monastic contemplative life in their world."[187] The Holy Father graciously

---

[183] Bochen,"Fourth and Walnut' Experience," *TME*, 160.

[184] Merton, *HGL*, 481-482.

[185] Merton, *HGL*, 482; cited in Shannon, *SL*, 182.

[186] Merton, *HGL*, 483.

[187] Ibid.

granted Merton's request to begin the gathering of intellectuals at Gethsemani. This apostolate occupied him for the rest of life, and led to many fruitful ecumenical exchanges, and eventually, interreligious dialogue at Gethsemani. It also led to significant studies of social issues, as will be examined later.

3.4 Life in the Hermitage and Journey to Asia (1966-1968)

Merton spent the fourth phase of his monastic life in the newer hermitage—the retreat house built on Mt. Olivet at Gethsemani—from August 1965 until his departure for Asia in the fall of 1968. In the hermitage, Merton was free to seek God in complete silence and solitude and continue writing undisturbed. In the solitary life in the hermitage, he was much more deeply connected to the world outside and began to take long, quiet looks at this world.

Life in the Hermitage

The longing to deepen his union with God through silence and solitude had led him to gradually seek a more solitary life as a hermit. Merton's vision of a hermitage on the grounds of Gethsemani where he could enjoy complete silence and solitude may be traced back all the way to 1949. At that time, he had expressed the desire to construct a little chapel in the woods, "a center where one might have little retreats in solitude and silence."[188]

Merton continued to express the desire to have more time for silence and solitude. In the beginning, Dom James did not want to grant Merton permission to live as a hermit in Gethsemani. When his request was denied, Merton resolved to leave the order. However, while the ecclesiastical authorities in Rome did not grant Merton permission to join another order, they were willing to allow him to live a more solitary life in the Gethsemani woods. Thus, a separate building, built in 1960 for retreats on the grounds, was given to Merton as a hermitage. He named it St. Mary's of Carmel.[189]

In the beginning he was spending only afternoons alone in the hermitage. On March 20, 1962, Merton spent his first full day in the

[188] O'Connell, "Hermitage," *TME,* 197.

[189] Ibid., 198.

hermitage. On October 13, 1964, he received permission to sleep there, without any special restrictions, though not necessarily all the time. On December 10, 1964, he celebrated the twenty-third year of the anniversary of his entry into the monastery at Gethsemani by cooking dinner for the first time in the hermitage. And six days later he set up the daily schedule to follow after becoming a full-time hermit, returning to the monastery at midday for his private Mass and dinner but spending the rest of the day in solitude. On the feast of St. Bernard, August 20, 1965, Merton was relieved of all responsibilities in order to become a full time hermit.[190] On July 16, 1967, he celebrated the first Mass in the hermitage. He made the hermitage accessible to both friends and strangers and it became a symbol of unity and love.

As he permanently settled into the hermitage, he was participating less and less in the activities of the monastery and spending more time, in study, prayer and meditation. In his various writings, he describes the daily schedule of the hermitage: "It was a day that began with early rising long before dawn, regular prayer, periods of meditation, manual work, study, writing, and the celebration of the liturgy."[191] Living alone in the hermitage enabled him to live with the rhythm of the days and hours, and to enjoy perfect harmony with the entire creation. Describing the joys of his vocation to solitude, he writes, "To pray and work in the morning and labor and rest in the afternoon, and to sit still again in meditation in the evening when night falls upon that land and when the silence fills itself with darkness and with stars. This is a true and special vocation."[192] Merton's life in the hermitage made him a better human being, Christian, and priest, helping him to grow in deep silence and solitude, prayer, meditation, and contemplation. In the eremitic life, he became an integrated

[190] Ibid., 197-200.

[191] Cunningham, 104.

[192] Merton, *Thoughts in Solitude*, 129; cited in Daniel J. Adams, *Thomas Merton's Shared Contemplation: A Protestant Perspective* (Kalamazoo, MI: Cistercian Publications, 1979), 263.

person, equipped to serve God's people in compassion and prophetic wisdom.

Falling in Love

His great temptation during this period was to abandon eremitic and monastic life altogether because of his love for a young nurse he met during the spring of 1966. He met her while he was undergoing treatment in St. Joseph Hospital in Louisville for a back injury. She had initially come to know him through his writings. Though there was a vast age difference between them—Merton was 51 and she was 25—nothing could hinder the unfolding of their relationship. Merton expresses that, "we are terribly in love, and it is the kind of love that can virtually tear you apart . . . I do so much want to love her as we began, spiritually . . . M. is terribly inflammable, and beautiful . . .tragically full of passion and so wide open."[193] Merton laments that in his love for her, "My response has been too total and too forthright, we have admitted too much, communicated all the fire to each other and we are caught. I am not as smart or as stable as I imagined." They communicated their love for one another through a series of letters, phone calls, and frequent meetings. This romantic love affair was a revolution within Merton. As Lipsey observes, "It was his revolution and the deepest of contradictions because he entered into the relation as a vowed monk, never abandoned his religious mind and heart, and yet lived their love affair with passionate intensity."[194] On June 13, 1966, their relationship was exposed when one of the brothers of the monastery overheard their phone conversation. The brother informed Dom James, who questioned the wisdom of Merton's solitary life. Merton records this experience the next day in his journal:

> I know he is mad and is waiting to give me the devil about it, which is only natural. I have to face the fact that I have been wrong and foolish in all this. Much as I love M., I should never

[193] Thomas Merton, *Learning to Love: Exploring Solitude and Freedom*, ed. Christine M. Bochen (New York: Harper Collins Publishers, 1997), 46. (Hereafter cited as *LL*).

[194] Lipsey, 227.

> have let myself be carried away to become so utterly imprudent. But I suppose I knew that. . . Well, it is clearly over now. I called her once more (she was desolate and so was I). She said, "I had the most terrible feeling something was wrong when I was waiting for you to call . . . Will we ever see each other again . . . What will I do without you? . . . How unfair it is, even inhuman . . . but we have both anticipated this . . ."[195]

Merton acknowledged his vulnerability before Dom James, who requested that Merton sever all connections with M. On September 8, 1967, in the presence of Dom James, Merton signed a solemn commitment to live in a solitary state for the rest of his life.[196]

After ending the relationship, Merton wrote "A Midsummer Diary," which was dedicated to M. In this essay, he describes himself as a "*lover*" of Margie, "passionate, tender, vulnerable, melancholy, full of longing, lonely, confused, and anguished." The dairy also depicts Merton as a "*hermit monk,*" one who was struggling to find meaning in this "passionate love and searching for ways to reconcile love and solitude, turning his loneliness for M. into a dimension of 'general loneliness' that is his 'ordinary climate' and insisting that 'love and solitude must test each other' in one who seeks solitude."[197] There had been a constant struggle between his actual self and ideal self after he began this relationship with M.

In sharing his deeply human love story, Merton invites all those who undergo similar struggles to discover the authentic meaning of love and to share their experience with others to enlighten them and deepen their spiritual lives. As Suzanne Zuercher reflects, "Merton has touched people in our time as we try in our own lives to discover

---

[195] Merton, *LL,* 82-83; cited in Lipsey, *Make Peace Before the Sun Goes Down*, 229-229.

[196] Merton, *The School of Charity*, Appendix 2: Two Private Vows, 419; cited in Lipsey, *Make Peace Before the Sun Goes Down,* 232.

[197] Merton, *Learning to Love,* xxi.

what it means to be committed creatures of the Creator and followers of Jesus Christ."[198]

Though they discontinued their relationship, it had brought many blessings to his life as a human being and a monk. This was his first adult experience of love. In it, he acknowledged the ability to love and to be loved as a normal human being, and to know deep joy in sharing himself with a woman. Zuercher observes that "it was Margie, more than any other person, or any other experience, who brought the spiritual master to embrace the fullness of his humanity."[199] In this relationship, he found healing from the wounds of the loss of his mother and his immature relationships with women in his previous life, and became aware of his human vulnerability as a religious.[200] "In his prophetic way," writes Zuercher, "he anticipated and chose to articulate some of the issues celibate women and men religious face." In this passionate love affair with Margie, Merton had deepened and authenticated his religious vocation and discovered the capacity to open to God and others more fully.

4. The Final Journey

Merton's reputation was growing because of his contributions to the world, the Church, and the society through his prolific writings and prophetic voice. Though throughout his monastic life Merton received many invitations from different parts of the world to deliver talks and attend conferences, Dom James did not encourage him in this regard. In 1967, Dom James resigned as abbot of the monastery and became a hermit. In 1968, under a new abbot Fr. Flavian Burns, Merton was able to travel to Asia and immerse himself for a short

---

[198] Suzanne Zuercher, *The Ground of Love and Truth: Reflections on Thomas Merton's Relationship with the Woman Known as "M"* (Chicago: In Extenso Press, 2014), 13.

[199] Ibid., 12.

[200] Mott, 348; cited in Donald Grayston, *The Camaldoli Correspondence: Thomas Merton and the Noonday Demon* (Eugene, OR: Cascade Books, 2015), 270-278. Margie Smith returned to Ohio and married to a medical doctor and raised sons. She did her advanced studies in nursing and was in contact with Louisville friends who were the friends of Merton.

while in the various religious traditions he had been studying for a long time.[201]

As he listened to the voice of God, his religious sphere expanded beyond Catholicism to an embrace of other religious traditions. The story of his historic journey is depicted in many of his writings, especially *The Asian Journal.* He found it fascinating to visit various places and meet distinguished scholars of other religions. At the same time, he was saddened and shocked to witness the overpopulation, poverty, starvation, and disease in different parts of India. As a social critic, Merton was stunned to see the sacred land corrupted and manipulated by Westerners.[202]

Merton had a desire to sink deep into the wellsprings of Eastern mysticism, and especially Buddhism. In Calcutta, Merton participated in the World Conference of Religions in 1968, in which Hindus, Sikhs, Muslims, Buddhists, Jains and Christians shared their faith. During the conference, while delivering the talk, Merton expressed, "I come as a pilgrim who is anxious to obtain not just information, not just 'facts' about other monastic traditions, but to drink from ancient sources of monastic vision and experience. I seek not only to learn more about religion and about monastic life but to become a better and more enlightened monk myself."[203] He became immersed in the rich religious traditions and spiritualities of the people of India.

On his journey to Asia, Merton met many Tibetan spiritual masters and spent fruitful time in prayer, meditation and dialogue. One of his significant encounters was with the Tibetan spiritual leader, the Dalai Lama. In his autobiography, *Freedom in Exile,* the Dalai Lama speaks of Merton with great approbation: "I could see he was a truly humble and deeply spiritual man. This was the first time I had been struck by such feeling of spirituality in anyone who

---

[201] Rakoczy, 25.

[202] Shannon, *SL*, 272-274.

[203] Rice, 131; Shannon, *SL*, 279; Thomas Merton, *Asian Journal of Thomas Merton,* edited from his original notebooks by Naomi Burton, Brother Patrick Hart and James Laughlin, Consulting editor Amiya Chakravarty (New York: New Directions Book, 1973), 313.

professed Christianity."[204] The Lama was delighted to meet Merton, and considers this meeting to be one of his "happiest memories . . . it was Merton who introduced me to the real meaning of the word 'Christian.'"[205] Merton found the Dalai Lama very human, "alert and energetic . . . simple and outgoing."[206] They discussed meditation, *Samadhi* (concentration), higher forms of prayer, Tibetan Mysticism, and the mysticism of Christian monks in monasteries. Merton recounts that the Dalai Lama kept insisting that no one can attain deep spiritual life without total dedication, continued effort, experienced guidance, and discipline.

In December, seven days before his death, Merton visited the Sri Lankan shrine at Polonnaruwa to see the amazing statues of the Buddha. Here he had a profound experience of *sunyata*, or emptiness, in which he was carried beyond all binary oppositions and the need for "well-established positions," to a place of silence, peace, and utter clarity.[207] As he recounts in *The Other Side of the Mountain*,

> Looking at these figures, I was suddenly, almost forcibly jerked clean out of the habitual, half-tied vision of things, and an inner clearness, clarity, as if exploding from the rocks themselves, became evident and obvious. . . All problems are resolved and everything is clear, simply because what matters is clear . . . everything is emptiness and everything is compassion. . . [208]

What he concluded about his Asian pilgrimage was surely prescient—he had come to the end of his journey having finally attained a measure of the illumination he sought throughout his life: "I mean, I know and have seen what I was obscurely looking for. I don't know what else remains but I have now seen and have

---

[204] 14th Dalai Lama, *Freedom in Exile: The Autobiography of Dalai Lama* (Toledo, U.S.A: Harper San Francisco, 1990), 189; cited in Shannon, *SL*, 274.

[205] Shannon, *SL*, 274.

[206] Rice, 126.

[207] Thomas Merton, *The Other Side of the Mountain: The End of the Journey*, ed. Patrick Hart (New York: Harper Collins Publishers, 1998), 323.

[208] Ibid., 323.

pierced through the surface and have got beyond the shadow and the disguise."[209]

After his rich experience of visiting the sacred sites in India, Merton travelled to Bangkok in Thailand for a conference with Catholic monastics, to share his thoughts on the future of the monastic life in Asia. The theme of his talk, given on December 10, 1968, was "Marxism and Monastic Perspectives." In it, he emphasized the differences and similarities between Marxism and Monasticism, contending that monastics and Marxists both make an important contribution to the world. While the Marxist assigns importance to the "material and economic structures of life," seeing religion as mystifying and alienating, the monk is "committed to bringing about a human transformation that begins at the level of consciousness."[210] After concluding his talk, he told the participants that questions would be engaged during the evening meeting and closed the session with the cryptic remark, "So I will disappear."[211]

Merton went to his room, and at about 3 P.M., Father Francois de Grunne, who had the room next to Merton's, heard the cry of someone and knocked at Merton's door, "but there was no response." Francois "looked through the louvers in the upper part of the door and saw Merton lying on the terrazzo floor. A standing fan had fallen on top of him."[212] The police confirmed through a test of the fan that a "defective electric cord was installed inside its stand" and that "the flow of electricity was strong enough to cause the death of a person if he touched the metal part."[213] Twenty-seven years ago to the day of his death, on December 10, 1941, Merton had arrived at the gates of

[209] Merton, *The Other Side of the Mountain,* 323; Merton, *The Asian Journal,* 233-236; Rackoczy, "The Dynamics of Discernment in the Life of Thomas Merton," 25.

[210] Merton, *The Asian Journal,* 329; See also in Forest, *Living with Wisdom,* 212.

[211] Ibid., 343; see also Forest, *Living with Wisdom,* 214.

[212] Forest, *Living with Wisdom,* 215.

[213] Ibid., 214-215.

Gethsemani with a heart full of longing for the life inside her walls, a life he would never forsake.

Merton's body was flown back to the United States along with those of American service members killed in Vietnam. The funeral Mass for Merton was conducted on December 17, in the late afternoon, in the Abbey Church at Gethsemani. On the cover of the booklet for the liturgy was a passage from *The Sign of Jonas:* "I have always overshadowed Jonas with My Mercy. . . . Have you lost sight of Me, Jonas My child? Mercy within mercy within mercy."[214] Death could not separate him from the Lord whom he had sought his entire life. In the beautiful words of the Trappist delegates at the Bangkok Conference: "In death Father Louis' face was set in a great and deep peace and it was obvious that he had found Him Whom he had searched for so diligently."[215]

Conclusion

This chapter has examined Thomas Merton's life, considering how the historical, social, cultural, educational, aesthetic, and spiritual forces in his environment shaped him as a contemplative monastic in the world, one who prophetically engaged the social and cultural realities of his era. Though he experienced deep insecurity, confusion, and restlessness in life, and sought the wisdom and beauty of the great mystical traditions of the East, his spirituality remained Christ-centered. The way in which Merton lived his consecrated life can serve as a vital resource for the renewal of religious life in India, as consecrated men and women of India seek to discover the true relevance and purpose of our mission. Merton shows us that consecrated life will be meaningful and fruitful only when it is rooted in a form of contemplation that engages the concrete historical realities of its time and place. Chapter Three will explore in greater depth the contemplative dimensions of Merton's spirituality.

[214] Ibid., 215.

[215] Rice, 138.

Chapter 3

The Contemplative Spirituality of Thomas Merton

Thomas Merton was ever grateful to God for the three major gifts he received in his life: his Catholic faith, his monastic vocation, and his call to be a writer—to share his faith and contemplative spirituality with others.[216] Contemplation is the foundation of Merton's spirituality. In his words,

> It is the highest expression of man's intellectual and spiritual life. It is that life itself, fully awake, fully active, fully aware that it is alive. It is spiritual wonder. It is spontaneous awe at the sacredness of life, of being. It is gratitude for life, for awareness and for being. It is a vivid realization of the fact that life and being in us proceed from an invisible, transcendent and infinitely abundant Source. Contemplation is, above all, awareness of the reality of that Source.[217]

In contemplation, Merton thus found his true identity in God as the source of his life.

---

[216] Thomas Merton, *The Road to Joy: The Letters of Thomas Merton to New and Old Friends Selected and Edited by Robert E. Daggy* (New York: Farrar, Straus, Giroux, 1989), 89.

[217] Thomas Merton, *New Seeds of Contemplation* (New York: New Directions, 1961), 1.

In this chapter, which examines Merton's contemplative spirituality, will unpack some key aspects of the foregoing description. Part One considers the essential elements of Merton's contemplative spirituality. These include his quest for silence, passion for solitude, search for God, and "prayer of the heart." Part Two examines the various thinkers and spiritual writers who influenced Merton's approach to contemplation: William Blake, Aldous Huxley, Thomas Aquinas, and St. John of the Cross. Part Three explores the various themes upon which Merton focused in contemplation: growth in the knowledge of Christ, *le pointe vierge* (the virgin point), discovery of the true self, the search for freedom, and wisdom— *sapientia.*

1. The Essential Element of Contemplation

The Meaning of Contemplation

According to Merton, in a world of science and technological development, human beings are disturbed and disoriented by the world they have created, and amidst these realities they feel internally empty and spiritually lost. To assuage this existential emptiness, they engage in meaningless pursuits in which they become alienated from themselves, others, and God. To address these conditions, Merton suggests the path of contemplation—to enter into one's interior world and thereby to encounter "the freshness and truth of [one's] own subjectivity, and to go on from there not only to God but to the spirit of other men." Merton sees contemplation as intimately related to the depth dimensions of all facets of life: "to art, to worship, to charity; all these reach out by intuition and self-dedication into the realms that transcend the material conduct of everyday life," and thereby contemplation connects one to the very source of life itself. In reconnecting the soul to itself, others, and God, contemplation provides the antidote to human alienation and spiritual emptiness.[218]

Through contemplation one touches the eternal source within. Encountering the divine in the core of one's being transforms a

[218] Thomas Merton, "Poetry and Contemplation: A Reappraisal," in *Thomas Merton: Selected Essays,* ed. Patrick F.O' Connell (Maryknoll, New York: Orbis Books, 2013), 25-26.

person to be fully awakened and active. This experience is beyond human comprehension and explanation. To enter the contemplative state, "one must in a certain sense die" in order to gain entrance into a higher life.[219]

Following Aquinas, Merton asserts that the *desire* for God is a prerequisite to the life of contemplation for the reason that "spiritual things are not received unless they are desired" (*Spiritualia non accipiuntur nisi desiderata*).[220] This desire for God includes the corresponding desire to *please* God that is born out of absolute trust, though in the darkness of unknowing. As we shall see below, for Merton, this darkness and unknowing is the very matrix of contemplation and union with God. Merton expresses this desire in his well-known prayer of trust:

> My Lord God, I have no idea where I am going.
> I do not see the road ahead of me.
> I cannot know for certain where it will end.
> Nor do I really know myself, and the fact that
> I think I am following Your will does not mean that I am
> actually doing so. But I believe that the desire to please You
> does in fact please you.
> And I hope I have that desire in all that I am doing.
> I hope that I will never do anything apart from that desire.
> And I know that, if I do this, You will lead me by the right
> road,
> though I may know nothing about it.
> Therefore I will trust You always though I may seem to be lost
> and in the shadow of death.
> I will not fear, for You are ever with me,
> and You will never leave me to face my perils alone.[221]

---

[219] Merton, *New Seeds*, 2.

[220] William H. Shannon, *Merton's Paradise Journey: Writings on Contemplation* (Cincinnati, Ohio: St. Anthony Messenger Press, 2000), 27.

[221] Thomas Merton, *Thoughts in Solitude* (New York: Farrar, Straus and Giroux, 1958), 79.

In this regard, desiring God presents a fundamental paradox: in order to desire God, one must have already known some measure of union with God, but to know such union, one must be moved by desire. However, in order to desire God, one must cease to occupy one's mind "with lower things." In the words of Aquinas, "As the tongue of a sick man cannot taste good things . . ., so the soul infected with the corruption of the world has no taste for the joys of heaven." To this dilemma, Merton poses contemplation—the retreat to the interior life—as the anodyne for the soul that is sickened and alienated from itself, others, and God by the "lower things" of this world. For Merton, the irrefutable proof of this love, that which distinguishes mediocrity from sainthood, the worldly person from the contemplative, lies in faithfully keeping God's word: "if anyone love me he will keep my word" (Jn 14:23). Here Merton again follows Aquinas, who declares: "It is obedience that makes a man fit to see God."[222] In this regard, William Shannon remarks, "desire based on some experience of love, love feeding desire and leading toward union, together with total uncompromising obedience to the will of Jesus—these are the dispositions needed in order to respond to the invitation, issued at Baptism, to achieve union with God in the experience of contemplation."[223]

Merton nevertheless affirms that true contemplation is not the fruit of human effort, but "is a religious and transcendent gift":

> It is the gift of God Who, in His mercy, completes the hidden and mysterious work of creation in us by enlightening our minds and hearts, by awakening in us the awareness that we are words spoken in His One Word, and that Creating Spirit (*Creator Spiritus*) dwells in us, and we in Him. That we are 'in Christ' and that Christ lives in us. That the natural life in us has been completed, elevated, transformed, and fulfilled in Christ by the Holy Spirit. Contemplation is the awareness and realization,

---

[222] Merton, *What Is Contemplation?* 70, 75, 77; Merton, "Poetry and Contemplation: A Reappraisal," 25.

[223] Shannon, *Thomas Merton's Paradise Journey, 28.*

> even in some sense *experience*, of what each Christian obscurely believes: 'It is no longer I that live but Christ lives in me.[224]

Thus, as the contemplative progresses in union with Christ, he/she becomes fully awakened, active, and alive. Merton affirms that the Christian call is "to respond to Him, to answer to Him, to echo Him, and even in some way to contain him and signify Him. . . It is a deep resonance in the inmost center of our spirit in which our very life loses its separate voice and resounds with the majesty and the mercy of the Hidden and Living One."[225] In contemplation, the Christian is transformed. Moreover, if we experience God in contemplation, we experience Him not for ourselves alone but also for others. The fruit of contemplation is not meant to be kept for oneself but to be shared with all by persons fully awakened in Christ.

2. The Characteristics of Merton's Contemplation

Quest for Silence

Silence was indispensable to Merton. According to him, silence was a requisite for growth in close relationship with God because it transforms one "to answer a call at the center of the heart."[226] In *Thoughts in Solitude*, Merton suggests that "If our life is poured out in useless words, we will never hear anything, will never become anything, and in the end, because we have said everything before we had anything to say, we shall be left speechless at the moment of our greatest decision."[227] Unless one is silent, one has difficulty hearing the voice of God. When one is confronted with silence, many existential questions arise regarding the commitments and genuineness of one's life. "In silence," writes Merton, "we face and admit the gap between the depths of our being, which we consistently ignore, and the surface

---

[224] Merton, *New Seeds*, 4-5.

[225] Ibid., 1.

[226] Thomas Merton, *An Invitation to the Contemplative Life*, ed. Wayne Simsic (Frederick, Maryland: The Word Among Us Press, 2006), 79.

[227] Merton, *Thoughts in Solitude*, 90.

which is untrue to our own reality."[228] There is a need in every person to return to the true self.

The desire for silence had grown in Merton from childhood. After his mother's death, his father, "whose artistic projects often took precedence over his fatherly responsibility," often left him alone (with relatives or in boarding school).[229] At times he was deeply forlorn and lonely, and at other times he embraced the condition of solitude as a part of his burden in life. While he was at Oakham, he often went to Brooke Hill, where he could be alone, and "think about things" by himself.[230] When he became a Catholic in 1938, he was attracted to a life in the Church which focused on silence and solitude. Shortly thereafter, his thoughts turned towards a religious order that emphasized silence. The Cistercian monastery at Gethsemani, which Merton joined in 1941, was committed to silence, and the monks communicated through sign language.[231]

The essence of Merton's emphasis on silence was the conviction that full mindfulness of God was not possible without silence and some degree of isolation. Silence, in his view, the primary function of monastic silence is "to preserve the *memoria Dei,* which is more than memory. It is total consciousness and awareness of God, which is impossible without silence, recollection, solitude, and a certain withdrawal."[232] Moreover, the silence of solitude also bridges the distance between one's mind and the things of God's world, in their full reality. Such silence "clears away the smoke-screen of words that

---

[228] Christine M. Bochen, "Silence and Solitude," *Thomas Merton: Essential Writings* (Maryknoll: Orbis Books, 2000), 75.

[229] William H. Shannon, Christine M. Bochen, Patrick F. O'Connell, "Solitude," *The Thomas Merton Encyclopedia* (Maryknoll, New York: Orbis Books, 2002), 443; (Hereafter cited as *TME*).

[230] William H. Shannon, *Silent Lamp: The Thomas Merton Storey* (New York, NY: The Crossroad Publishing Company, 1992), 62; (Hereafter cited as *SL).*

[231] Shannon, "Solitude," *TME,* 443.

[232] Thomas Merton, *Come to the Mountain: New Ways and Living Traditions in the Monastic Life* (Colorado: St. Benedict's Monastery, 1964), 46.

man has laid down between his mind and things. In solitude, we remain face to face with the naked beings of things."[233]

As noted in the previous chapter, Merton tasted such solitude in the abandoned tool shed in the woods given him by Dom James, which he named "St. Ann's Hermitage." In the autumn of 1952, he wrote in his journal, "I am now almost completely convinced that I am only really a monk when I am alone in the old toolshed Reverend Father gave me."[234] In the silence of the landscape, he found the authenticity and grounding he had sought his entire life, and it healed him and made him whole.

In 1965, he was given a permanent building as a hermitage about a mile from the monastery. He enjoyed the silence of his hermitage though it was interrupted to some degree by occasional visitors. When he left for Asia in 1968, one of Merton's desires was to find a place of more "secure solitude where he could live apart from the monastery, but still as a monk of Gethsemani."[235] Sadly, this dream remained unrealized because of his untimely death.

Desire for Solitude

Merton's understanding of solitude was multifaceted and according to one author, included "loneliness, hiddenness, anonymity, rejection, secrecy, emptiness, poverty, egolessness, detachment, freedom, utter Otherness, and above all, the undivided unity of love."[236] One is called to live in solitariness not by solving the contradictions in life but to live with them and to rise above them. "In solitude," writes Merton, "we remain face to face with the naked being of things. And yet, we find that the nakedness of reality which we have feared is neither a matter of terror nor for shame. It is clothed in the friendly

---

[233] Merton, *Thoughts in Solitude*, 82.

[234] Thomas Merton, *A Search for Solitude,* The Journals of Thomas Merton, vol. 3, 1952-60, ed. Lawrence S. Cunningham (San Francisco: Harper San Francisco, 1996), 14.

[235] Shannon, "Solitude," *TME*, 443-444.

[236] Vazhakoottathil, 159.

communion of silence, and this silence is related to love."[237] Solitude calls one to a deep encounter with oneself.

Vazhakoottathil observes, "Solitude was a driving passion in [Merton's] life, because it was in solitude that he sought and found God."[238] Merton wrote, "I have only one desire and that is the desire for solitude—to disappear into God, to be submerged in His peace, to be lost in the secret of His face."[239] Similarly, he wrote, "everything in me cries out for solitude and for God alone," though he would also reflect on the possibility that he perhaps lacked full understanding of what it meant to have a "purely contemplative vocation." This passage from *The Sign of Jonas* reflects his struggle to come to terms with the fact that his burning desire for an utterly solitary life seemed not to be the life God had chosen for him in a communal monastery.

Merton holds that to be a true solitary, one needs to develop internal and external solitude. Internal solitude enables the person to discover the true self.[240] It involves the

> actualization of a faith in which a man takes responsibility for his own inner life. He faces its full mystery, in the presence of the invisible God. And he takes upon himself the lonely, barely comprehensible, incommunicable task of working his way through the darkness of his own mystery until he discovers that his mystery and the mystery of God merge into one reality, which is the only reality.[241]

In interior solitude, one discovers one's true identity: "*me as I am known by God, and as God intended me to be.*"[242] Interior solitude invites the person to be united with God and others at a deeper level.

For Merton, external or physical solitude meant "place, space, geographical separation from someone or something, a 'getting away'

---

[237] Merton, *Thoughts in Solitude*, 81-82.

[238] Vazhakoottathil, 158.

[239] Thomas Merton, *Sign of Jonas* (New York: Harcourt, Brace and Company, 1953), 17-18.

[240] Merton, "Notes for a Philosophy of Solitude," in *TME,* 68.

[241] Ibid.

[242] Vazhakoottathil, 160; (Italics in original in Vazhakoottathil).

or a 'going apart.'" However, for him, it was the interior solitude that was crucial. This conviction caused him to declare, in *Seeds of Contemplation*, that ultimately, "there is no solitude except interior solitude."[243] Moreover, external solitude can become deceptive when one seeks only to escape from the realities of the world. Physical solitude has the potential to become "false or dangerous, full of self-hatred and life-denial, a flight from responsibility, or spiteful separation from one's fellow man."[244] Significantly, for Merton, external solitude is not an absolute requirement for the cultivation of the interior life of solitude. As he explains,

> To love solitude and to seek it does not mean constantly traveling from one geographical possibility to another. A person becomes a solitary at the moment when, no matter what may be one's external surroundings, one is suddenly aware of one's own inalienable solitude and sees that he or she will never be anything but solitary. From that moment, solitude is not potential—it is actual.[245]

True solitude enables one to reach out to others in love, prayer, and acts of charity. For Merton "True solitude is not mere separateness. It tends only to *unity*."[246] In merging with God, the true solitary is ultimately allied with others: "The solitary of whom I speak is called not to leave society but to transcend it: not to withdraw from the fellowship with other men but to renounce the appearance, the myth of union in diversion in order to attain to union on a higher and more spiritual level—the mystical level of the Body of Christ."[247] Though at times the solitary may experience physical aloneness, he/she is called to be united with God and to others on a deeper and more mystical level.

---

[243] Thomas Merton, *Seeds of Contemplation*, (New York: Dell, 1960), 42: cited in Vazhakootathil, *Thomas Merton's Mystical Quest for the Union with God*, 159.

[244] Vazhakootathil, 159.

[245] Merton, *Thoughts in Solitude*, 81.

[246] Merton, "Notes for philosophy of Solitude," in *TME*, 71.

[247] Ibid., 69.

Seeking God

The concept of the "search" captures an essential element in the contemplative life of Merton. He was a perpetual seeker of God who was influenced by the teaching of St. Benedict "to seek God." Merton lived this vocation with a firm heart: "This one thing that most truly makes a monk what he is, is that irrevocable break with the world and all that is in it, in order to seek God in solitude."[248] In *Seeds of Contemplation*, Merton elucidates his true understanding of what seeking God meant for him:

> To withdraw from illusion and pleasures, from worldly anxieties and desires … to keep my mind free from confusion . . . to entertain silence in my heart and listen for the voice of God; to cultivate an intellectual freedom from concepts and the images of created things . . . to rest in humility and to find peace in withdrawal from conflict and competition with [others] . . .; to turn aside from controversy and put away heavy loads of judgment and censorship and criticisms.[249]

Jonathan Montaldo affirms that "always stretching forward in his search for a deeper experience of God and of what it might mean to be a more complete human being was a continuing element in Merton's monastic life."[250] Merton's poem entitled "The Biography," exemplifies his enduring search for the Divine.

Christ from my cradle, I had known you everywhere,

And even though I sinned, I walked in you, and knew
You were my world:
You were my France and England,
My seas and my America:
You were my life and air, and yet I would not own You.
Oh, when I loved You, even while I hated You,
Loving and yet refusing You in all the glories of Your universe

---

[248] Thomas Merton, *No Man is an Island* (New York: Dell, 1957), 148; see also Elena Malits, *The Solitary Explorer: Thomas Merton's Transforming Journey* (San Francisco: Harper and Row Publishers, 1980), 68.

[249] Merton, *Seeds of Contemplation*, 30-31.

[250] Atkinson and Montaldo, *Soul Searching*, 7.

> It was Your living Flesh I tore and trampled, not the air and earth...
> If on Your Cross Your life and death and mine are one,
> Love teaches me to read, in You, the rest of a new history.
> I trace my days back to another childhood,
> Exchanging as I go,
> New York and Cuba for Your Galilee,
> And Cambridge for your Nazareth,
> Until I come again to my beginning,
> And I find a manger, star and straw,
> A pair of animals, some simple men,
> And thus I learn that I was born,
> Now not in France, but Bethlehem.[251]

This poem lays bare his soul in its inexorable search for and encounter with God. As Shannon expresses it, Merton "had passed through a mystical 'Straits of Dover' and found a new symbol that, from then on, would bring richness of meaning to his life: the Gospel of Jesus Christ, which began quite explicitly, to teach him how to walk the 'holy way' on which Christ's life and his would intersect."[252] Finding Christ was the new path that Merton chose for his life.

Prayer of the Heart

Though he was a spiritual master, Merton did not write much about his personal experience in prayer, perhaps, as Wayne Simsic suggests, because he found it unnecessary to do so given that his was a "prayer of the heart," which lacked any particular technique or form, and used few, if any words. Instead it consisted of resting in God, whom we find in the depths of our being, and waiting expectantly in faith, trust, and love, with "a willing, attentive heart."[253] This for Merton was the essence of contemplative prayer.

---

[251] Thomas Merton, *Collected Poems* (New York: New Directions, 1997), 104-105.

[252] Shannon, *SL*, 95. Shannon explains that for Merton, "passing Dover Castle meantpassing a symbol that stood at the crossroads of his life up to that point," *SL*, 77.

[253] Merton, *An Invitation to the Contemplative Life*, 65.

Though Merton was not wont to describe his manner of prayer, he once did so in a letter to Abdul Aziz, a Sufi from Pakistan with whom he corresponded: "I have a very simple way of prayer. It is centered entirely on attention to the presence of God and to His will and His love. That is to say it is centered on *faith* by which alone we can know the presence of God." It is the experience of the invisible presence of God beyond human comprehension. Merton thirsted in his heart "to recognize totally the nothingness of all that is not God. My prayer is then a kind of praise rising up out of the center of Nothing and Silence." Merton believed that if God wills it, God can change the nothingness into clarity and if God does not will it, the nothingness will remain an obstacle. He explained that his prayer did not consist of "thinking about" something, "but a direct seeking of the Face of the Invisible, which cannot be found unless we become lost in Him who is Invisible."[254]

For Merton, it was not the technique of prayer that was important but the experience of God. Therefore, as the master of novices at Gethsemani, he did not offer any specific prescription for prayer except the *lectio divina*. In a letter to his friend and fellow spiritual writer Etta Gullick, he wrote, "I try to make them love the freedom and peace of being with God alone in faith and simplicity, to abolish all divisiveness and diminish all useless strain and concentration on one's own efforts and all formalism: all the nonsense of taking seriously the apparatus of an official prayer life, in the wrong way. . ."[255] Merton guided the novices and others to walk with God in the activities of one's daily routine.

In March 1966, Gullick suggested to Merton that he should write an essay or book on "progress in prayer." However, Merton was somewhat hesitant to do so on the grounds that one's progress in prayer cannot be measured. Attempting to measure progress in prayer can lead one to a hyper-awareness of one's own efforts in prayer.

---

[254] Thomas Merton, *The Hidden Ground of Love: The Letters of Thomas Merton on Religious Experience and Social Concerns,* ed. William Shannon (New York: Farrar, Straus and Giroux, 1985), 63-64; (Hereafter cited as *HGL*).

[255] Merton, *HGL,* 368; cited in Shannon, "Prayer," *TME,* 365.

He suggests rather, that "progress in prayer comes from the Cross and humiliation and whatever makes us really experience our total poverty and nothingness, and also gets our mind off ourselves."[256] True progress in prayer consists in our ability to depend on God in our emptiness. One needs to begin the journey to God in prayer from where one is. Though many are not aware of this great truth, each person possesses everything in Christ. One must take sufficient time to listen and to experience God's presence. As Merton writes, "Every moment is God's own good time, his *kairos*."[257] Therefore, one is invited to pray at every time, in every place, with a deep yearning for the simple presence of God.

3. Influence of Merton's Understanding on Contemplation

Merton grew gradually in contemplation through the influence of many spiritual masters, thinkers and writers. In this section I will consider four noteworthy people in this regard: William Blake, Aldous Huxley, Thomas Aquinas and John of the Cross.

William Blake

William Blake's influence is noteworthy in shaping Merton's contemplative spirituality. As Merton reflects, "I think my love for William Blake had something in it of God's grace. It is a love that has never died, and which has entered very deeply into the development of my life." Owen Merton first introduced Merton to Blake when Merton was a child. He remembers that "Father had always liked Blake, and had tried to explain to me what was good about him when I was a child of ten."[258] As a mystic, Blake saw beyond external reality to the timeless realm of the divine, finding God's presence in every facet of creation, as one of his famous quatrains reflects:

To see a World in a grain of sand,
And a Heaven in a wild flower,

---

[256] Ibid., 376.

[257] Shannon, "Prayer," *TME,* 366.

[258] Merton, *SSM*, 85.

Hold Infinity in the palm of your hand,
An Eternity in an hour.[259]

As a visionary, Blake perceived this divine presence in all things through the lens of his imagination. In Blake's view, the imagination "was not just a faculty of the mind but a divine reality." Blake called the imagination "vision," which is equal to the eternal world. This gift of apprehending divine reality through the natural world was open to everyone, Blake insisted, though most people remain unaware of it because of their habitually limited ways of thinking and behaving. However, "if the doors of perception were cleansed everything would appear to man as it is, infinite. For man has closed himself up till he sees all things through narrow chinks of his cavern."[260] He insisted that although people see things according to their conditioning, for the visionary, "Nature is Imagination itself."[261]

For Blake, God's presence pervaded all eternity with "love and beauty." To understand the depths of God's goodness, the human mind must transcend to the realm of God, a movement which is facilitated by art and prayer. Merton saw that for Blake, "The interior light given the artist by God must be cherished, that it may strengthen and come to burn brilliantly in the end." Mature art requires the vital discipline of contemplation, which involves "a kind of asceticism that

---

[259] William Blake, opening to "Auguries of innocence," in *Selected Poems of William Blake* (Oxford: Oxford University Press, 1927), 107, cited in James Harpur, *Love Burning in the Soul: The Story of the Christian Mystics, from Saint Paul to Thomas Merton* (Boston: New Seeds, 2005), 193. "Merton knows that God must be met in the present moment, which he has learned from Blake is a doorway opening to eternity. But what sounds simple is difficult because the awareness of passing time is a barrier to the experience of the moment of time," Lee Price, "Thomas Merton, William Blake, and I Contemplate Eternity," *21 Essays*, (February 16, 2015); accessed January 17, 2018, http://21essays.blogspot.com/2015/02/thomas-merton-william-blake-and-i.html.

[260] William Blake, "The Marriage of Heaven and Hell," *Wiiliam Blakes Poems*, 146, (November 28, 1757–August 12, 1827); accessed February 5, 2018, https://www.poemhunter.com/poem/the-marriage-of-heaven-and-hell-2/; cited in Harpur, 193-94.

[261] Harper, 193.

is self-sacrifice, sacrifice of immediate physical goods for the good of the spirit, for the success of the work of art."[262]

Merton found in Blake a genuinely holy and good man, full of faith and love for God, under whose influence Merton would "one day come, in a round-about way, to the only true Church, and to the One Living God, through His son, Jesus Christ." Through the influence of Blake, Merton realized that the only way to live was to be in a world "charged with the presence and reality of God."[263]

Aldous Huxley

During his studies at Columbia, two books in particular made a great impact on Merton's faith journey. The first was Etienne Gilson's *The Spirit of Medieval Philosophy,* which led him to believe in the real existence of "God as being." The second was Aldous Huxley's *Ends and Means,* which was introduced to Merton by his close friend Robert Lax. In reading this book, Merton's eyes were opened to "mysticism and the possibility of real, experimental contact with God."[264]

Though Huxley expressed a clear preference for Eastern mysticism, he recognized that "the mystical vision was by no means absent from Christian faith." Huxley held that there were two realms—the world of "greed, violence, ambition, and materialistic values," and a higher realm of spiritual or transcendental values.[265] Moreover, this realm is accessible to human experience through the practice of "prayer and asceticism." Huxley, however, did not emphasize the "physical angle of mortification and asceticism," but rather the need for personal detachment. For him, the process of negation was not an end in itself, but "a freeing, a vindication of our real selves, a liberation of the spirit from limits and bonds that were intolerable, suicidal—from a servitude to flesh that must ultimately destroy our whole nature and society and the world as well." When the spirit is freed and able

---

[262] Thomas Merton, "Blakes Ideas on the Place of Nature in Art," in *The Literary Essays of Thomas Merton,* ed., Patrick Hart (New York: New Directions, 198), 425, 448.

[263] Merton, *SSM,* 88, 191.

[264] Bochen, "Conversion," *TME,* 88.

[265] Ibid., 87-88.

to return to "its own element," it finds it is not alone, but in the presence of the "absolute and perfect Spirit, God." As a consequence, one enters into union with this perfect Spirit, a union that is not "vague and metaphorical," but "a matter of real experience." In 1937, as Merton faced both his own existential crises and the "general crisis" of a world on the brink of war, he welcomed the insights contained in *Ends and Means* as a revelation of his "need for a spiritual life, an interior life, including some kind of mortification."[266]

Thomas Aquinas

While he was studying at Columbia, Merton became familiar with Thomas Aquinas through the influence of his professor Daniel Walsh. Walsh offered a course on Aquinas in the graduate school of philosophy, and through this course, Merton came to know the *Summa Theologica*, the "monument" to Aquinas' "genius and to his sanctity."[267] Merton realized that Aquinas was not only a systematic theologian but also a mystical theologian, whose doctrines and teachings influenced Merton's understanding of contemplation. For Aquinas, union with God occurs through the activity of the intelligence. In *The Ascent to Truth*, Merton writes,

> Saint Thomas, like all Christian theologians, knows perfectly well that the consummation of man's destiny is love and that the way to divine union is the way of theological virtues, through the night of faith. Hence, the paradox that the intellectualism of Thomas Aquinas turns out, after all, to be the supreme criterion of true mysticism, because there is no such thing as sanctity that is not intelligent.[268]

Following Aquinas, Merton thus understood that union with God is fulfilled in an operation of the human intelligence through which God nevertheless acts. In this act, "the mind and will of man are moved passively by God, and it is that sense that 'God alone

---

266 Merton, *SSM,* 185-187.

267 Thomas Merton, *The Ascent to Truth* (New York: Harcourt, Brace and Company, 1951), 323.

268

acts.'" In brief, humans become agents of grace only through the power of God, though human effort is necessary. As Merton notes, "God alone can give us perfect happiness by raising us to union with Himself. Our cooperation with His grace is demanded of us. There must be action on both sides. He will not give Himself to us unless we give ourselves to Him."[269]

Aquinas also inspired Merton to integrate contemplation into active life. For Aquinas, contemplation must, as Merton understands it, lead the soul to "overflow and communicate its secrets to the world." According to Aquinas, fruitful union with God in contemplation is the basis of all other loves, and establishes one "in the very heart of all spiritual fecundity."[270]

John of the Cross

Merton was deeply influenced by St. John of the Cross, the great mystic of the Spanish Carmelite Order. He wrote an entire book, *The Ascent to Truth*, on the theology and spirituality of John of the Cross. Merton notes that John of the Cross was so inspired by Aquinas that, "his doctrine of complete detachment from creatures in order to arrive at union with God, [is] sometimes quoted word for word from Saint Thomas."[271] Daniel Adams, reflecting on the approach of these two great saints, argues that "Aquinas took a theological approach to contemplation while John of the Cross tended to be more mystical."[272] In his essay simply entitled "St. John of the Cross," Merton names St. John as one of his favorite saints:

---

[269] Ibid., 325, 135-136.

[270] Merton, *SSM*, 415.

[271] This doctrine is elucidated in the opening questions of the *Prima Secundae* that outline the "supreme contemplation" which is humanity's final end. See Merton, *The Ascent to Truth*, 132.

[272] Daniel J. Adams, *Thomas Merton's Shared Contemplation: A Protestant Perspective*, Cistercian Studies, Series: Number Sixty Two (Kalamazoo, Michigan: Cistercian Publications, 1979), 132. This statement by no means obviates the fact that Aquinas was also a mystical theologian; the two theologians simply expressed their approaches to mysticism in different ways. Though John of the Cross was influenced by Thomas Aquinas in some ways, especially in his method of explication, their ideas as such were arguably quite different. For some of the

> He is the patron and the protector and master of those whom God has led into the uninteresting wilderness of contemplative prayer. . . He is the patron of those who pray in a certain way in which God wants them to pray, whether they happen to be in the cloister, the desert, or the city. . . I would venture to say that he is the father of all those whose prayer is an undefined isolation outside the boundary of "spirituality." He deals chiefly with those who, in one way or another, have been brought face to face with God in a way those methods cannot account for and books do not explain. He is in Christ the model and the maker of contemplatives wherever they may be found.[273]

Merton followed John's teaching on detachment and the dark night. In contemplation, St. John entered into mystical union with Christ, which he attained by purifying his senses and soul, and accepting the dark-night experience of the cross. According to him, for a soul to enter into mystical union with Christ, one must detach oneself from all impediments. The cross is one way in which a soul detaches itself from all created realities and attaches itself to God. As St. John avers, "For if a man resolve to submit himself to carrying this cross—that is to say, if he resolve to desire in truth to meet trials and to bear them in all things for God's sake—he will find in them great relief and sweetness wherewith he may travel on this road, detached from all things and desiring nothing."[274] When a soul is purified of all desires, God infuses God's Spirit into the soul: "In order to possess Him Who is all, one must renounce the possession of anything that

---

differences, see Iain Matthew, *The Impact of God: Soundings from St John of the Cross* (London, NWI: Hodder and Stoughton, 1995), 121, 130; the two differ, for example, in their reasons for the Incarnation; whereas for Thomas, the Word became flesh because of sin, for John, the Word became flesh out of the Father's love for creation and His desire to share His Son with the world in love and intimacy: in the Son's movement from the Father into the world and his return to Father, "the Son intends a cosmic sweep in which he will embrace his bride 'tenderly[. . .]give her his love,' and lift her into the life of the Father," (from *Ballads* 155-6, 165-6), 121.

[273] Merton, "St. John of the Cross," in *TME*, 22.

[274] Ibid., 19-20.

is less than God."[275] All tangible and enjoyable things are considered to be less than God.

For Merton, John's entire theology was recapitulated in these two words: *Todo y Nada.* All and nothing: *Todo*—all—is God, and in God one possesses everything. In order to possess God, one needs to empty oneself of everything that is not of God—*Nada*. The content of renunciation depends on two dimensions: "submission to authority and a turning away even from genuine religious experiences."[276] Merton considers that for St. John, submission to authority entails humility, obedience, interior detachment, without which spiritual liberty can never be attained.

With regard to detachment from religious experiences, St. John insists that, "under every circumstance we must turn away even from genuine visions, revelations, raptures, locutions, and so on in order to rest in 'pure faith,' which is the only proximate means of union with God."[277] Religious experience is only a pathway to knowing and experiencing God, one that prepares the soul to enter into the mystical union of possessing God. In this regard, Merton warns of becoming attached to one's own spiritual practices, and cautions that one must not place undue emphasis on religious fervor in itself, which can be "one of the most dangerous obstacles" for the one who is called to true contemplation. This is so because the difference is often not clearly understood between "mystical contemplation in the proper sense and all these accidentals, these experiences, these manifestations and curiosities, which may or may not be supernatural, and which have no essential connection with sanctity or with the pure love which is at the heart of true contemplation."[278]

---

[275] Merton, *The Ascent to Truth*, 53.

[276] Adams, 133.

[277] Merton, *The Ascent to Truth*, 249-250.

[278] Merton, *NSC*, 247.

4. Important Themes in Merton's Contemplation

Growth in the knowledge of Jesus Christ

Merton's growth in the knowledge and experience of Jesus Christ is the foundation of his contemplative spirituality. He grew in his Christocentric faith by imbibing the writings of the great Christian contemplatives and mystics and by spending time in prayer. As noted previously, his first awakenings to Christ occurred when he was eighteen years old, while visiting Rome for the first time. He recalls that in Rome, at the church of Saints Cosmas and Damian, he was deeply taken with a "great mosaic, in the apse, of Christ coming in judgment in a dark blue sky, with a suggestion of fire in the small clouds beneath His feet." The ancient churches awakened Merton's imagination and stirred a deep though inchoate longing in him to know this Christ whom he encountered in Rome: "And now for the first time in my life I began to find out something of Who this Person was that men called Christ. It was obscure, but it was a true knowledge of Him, in some sense, truer than I knew and truer than I would admit."[279]

Later, however, he would come to insist that even beyond the images of Christ the imagination is able to conjure, a mere invocation of the name of Jesus, or a simple awareness of his loving presence in our souls, "is a thing more real and more valuable by far than anything we can arrive at by our interior senses alone, for the picture of Jesus we may have in our imagination remains nothing but a picture, while the love that His grace produces in our hearts can bring us into direct contact with Him as He really is."[280] In reading the Gospels, one not only gets the picture of Christ, but is also invited to enter into an intimate relationship with Him who dwells in human souls through faith.[281] Merton discovered the personal presence of the Risen Christ, shining in the depths of one's being:

[279] Merton, *SSM*, 108, 100.

[280] Merton, *NSC*, 155.

[281] Merton, *Seeds of Contemplation,* 94.

> As a magnifying glass concentrates the rays of the sun into a little burning knot of heat that can set fire to a dry leaf or a piece of paper, so the mysteries of Christ in the Gospel concentrate the rays of God's light and fire to a point that sets fire to the spirit of man. And this is why Christ was born and lived in the world and died and returned from death and ascended to His Father in heaven. . . Through the glass of His Humanity He concentrates the rays His Holy spirit upon us so that we feel the burn, and all mystical experience is infused into the soul through the Man Christ.[282]

Being a Christian means not only believing in Christ, but also living as Christ lived, seeking to become united with him. The Christian is called to encounter Christ in the ordinary daily activities of life. Merton notes, "The work, the family, the simple consolations, and the ordinary sufferings of Christians are lived in a new Spirit, and filled with love and faith that seek only God's will, not personal profit and gratification."[283] Christians are called to find the presence of Christ in everything and in everyone.

Le Point Vierge

A crucially important concept for Merton is "*Le Pointe Vierge*," which literally means "the virgin point," though ultimately, the term cannot be translated. For him, it is "a metaphor for the place deep within that is the point of our encounter with God."[284] Merton noted the concept of *le pointe vierge* through reading Louis Massignon, a French scholar who wrote on the Sufi tradition. Merton writes, "Massignon has some deeply moving pages in the *Mardis de Dar-es-Salam*: About the desert, the tears of Agar, the Muslims, the '*point vierge*' of the spirit, the center of our nothingness where, in apparent despair, one

---

282 Ibid., 91.

283 Thomas Merton, *Honorable Reader,* ed. Robert E. Daggy, Forward by Harry James Cargas (New York, NY: The Cross Road Publishing Company, 1981), 99.

284 Christine M. Bochen, *Thomas Merton: Essential Writings* (Maryknoll, New York: Orbis Books), 60-61.

meets God—and is found completely in His mercy."[285] Massignon focused on encountering God in the depths of one's being, a concept which evoked in Merton a desire to experience God in such a way within himself.

Monica Weis explains that Merton's concept of *lepoint vierge* holds a surplus of meaning. It can signify, as in *Conjectures of a Guilty Bystander*, the break of dawn, the cusp of light and darkness—the moment of transition. As Merton writes,

> The first chirps of the waking day birds mark the '*point vierge*' of the dawn under a sky as yet without real light, a moment of awe and inexpressible innocence, when the Father in perfect silence opens their eyes. They begin to speak to Him, not with fluent song, but with an awakening question that is their dawn state, their state at the '*point vierge*. Their condition asks if it is time for them to 'be.' He answers 'yes.' Then, they one by one wake up, and become birds. They manifest themselves as birds, beginning to sing. Presently they will be fully themselves, and will even fly.[286]

Indeed, in this "most wonderful time of day," all creation, in its innocence, asks once again for permission "to be," as on the very first morning of creation. *Lepoint vierge* can also mean a "moment of poise," when anything is possible and the outcome may hold cosmic implications, such as in Shakespeare's *A Midsummer Night's Dream*, "when fairy magic can alter the expected rhythm of the world."[287]

The still point within ourselves wherein we encounter the divine has its counterpart in nature, which, in every singular and minute detail, discloses something of the holy within the ordinary, in that "mysterious, cosmic dance," in which "the Lord plays and diverts

---

[285] Thomas Merton, *Conjectures of a Guilty Bystander* (Garden City, New York: Image Books, 1966), 151; (Hereafter cited as *CGB*).

[286] Ibid., 131.

[287] Monica Weis, *The Environmental Vision of Thomas Merton* (Lexington, Kentucky: The University Press of Kentucky, 2011), 60-61.

Himself in the garden of his creation."[288] Merton asserts that if we can only let go of any preconceived notion of what it all means, we can follow God in this dance.

> We do not have to go very far to catch echoes of that game, and of that dancing. When we are alone, on a starlit night; when by chance we see the migrating birds in autumn descending on a grove of junipers to rest and eat; when we see children in a moment when they are really children; when we know love in our hearts; or when, like the Japanese poet Basho we hear an old frog land in a quiet pond with a solitary splash—at such times the awakening, the turning inside out of all values, the 'newness,' the emptiness and the purity of vision that make themselves evident, provide a glimpse of the cosmic dance.[289]

It is at the center of our being—*le point vierge*—that we enter that dance with the rest of creation. And it is the sustaining spark of divinity within that allows us to recognize our unity with each other and with God's self.

Finally, Merton's spiritual awakening at the intersection of Fourth and Walnut in Louisville in March 1958 demonstrates another instance of *le point vierge*. Here he experienced a profound awakening to his unity with all the other pedestrians on that street corner, and saw them all "walking around shining like the sun."[290] In this moment, he saw into "the secret beauty of their hearts . . . where neither sin nor desire nor self-knowledge can reach, the core of their reality, the person that each one is in God's eyes." In this awakening, he recognized that his own solitude belonged as much to them as to himself, and was thus disabused of any illusions of difference or separation from them. He, like all the others, was "a member of a

---

[288] Merton, *NSC*, 296; see also Jason M. Brown, "Thomas Merton, Wildness and the sacramental Power of Place," ed. Deborah Pope Kehoe and Joseph Quinn Raab, *The Merton Annual*, Studies in Culture, Spirituality, and Social Concerns, Volume 29 (2016): 86- 87.

[289] Merton, *NSC*, 296-297.

[290] Merton, *CGB*, 157.

race in which God Himself became incarnate."[291] This epiphany led Merton to the recognition of the divine spark within all people:

> At the center of our being is a point of nothingness which is untouched by sin and by illusion, a point of pure truth, a point or spark which belongs entirely to God, which is never at our disposal, from which God disposes of our lives, which is inaccessible to the fantasies of our mind or the brutalities of our own will. This little point of nothingness and of *absolute poverty* is the pure glory of God in us. It is so to speak His name written in us, as our poverty, as our indigence, as our dependence, as our sonship. It is like a pure diamond, blazing with the invisible light of heaven.[292]

For Merton, this moment of epiphany disclosed the reality of the divine within the human, marking the moment of his "return to the world" and thereby transforming his understanding of his own vocation to monastic life. As he wrote to Pope John XXIII in the autumn of that year, "this poor world has a right to a place in my solitude." To enter into the realm of contemplation one must be prepared to engage the concrete realities of this world rather than retreating from them, and thus to see the world at large through a sacramental imagination. Merton came to see that "the whole world and all the incidents of life tend to be sacraments—signs of God, signs of God's love working in the world."[293] Through this event, he had become deeply conscious that he was not separate from other human beings, all of whom carried that sacred spark within, and therefore, he shared the responsibility for building a just future for all.

Discovering the "True Self"

Merton's contemplative life was filled with various life-transforming experiences that led him on a quest to deepen the knowledge of

---

[291] Ibid.

[292] Ibid., 158.

[293] Merton, "Poetry and Contemplation: A Reappraisal, in *The Literary Essays of Thomas Merton*, 345.

his identity. James Finley observes that "Merton's *whole spirituality*, in one way or another, pivots on the question of ultimate human identity."[294] According to Merton scholar Daniel P. Horan, Merton's faith journey revolved around answering two questions: "who am I and who is God?" These questions are interconnected because the identity of each person ultimately lies in God.[295]

For Merton, every person is called to recognize that they are created in the image and likeness of God. However, the true self, which bears the image of God, is often tarnished, hidden beneath the mask of the "false self." In his description of the false self, he writes:

> Every one of us is shadowed by an illusory person: a false self. This is the man that I want myself to be but who cannot exist, because God does not know anything about him. . . . My false and private self is the one who wants to exist outside the reach of God's will and God's love—outside of reality and outside of life. And such a self cannot help but be an illusion. . . .A life devoted to the cult of this shadow is what is called a life of sin.[296]

All sin, therefore, ultimately arises from the insatiable demands of the false self and its claims to being "the fundamental reality of life to which everything else in the universe is ordered." Out of devotion to the false self, I thus "use up my life in the desire for pleasures and the thirst for experiences, for power, honor, knowledge and love, to clothe this false self and construct its nothingness into something objectively real." The false self binds one by setting up comparisons between the self and others, and often blocks one's path of achievement in life.[297] The false self prevents people from discovering their true identity and dignity in God. In contrast, the true self opens the person to God. It enables one to accept one's talents, skills, and any other gifts

---

[294] James Finley, *Merton's Palace of Nowhere* (Notre Dame, IN: Ave Maria Press, 1978), 21 (Italics added); cited in Daniel P. Horan in *The Franciscan Heart of Thomas Merton: A New Look at the Spiritual Inspiration of His Life, Thought, and Writing* (Notre Dame, Indiana: Ave Maria Press, 2014), 96.

[295] Horan, 96.

[296] Merton, *NSC*, 34.

[297] Ibid., 35, 45.

from God with gratitude. The true self is discovered only in deep relationship with and love for God. At the same time, we ourselves have a crucial role in the unfolding of our identities:

> Our vocation is not simply to *be*, but to work together with God in the creation of our own life, our own identity, our own destiny. . . The secret of my full identity is hidden in Him. He alone can make me who I am, or rather who I will be when at last I fully begin to be. But unless I desire this identity and work to find it with him and in him, the work will never be done.[298]

By working out our own identity in God, Merton meant "working out our own salvation," which requires "sacrifice and anguish, risk and many tears." It calls for "close attention to reality at every moment, and great fidelity to God" as God discloses God's presence in "the mystery of each new situation." Through contemplation, one understands the work God desires to do in the individual: "*The seeds that are planted in my liberty at every moment, by God's will, are the seeds of my own identity, my own reality, my own happiness, my own sanctity.*"[299] In this regard, we become contemplatives when God discovers Himself in us.

Search for Freedom

For Merton, contemplation led to freedom. As he developed as a contemplative, he grew in authentic freedom. Shannon divides this process into three phases. In the first phase, during his youth at Clare College, Merton was controlled by his passions and desires, which led him to moral degradation and spiritual emptiness. The second phase began with his conversion experience at Columbia in 1938, which led to his reception of the sacraments of baptism, reconciliation and Eucharist. In accepting the Catholic faith, Merton awakened to a new path of freedom, which led him to enter the monastery at Gethsemani in 1941. Reflecting on the first day of his entry into the monastery, when Brother Matthew closed the gate behind him, he writes that

[298] Merton, *NSC*, 32.

[299] Ibid., 33. (Italics in Original).

at that moment, his "freedom had already begun."[300] The freedom of enclosure within the four walls meant the freedom to observe the rules and regulations stipulated by the authorities of the monastery. In his early days of monastic life, he embraced the dictum, "Obey your superiors and you will be using your freedom properly. You will be carrying out the will of God." Such "freedom," however, fostered excessive dependency on his superiors, effectively blocking his individual freedom and leading to a kind of "moral rigidity."[301] As he lived the monastic way of life, and grew in contemplative spirituality and prayer, his understanding of freedom began to change.

In the third phase, Merton discovered that true freedom is an inner reality guided much more from within than from without. He began to experience freedom from within as the fruit of contemplative prayer and meditation. He held that humans, whom God created in love and innocence, had lost their capacity, through original sin, to see reality as it is—as God sees it. This led them to struggle with a vast array of illusions that masked the truth, deformed their vision, and enslaved them. The decisive question for Merton, therefore, was not about happiness, but about freedom—"how can I be free?"[302] Authentic freedom, he asserted, is attained only in relation to God and submission to God's will.

> All good, all perfection, all happiness, are found in the infinitely good and perfect and blessed will of God. Since true freedom means the ability to desire and choose, always, without error, without defection, what is really good, then freedom can only be found in perfect union and submission to the will of God. If our will travels with His, it will reach the same end, rest in the same peace, and be filled with the same infinite happiness that is His. Therefore, the simplest definition of freedom is this: it means the ability to do the will of God. To be able to resist His will is not to be free.[303]

---

[300] Merton, *SSM,* 372-373; see also Shannon, "Freedom," *TME*, 164.

[301] Shannon, "Freedom," *TME*, 164.

[302] Simsic, 15.

[303] Merton, *NSC*, 200-201.

One attains true freedom, therefore, in cooperating with God's grace and doing God's will. It follows that "If we never encounter him, our freedom never fully develops."[304] The person deeply united with God grows in the fullness of freedom.

Wisdom—*Sapientia*

Particularly in the final decade of his life, Merton associated "the ability to perceive the sacredness of the ordinary [and] the unity of the disparate . . ., with the gift of wisdom."[305] In his essay "Gandhi and the One-eyed Giant," Merton describes wisdom as a way of knowing "which transcends and unites . . . which dwells in body and soul together and which, more by means of myth, of rite, of contemplation, than scientific experiment, opens the door to a life in which the individual is not lost in the cosmos and in society but found in them." This is the kind of wisdom that, even in its so-called secular or profane form, makes all life sacred and meaningful. Wisdom became increasingly important to Merton in the last decade of his life for four notable reasons. First, it rooted him solidly in his own tradition of Christian contemplation. Second, it served as an important point of encounter with the religious traditions of the East. Third, it gave him a theological grounding for his sacramental vision of creation, and fourth, it provided an "alternative perspective to the analytical, quantitative, exploitative approach to the uniqueness of scientific rationalism."[306] Scripture provided Merton with sources of reflection on *sapientia*. As a Cistercian, he deemed wisdom to be the most important of the seven gifts of the Holy Spirit named in Isaiah 11. Through the Pauline writings of 1 Corinthians, he pondered the contrast between human and divine wisdom, and found the wellspring of wisdom in "the personified figure of Wisdom as the creative agent

---

[304] Basil Pennington, *Thomas Merton Brother Monk: The Quest for True Freedom* (New York: Harper and Row Publishers, 1987), 28.

[305] O'Connell, "Wisdom," *TME*, 533.

[306] Thomas Merton, "Gandhi and the One-Eyed Giant," in *Gandhi on Non-Violence*, Selected Texts from Mohandas K. Gandhi's Non-Violence in Peace and War, ed. with an Introduction by Thomas Merton (New York: New Directions Publishing Corporation, 1965), 1; cited in O'Connell, "Wisdom," *TME*, 533.

of God in Proverbs 8 and the Wisdom of Solomon."[307] As O'Connell notes, the figure of Wisdom became "identified implicitly in the New Testament and explicitly by the Church Fathers with the Logos of John's Gospel, the pre-existent Word of God through whom all things were made and who takes on human nature in the person of Jesus."[308] Merton portrays wisdom as the feminine face of God in his poem *Hagia Sophia*:

> Sophia, the feminine child, is playing in the world, obvious and unseen, playing at all times before the Creator. Her delights are to be with the children of men. She is their sister. The core of life that exists in all things is tenderness, mercy, virginity, the Light, the Life considered as passive, as received, as given, as taken, as inexhaustibly renewed by the Gift of God. Sophia is Gift, is Spirit, *Donum Dei.* She is God-given and God Himself as Gift.[309]

The feminine figure of Wisdom is compassionate and tender in contrast to a utilitarian orientation to life, in which everything must have "a clearly defined purpose." Merton saw "contemplative wisdom" as "a living contact with the Infinite Source of all being, a contact not only of minds and hearts, not only of 'I and thou,' but a transcendent union of consciousness in which man and God become, according to the expression of St. Paul, 'one spirit.'"[310]

Christopher Pramuk, in his article "Theodicy and the Feminine Divine: Thomas Merton's 'Hagia Sophia' in Dialogue with Western Theology," further reflects that, for Merton Sophia "is not just the feminine face of a masculine God, or a masculine God with feminine

---

[307] O'Connell, "Wisdom," *TME,* 533.

[308] I credit O'Connell for these four categories, which provide a helpful organizing structure for understanding the importance of wisdom in Merton's later spirituality; O'Connell, "Wisdom," *TME,* 533-535.

[309] Merton, *The Collected Poems of Thomas Merton,* 368; see also O'Connell, *TME,* 535.

[310] Thomas Merton, *Faith and Violence* (Notre Dame, Indiana: University of Notre Dame Press, 1968), 222; cited O'Connell, "Wisdom," *TME,* 534.

attributes . . . but an active power permeating all things."[311] Through the affirmation of the feminine dimension of God, Merton seeks to "articulate a mode of divine presence hidden in and responsive to the crisis of his times: a mode of presence faithful to the revelation of God and humanity fully alive in Jesus, and at the same time, a vision of Christian hope, a kind of God-talk . . . that will resonate in a key familiar to others beyond Christianity and Catholicism."[312]

Merton's rootedness in Christian contemplation led him to discover the wisdom in other religious traditions. Despite his decisively Christocentric approach to wisdom, he recognized that other religions, notably those of the East, also had at their core a vital tradition of mysticism and wisdom. He writes, "In all religions it is more or less generally recognized that this profound 'sapiential' experience, call it gnosis, contemplation, 'mysticism,' 'prophecy,' or what you will, represents the deepest and most authentic fruit of the religion itself." The wisdom tradition at the heart of every religion is grounded in contemplation and is particularly evident in Zen. For Merton "Zen has much to say not only to a Christian but also to a modern man. It is nondoctrinal, concrete, direct, existential, and seeks above all to come to grips with life itself, not with ideas about life, still less with party platforms in politics, religion, science, or anything else." Merton describes the true purpose of Zen as "awakening a deep ontological awareness, a wisdom-intuition (*Prajna*) in the ground of the being of the one awakened"[313]

For Merton, the whole creation bears the imprint of and thus discloses sacramentally the divine wisdom of God. He writes: "The

---

[311] Christopher Pramuk, "Theodicy and the Feminine Divine: Thomas Merton's "Hagia Sophia" in Dialogue with Western Theology," in *Theological Studies,* Vol. 77(1), (2016): 56; see also Christopher Pramuk, *At Play in Creation: Merton's Awakening to the Feminine Divine* (Collegeville, Minnesota: Liturgical Press, 2015), 27; *Sophia: The Hidden Christ of Thomas Merton* (Collegeville, Minnesota: Liturgical Press, 2009).

[312] Pramuk, "Theodicy and the Feminine Divine: Thomas Merton's "Hagia Sophia" in Dialogue with Western Theology," 56.

[313] Thomas Merton, *Zen and the Birds of Appetite* (New Directions Paper book, 32), New Directions, Kindle Edition.

forms and individual characters of living and growing things, of inanimate beings, of animals and flowers and all nature, constitute their holiness in the sight of God. Their inscape is their sanctity. It is the imprint of His wisdom and His reality in them." Merton called this mode of wisdom "sophianic," indicating "the central wisdom that comes in tune with the divine and cosmic music." There is a revelatory dimension in the deepest patterns of order within the structures of reality themselves. This cosmic order is prior to, though in complete harmony with, the revelation of Scripture and the incarnation. This "cosmic revelation" is the key to integrating Christian wisdom not only with Eastern religions but also with pre-Christian Western thought and even with artists who, though they may not be Christian, share a basic sapiential awareness. Compared to *sapientia* (the wisdom of God), *scientia* (scientific knowledge) is "objective, analytical, abstract, and quantitative." Though it "has a legitimate, indeed indispensable role to play in human life," when it seeks to control wisdom by claiming to be the only valid form of knowledge, and negates the questions raised by wisdom as insignificant, then it becomes a problem.[314] As Merton writes in *Faith and Violence*, "Without wisdom, without the intuition and freedom that enable man to return to the root of his being, science can only precipitate him still further into the centrifugal flight that flings him, in all his compact and uncomprehending isolation, into the darkness of outer space without purpose and without objective."[315]

According to Merton, "neither the ancient wisdoms nor the modern sciences are complete in themselves." They are not

---

[314] Merton, *NSC*, 30, 535; Merton derived the concept of "inscape" from Gerard Manley Hopkins, who deeply influenced Merton's sacramental view of created realities. For Merton inscape means that "each particular being, in its individuality, its concrete nature and entity, with all its own characteristics and its private qualities and its own inviolable identity, gives glory to God by being precisely what He wants it to be here and now, in the circumstances ordained for it by His Love and His infinite Art."

[315] Thomas Merton, *Faith and Violence: Christian Teaching and Christian Practice* (Kindle Locations 3058-3060), University of Notre Dame Press, Kindle Edition.

independent entities but are interconnected. Wisdom without the appropriate scientific knowledge is unable to understand fully the "sapiential meaning of the created and material cosmos." Science without wisdom enslaves humans within a "world of unrelated objects in which there is no way of discovering (or creating) order and deep significance in man's own pointless existence."[316] Without wisdom, and with scientific knowledge alone, it is impossible for humans to be united with God and to live an integrated life. However, when *scientia* is incorporated with wisdom, it advances, "personal, social, and cosmic harmony."[317]

Conclusion

Merton's search for God in contemplation is foundational to his spirituality. His longing for silence and solitude in contemplation led him to encounter God, and to be conscious of the presence of God everywhere, at every moment and in every person. In his writings, he opens the riches of wisdom from his contemplative journey to nurture the spirituality of others. Merton invites every spiritual seeker to silence, solitude, and contemplation, to find Christ's divine presence hidden within and thereby to return to one's true self. He has left a legacy not only for those in consecrated life, nor merely for Christians, but for all humanity. The following chapter considers Merton's call to the prophetic dimensions of contemplative life.

---

[316] Merton, "Gandhi on Non-Violence," 1.

[317] O'Connell, "Wisdom," *TME,* 535.

Chapter 4

The Prophetic Spirituality of Thomas Merton

As a Christian spiritual leader of the twentieth century, Merton sought to find a balance between contemplation and social justice. His contemplative experience led him, out of love for God and God's creation, to give voice to the prophetic dimensions of the Christian message. He believed that contemplation and action for social transformation must go hand-in-hand, making him a vanguard of the modern-day emphasis on the intersection of faith and political life. Though he was a monk, he realized that he was called to go beyond the confines of his monastic life and to engage prophetically in the life of the society. As a prophet, he shared his passion for justice with the broken world through his writings, many of which denounced the injustices within the culture and society. His message was at once "deeply spiritual" and "profoundly political." And "it broke loose of any categories or ideologies: it was human to the core." Merton is therefore a role model for a contemporary, contemplative-prophetic life.[318]

This chapter explores Merton's contribution as a prophet to the world, the church, and the American society. Part One engages Merton's prophetic awakening and vocation. Part Two explores the roots of Merton's prophecy, which include the biblical foundations

[318] John Dear, *The Sound of Listening: A Retreat Journal from Thomas Merton's Heritage* (New York: Continuum Publishing Company, 1999), 10.

and William Blake's prophetic vision. Part Three analyzes the influence of contemporary prophets, notably Dorothy Day and the Baroness Catherine de Hueck, on Merton's prophetic vision. Part Four explores Merton's reading of the signs of the times, considering the influences of Gandhi and Martin Luther King Jr. on his approach to nonviolence, racism in the United States, his views on peace and nuclear war, his denunciation of the Vietnam War and his prophetic contribution to Church.

1. Merton's Prophetic Call

Merton's prophetic call was not immediately evident in the early years of his life, but was "germinating, awaiting release at the opportune moment." "Fidelity to God" was the source of Merton's prophetic spirituality. He held that one need not explicitly play the role of a prophet; rather, by simply remaining faithful to God in all things, one becomes a sign of contradiction in the world and the church against the values that oppose God's justice and mercy.[319] He came to believe that every monk has a vocation in this world to be a prophetic voice.

Merton's prophetic spirituality was firmly grounded in the charismatic dimensions of the spiritual life, which link inextricably the realms of the contemplative and the prophetic. This spirituality "insists on personal experience as a crucial component in the spiritual quest, [and] in Merton's view, it seeks to foster a prophetic ear—a way of listening to and discerning God's voice and will."[320] His mystical experience at Fourth and Walnut on March 18, 1958, in which he experienced a oneness with the rest of humanity, marked the culmination of his long, gradual awakening to a prophetic call: "In Louisville, at the corner of Fourth and Walnut, in the center of the shopping district, I was suddenly overwhelmed with the

[319] Ephrem Arcement, *In the School of Prophets: The Formation of Thomas Merton's Prophetic Spirituality* (Collegeville, Minnesota: Cistercian Publications, 2015), 200, 204.

[320] Ibid., 203-204. For Merton, the term *charismatic* meant "the experiential dimension of the spiritual life, encompassing the whole person and leading toward total availability to the spontaneous movements of the Spirit."

realization that I loved all those people, that they were mine and I theirs, that we could not be alien to one another even though we were total strangers."[321] This experience awakened Merton's deep need to express himself prophetically: "It was a mystical insight that reconciled his early passion for justice with his equally passionate desire for solitude."[322] It was an invitation for Merton to return to the world as a transformed monk to serve humanity in compassion and love. William Shannon explains that Merton was drawn back to the world because

> [h]e saw a world full of men and women blinded by illusion, not knowing who they were or what destiny lay in store for them. It was a world benumbed by a technological culture that conspired to hide from people the truth of their humanness and their right to be truly free. He had responsibility to that world that he could not shirk simply because he lived in a monastery.[323]

Merton's inner eyes were opened through this mystical experience. In a letter to Pope John XXIII in November 1958, he put words to his new vision of himself and his place in the world:

> It seems to me that, as a contemplative, I do not need to lock myself into solitude and lose all contact with the rest of the world; rather this poor world has a right to a place in my solitude. It is not enough for me to think of the apostolic value of prayer and penance; I also have to think in terms of a contemplative grasp of the political, intellectual, artistic and social movements in this world—by which I mean sympathy for the honest aspirations of so many intellectuals everywhere in the world and the terrible problems they have to face.[324]

As a contemplative, Merton came to recognize his responsibility to make the world part of his spirituality and to reach out to humanity in compassion and love. He explained to Pope John that he had begun

---

[321] Merton, *CGB,* 140-14.

[322] Arcement, 201.

[323] Shannon, *SL,* 178.

[324] Merton, *HGL,* 482.

to exercise "an apostolic friendship" with "a circle of intellectuals"—artists, writers, publishers, and poets. He even proposed the idea of a monastic foundation "whose purpose would be to exercise a contemplative apostolate of this kind"—perhaps in South America. As Paul Dekar comments, "Whatever the circumstances that led Merton to Gethsemani, his wild youth, his sexual adventures as a young person, his concern about war, his horror at a world marked by genocide and other evils, withdrawal from society freed him to be open to a new world of possibility for embracing and serving others."[325] Merton's prophetic call was thus awakened as he sought to live out his contemplative spirituality.

2. The Roots of Merton's Prophecy

Biblical Foundations

Merton drew his prophetic insights from the Scriptures. Reflecting on the prophetic figures of the Bible, he asserts, "A prophet is one who lives in direct submission to the Holy Spirit in order that, by his life, actions and words, he may at all times be a sign of God in the world of men. Christ the Incarnate Word was of course the supreme Prophet, and all sanctity participates in this prophetic quality. Their submission to God is not merely a matter of charismatic accident but of perfect fidelity to grace."[326] For Merton, the foundation of prophecy in the Bible is rooted in the "vocation of Israel." God loved the people of Israel and established a covenantal relationship with them on Mount Sinai (Ex.19:5-6). Through this covenant, God entered into an intimate relationship with them. This covenantal relationship revealed the faithfulness of the Lord in the Exodus journey. As the chosen instruments of God, the prophets of Israel had a mission to remind the people to remain faithful to God in their journey to the Promised Land. Prophets such as Moses, Elijah, Jeremiah, John the Baptist, and others were solitaries, desert figures, and voices crying

---

[325] Paul R. Dekar, *Thomas Merton. Twentieth-Century Wisdom for Twenty-First-Century Living* (Eugene, OR: Cascade Books, 2011), 60.

[326] Thomas Merton, *Disputed Questions* (New York: Harcourt Brace Jovanovich, 1960), 223. (Hereafter cited as *DQ*).

in the wilderness.[327] The ultimate goal of the prophets was to restore right relationship in all spheres of life. In *Disputed Questions,* Merton reflects on the core message of prophecy:

> Return to the spirit of your days in the desert! Recovery of the spirit of the desert meant a return to fidelity, to charity, to fraternal union; it meant destruction of the inequalities and oppressions dividing rich and poor; conversion to justice and equity meant the return to the true Sabbath. For the law of the desert was the law of peace, direct dependence on the Lord, silence, trust, forgiveness of debts, restoration of unity, purity of worship.[328]

The prophets were called by thc Lord to liberate those who were oppressed and to restore the entire creation in unity and love. For this, however, they were often ridiculed, humiliated, condemned, abandoned, persecuted or killed by the political and religious leaders. Merton believed that prophecy and prophetic action are fulfilled in Jesus, who was filled with the Spirit and led by the Spirit into the wilderness to challenge the dominion of the evil spirit. He proclaimed the good news of liberation to the poor and downtrodden. As a consequence of his fidelity to his mission, Jesus was rejected, tortured, and crucified. For the Christian, prophecy means "participation in the identity and mission of Jesus."[329]

For Merton, the role of the prophet in the contemporary world is the same as that of the biblical prophets: the identification and denunciation of idolatry. Today, humans worship the idols of material wealth, possessions, comfort, and religious or political power. Ideologies become gods when people dedicate their time, devotion, unreasonable loyalty, energy and vitality to these idols. In the contemporary world, the prophetic role is to recognize personal idolatries and to address them in order to help people to be liberated from within. Merton assumes that the true liberation of the prophet

---

327 Patrick F. O'Connell, "Prophecy," *TME*, 372.

328 Merton, *DQ*, 223; see also in O'Connell, "Prophecy," *TME*, 372.

329 Ibid.

depends on the humility to be rooted in God's presence, which gives him/her "the courage to speak and act prophetically."[330]

William Blake's Prophetic Vision

Merton first reflected on prophecy at the age of twenty three, while studying the works of Blake. In a letter to Robert Lax, he wrote, "I have studied William Blake, I have measured him with a ruler, I have sneaked at him with pencils and T squares, I have spied on him from a distance with a small spyglass, I have held him up to mirrors, and will shortly endeavor to prove the prophetic books were all written with lemon juice and must be held in front of a slow fire to be read."[331] Merton thoroughly studied Blake and was deeply compelled by his prophetic imagination. For Blake, "imagination is the faculty by which man penetrates ultimate reality and religious mystery." The imagination is essential to understanding reality, and Blake had the capacity to see it as it existed.[332]

Merton considered Blake a prophet in the sense that he "'utters' and 'announces' news about man's own deepest trouble—which is man himself."[333] In the midst of this trouble, however, the prophetic imagination envisions a hope-filled future marked by justice and peace. In Merton's view, "The revolutionary energy of Blake and his impassioned fight for charism and vision against dogma and institution make him an obvious saint for radical Christians." For Merton, Blake is a "seer—a visionary," because he "boldly asserted his own imaginative vision in the face of ridicule and misunderstanding." Blake was ablaze with prophetic anger against "the blind complacencies of rationalism,

---

330 Merton, *Faith and Violence*, 154; cited in O'Connell, "Prophecy," *TME*, 373.

331 Thomas Merton, *The Road to Joy: The Letters of Thomas Merton to New and Old Friends. Selected and edited by Robert E. Daggy* (New York: Farrar, Straus and Giroux, 1989), 142. (Hereafter cited as *RJ*).

332 Arcement, 12; for details on Blake's influence on Merton, see chapter 2, 63 and chapter 3, 119-121.

333 Merton, "Blake and the New Theology," *The Literary Essays of Thomas Merton*, 3.

of Enlightenment deism, and of the established Churches,"[334] and criticized any spirituality or institution which diminished, distorted, or sought to control the human experience of God. Blake's prophetic critique of institutional religion enabled Merton to later evaluate critically the institution of monasticism.

Influenced by Blake, Merton wrote two anti-poetry books—*Cables to the Ace, or Familiar Liturgies of Misunderstanding* and *The Geography of Lograire*. The prophetic role of anti-poetry is to parody the hollowness and absurdity of "modernity's suppressed imagination and spirit." By demonstrating that "words have become empty and meaningless—only noise," anti-poetry discloses society's deep need for silence and integrity, and seeks to foster a higher consciousness.[335] Blake's prophetic mysticism enabled Merton to be an authentic contemplative prophet of the twentieth century, to challenge the injustices prevalent in the society and the church.

3. The Influence of the Contemporary Prophets

Baroness Catherine de Hueck

As part of the program Merton was teaching for the summer school students at St. Bonaventure, famous speakers were made available to share their knowledge with the students. One of the speakers was the Baroness Catherine de Hueck, a wealthy Russian woman who had set up Friendship Houses in Toronto and Harlem. Friendship House was an interracial apostolate which sought to improve race relations and awaken Christians to respond to racial and economic injustice. She communicated a powerful and simple message: "If Catholics could just see Harlem—this place of unrelieved poverty and sickness, where an abandoned race of people was being crushed and perverted, morally and physically, under the burden of colossal economic injustices—they would not be able to stay away. They would want to come there to serve Christ suffering in his members."[336]

This message had a powerful impact on Merton. He spent two weeks

[334] Merton, "Blake and the New Theology," 3-4.

[335] Arcement, 20.

[336] Shannon, *SL*, 113.

immersed in the work of Friendship House. Harlem was a world by which Merton had been largely untouched as a student at Columbia, a "world of poverty and perversity, bred—he felt—by the sins of white people. It was especially the world of abused children, crowded together like sardines in tenement rooms where 'evil' takes place hourly and inescapably before their eyes."[337] In the poem "Aubade—Harlem," Merton expressed his bitter pain and anger against the injustices done to the poor people of Harlem:

> Across the cages of the keyless aviaries,
> The lines and wires, the gallows of the broken kites,
> Crucify, against the fearful light,
> The ragged dresses of the little children.
> Soon, in the sterile jungles of the water pipes and ladders,
> The bleeding sun, a bird of prey, will terrify the poor,
> These will forget the unbelievable moon.[338]

In this poem, Merton pictures the poor of Harlem as birds locked in a cage, surrounded by wires and lines. He raised his voice against the injustices perpetrated against them, and carried their pain, which he saw as the agony of Christ himself:

> Daylight has driven iron spikes,
> Into the flesh of Jesus' hands and feet:
> Four flowers of blood have nailed Him to the walls of
> Harlem.[339]

Merton was deeply conflicted after his experience in Harlem—whether to join the monastery or to serve the poor in Harlem. On November 23, 1941, Merton attended a retreat for Friendship House volunteers, which was guided by Father Paul Hanley Furfey, a professor of sociology and social justice activist from the Catholic University in Washington, DC.[340] The theme of the retreat was the

---

337 Ibid., 114.

338 Thomas Merton, "Aubade—Harlem," for Baroness G.de Hueck, *The Collected Poems of Thomas Merton* (New York: New Directions, 1977), 82.

339 Ibid.

340 Albert J. Raboteau, *American Prophets: Seven Religious Radicals and their Struggle for Social and Political Justice* (Princeton and Oxford: Princeton University Press, 2016), 125-126.

Mystical Body of Christ, which in Merton's view, is the one infinite source of life that nourishes both Friendship House and the Trappists. After the retreat, which emphasized the social implications of the Mystical Body in relation to racial injustice, Merton returned home with fire in his heart (though Furfey had mentioned nothing about the Trappists). Nevertheless, after much inner turmoil, he "chose Gethsemani over Harlem."[341]

Though Merton chose the monastic life, he never forgot the racial issues and poverty that touched him in 1941 in Harlem. The Baroness was the first person to whom Merton communicated after his entry to the monastery regarding his decision to become a monk. He wrote: "[I]t will no doubt be hard, but at least I will know there is nothing keeping me from my God anymore—I can belong entirely to Him by simply consenting to each trial as it presents itself, and that is enough! It is everything. I only want to belong entirely to Him. I will never forget FH in my prayers!"[342] His experiences at Friendship House would forever infuse his contemplative life with prophetic fire.

Dorothy Day

Dorothy Day, the founder of the Catholic Worker movement in the United States, influenced Merton to work for social justice. Merton and Day were among the four great Americans, along with Abraham Lincoln and Martin Luther King Jr., whom Pope Francis recognized in his address to the U.S. Congress on September 24, 2015. The Pope highlighted Day's untiring work for "social justice and the rights of persons," and extolled Merton as "a man of prayer . . . who challenged the certitudes of his time and opened new horizons for souls and for the Church. He was also a man of dialogue, a promoter of peace between peoples and religions."[343]

---

[341] Raboteau, 125-126; Merton, *HGL,* 10.

[342] Robert A. Wild, ed. *Compassionate Fire: The Letters of Thomas Merton and Catherine de Hueck Doherty* (Notre Dame, Indiana: Ave Maria Press, 2009), 26.

[343] Pope Francis, "Address of the Holy Father to a Joint Session of the United States Congress September 24, 2015," *The Merton Annual* 28 (2015) 22-23; see

Day's deep concern for the poor prompted her to establish the Catholic Worker movement in 1932 along with Peter Maurin, and to become a voice for the voiceless through her writings. Though Merton and Day never met in person, their friendship revolved around a two-decades-long correspondence, through which they shared "their mutual commitment to peace and non-violence and a love of literature," notably Russian literature. In the 1960s, Merton began to contribute regularly to the Catholic Worker newspaper.

Merton and Day's correspondence is thought to have begun in 1956. Upon reading the *Seven Storey Mountain* in 1959, Day was not overly impressed. She saw Merton's interpretation of religious life as being confined inside the walls of Gethsemane, and his worldview "narrow and limited."[344] In her diary entry of February 22, 1959, she wrote that Merton "has plunged himself so deeply in religion that his view of the world and its problems is hateful and scornful."[345] However, as Merton began to embrace a more active role in non-violence, peacemaking, and social justice, Day and Merton grew closer.

They began a significant exchange around social issues. Merton lauded her prophetic role in the American society and church and was deeply inspired by her passion for peace and justice. He assured her of his support and solidarity in her work for peace:

> I am touched deeply by your witness for peace. You are very right in going at it along the lines of [Gandhi's] Satyagraha. I see no other way, though of course the angles of the problem are not all clear. I am certainly with you on taking some kind of stand and acting accordingly. . . So don't worry about whether or not in every point you are perfectly right according to everybody's books: you are right before God as far as you can go and you are

---

also Thomas Spencer, "I Must Pray to Him for Aid Now': Thomas Merton's and Dorothy Day's Diaries," in *The Thomas Merton Seasonal*, A Quarterly Review, Vol. 41, No. 1, (Spring 2016), 7-8.

[344] Spencer, 3-4.

[345] Dorothy Day, *The Duty of Delight: The Diaries of Dorothy Day*, ed. Robert Ellsberg (Milwaukee: Marquette University Press, 2008), 250, cited in Spencer, 4.

> fighting for a truth that is clear enough and important enough. What more anybody can do?[346]

For Merton, Day embodied the authentic meaning of the Gospel: a deep love for the poor and forgotten of the world. It may be said that "they lived parallel lives ultimately pointed in the same direction: toward the inner and outer peacemaking that comes from radically seeking God's Presence and Love in all things."[347]

4. Reading the Signs of the Times

In the manner of a true prophet, Merton read the signs of the times. He was deeply disturbed by the injustice happening in American society. As Anthony Padovano notes, Merton "makes contact in his writing with the cataclysmic events of his era: world wars and nuclear arsenals, social violence and church reform, cultural upheavals and social revolutions. Tranquility is not easy in such a time, even for a hermit."[348] However, as Paul Pearson, the former director of the Merton Center at Bellarmine University, observes: "In facing the darkness of the bomb, our ecological degradation of the planet, our unbridled, rampant technology, the breakdown of community and ultimately of communion between people, Merton continually stresses that the Christian vision is greater than the darkness which all too frequently seems ready to overwhelm us."[349] During Merton's lifetime, several trends threatened the quality of human life. He took up the key issues of war, the nuclear arms race, racism and poverty. Believing that the true contemplative must not become disassociated from the devastating consequences of the sin of the world, Merton avowed: "The contemplative life in our time is therefore necessarily modified by the sins of our age. They bring down upon us a cloud

---

[346] Merton, *HGL,* 136.

[347] David Hoover and Sharon Halsey, "Thomas Merton & Dorothy Day: Pilgrims and Prophets of Peace," accessed January 24, 2018, Hooverhttp://www.inscapeministries.com/images/MertonDayWEB.pdf.

[348] Antony T. Padovano, *The Human Journey: Thomas Merton Symbol of a Century* (Garden City, New York: Doubleday & Company, INC., 1982), 22.

[349] Dekar, xii.

of darkness far more terrible than the innocent night of unknowing. It is the dark night of the soul which has descended on the whole world."[350]

Merton could see that the horrors of the twentieth century and the cruelty of human beings were manifesting darkness within society, and therefore he stood and faced the darkness and encouraged others to do the same. As Paul Dekar writes, "Welling up with compassion for a world caught up in pursuit of the false self, a world of hallucinogenic drugs, consumerism, propaganda, technology, and war, Merton sought to bring people to their senses."[351] As a contemplative prophet, Merton engaged the signs of the times that remained obscure to most. In so doing, he confronted the world, American society, and the Church through his writings on violence, nuclear war, the Vietnam War, and racism.

Conquering Violence through Nonviolence

During the twentieth century, the world grew increasingly violent. According to Merton, "the problem of violence today must be traced to its root: not the small-time murderers but the massively organized bands of murderers whose operations are global. . . . Violence today is *white-collar violence, the systematically organized bureaucratic and technological destruction of man*."[352] Merton believed that structural violence could only be overcome through the means of nonviolence.

For Merton, "nonviolence is not simply a way of proving one's point and getting what one wants without being involved in behavior that one considers ugly and evil." Rather, it is possibly "the most exacting of all forms of struggle, not only because it demands first of all that one be ready to suffer evil and even face the threat of death without violent retaliation, but because it excludes mere transient self-interest from its considerations." He held that Christian nonviolence is "perhaps the only really effective way of transforming human beings

---

[350] Thomas Merton, *The Inner Experience: Notes on Contemplation*, ed. with an introduction by William H. Shannon (San Francisco: Harper San Francisco, 2003), 121-122; cited in Dekar, xi.

[351] Dekar, 104.

[352] Merton, *Faith and Violence,* 3-6. (Italics in original).

and human society." In order to be truly transformative, however, it must be free of reliance on all uses of unjust power. The power of nonviolence is rooted in humility, vulnerability, and powerless, trusting in "the hidden power of the Gospel" and the reality of Christ's victory over sin and death. It implies "a particular understanding of the power of human poverty and powerlessness when they are united with the invisible strength of Christ."[353] Merton further writes:

> In resume, the meekness and humility which Christ extolled in the Sermon on the Mount and which are the basis of Christian nonviolence are inseparable from an eschatological Christian hope which is completely open to the presence of God in the world and therefore to the presence of our brother who is always seen, no matter who he may be, in the perspectives of the Kingdom. Despair is not permitted to the meek, the humble, the afflicted, the ones famished for justice, the merciful, the clean of heart and the peacemakers. All the beatitudes 'hope against hope,' bear everything, believe everything, hope for everything, endure everything (I Cor. 13:7).[354]

For Merton, the beatitudes are the manifestation of Christ's love for humanity. In turn, the Christian takes upon his own shoulders the yoke of the savior, meek and humble of heart. This yoke is the burden of the world's sin with all its confusions, and all its problems. Christians, in "humility and faith," are called to be completely available to their brothers and sisters. Nonviolence is a gift that Christians can offer to the world by following the true path of Christ and thereby transforming the world into a place of love and peace.

Gandhi's Satyagraha

Gandhi was key to Merton's understanding of nonviolence. Merton's acquaintance with Gandhi began when he was studying at Oakham School in 1931, where he defended Gandhi in a school debate. In

---

[353] Christine M. Bochen, "The Way of Nonviolence," *Thomas Merton: Essential Writings*, Selected with an Introduction by Christine M. Bochen (Maryknoll, New York: Orbis Books, 2000), 123-126.

[354] Bochen, *Thomas Merton: Essential Writings,* 134.

the 1950s, he studied Gandhi's writings on non-violence in depth and produced two articles on Gandhi's spirituality of nonviolence: "A Tribute to Gandhi," and "Gandhi and the One-Eyed Giant." In 1965, Merton published *Gandhi on Non-Violence*. In this book, Merton suggests that for Gandhi, the traditional Indian understanding of *ahimsa,* or nonviolence is the basis of "human life and action." Ahimsa is rooted in the realization of the unity of all reality. Gandhi discovered a new concept to explain the true significance of nonviolence, which he termed *satyagraha*, meaning firmness or "persistence in the truth."[355] In Merton's view, "a *Satyagrahi* is one who is totally dedicated to the transformation of his own life, of his adversary, and of society by means of love."[356] Satyagraha promotes an inclusive spirituality of love and acceptance of everyone. Gandhi found in Jesus Christ a true model of nonviolence. In his view, Jesus was the most active resister known perhaps to history. This was non-violence par excellence.

Furthermore, for Gandhi, "nonviolence was not simply a political tactic which was supremely useful and efficacious in liberating his people." Rather, "the spirit of non-violence sprang from *an inner realization of spiritual unity in himself.*"[357] Merton further explains:

> Gandhi recognized, as no other world leader of our time has done, the necessity to be free from pressures, the exorbitant and tyrannical demands of a society that is violent because it is essentially greedy, lustful, and cruel. Therefore, he fasted, observed days of silence, lived frequently in retreat, knew the value of solitude, as well as of the totally generous expenditure of his time and energy in listening to others and communicating with them.[358]

---

[355] Merton, "Gandhi on Non-Violence: A Selection from the Writings of Mahatma Gandhi," Shannon, *TME*, 168-169.

[356] Merton, *Gandhi on Non-Violence,* 35.

[357] Ibid., 6; (Italics in Original).

[358] Thomas Merton, "A Tribute to Gandhi," *Selected Essays*, ed. with an Introduction by Patrick F. O'Connell (Maryknoll, New York: Orbis Books, 2013), 183.

Merton appreciated that Gandhi's deep rooted spirituality led him to live a contemplative, disciplined, and nonviolent life. Motivated by Gandhi, Merton believed that if one wishes to work for peace and non-violence, one must first be rooted within oneself, doing one's "inner work, and then it will spread far and wide in the Spirit of God."[359] Merton realized that spiritual discipline was the "foundation of Gandhi's active nonviolence. Gandhi overcame the violence within himself and in society through nonviolence, the fruit of his spiritual discipline. Merton therefore considered Gandhi a role model for nonviolence in that his life was marked by wholeness and wisdom, an integrity and a spiritual consistency.

Martin Luther King, Jr.

Merton was inspired by the leadership of Martin Luther King, Jr., who fought against racism using the "nonviolent philosophy of Gandhi." David Givey comments that "such leadership accepted suffering, not only to gain freedom for black people but also to save white people's souls by showing them their sins of injustice."[360] For both King and Gandhi, nonviolence was the only method that respected the dignity, and indeed the sacredness, of the person. They criticized the existing "attitudes and behaviors" that curtailed "human freedom" and deadened human consciousness. They especially rejected the human struggle for "power, status, and wealth—and consumerism," which treats humans as objects and uses interpersonal relationships for "manipulation and exploitation."[361] King urged people to move from a thing-oriented society to a person-oriented society. King's civil rights movement was based on the spirit of Christian nonviolence. Merton admired King and encouraged white Americans to read and ponder his words.

---

[359] John Dear, *Thomas Merton, Peacemaker: Meditations on Merton, Peacemaking, and the Spiritual Life*. (Maryknoll, New York: Orbis Books, 2015), 18.

[360] David W. Givey, *The Social Thoughts of Thomas Merton: The Way of Nonviolence and Peace for the Future* (Winona, MN: Anselm Academic, 2009), 93.

[361] Raboteau, *American Prophets,* 155.

For Merton, like King, commitment to nonviolence affirmed the preciousness of each human life—an intuition rising out of his own contemplative experience of the presence of God at the still point (*le pointe vierge*) of each person. King emphasized that "every man is somebody, because he is a child of God." This universal identity is shared by all, because "every human being has etched in his personality the indelible stamp of the Creator."[362] And he held that if any human person is treated as a means to an end, the image of God is abused in him and consequently and proportionately lost by those who inflict this abuse. For King and Merton alike, the "interrelatedness of human beings—the hidden wholeness that binds us all together," is the basis of our responsibility to enact social justice.[363]

Challenging Racism in the United States

According to Merton, Christians in the United States often failed to recognize their *kairos* time, those moments of truth, urgency and "providential decision," in which the time comes for a decisive response to a grave moral or social evil in society. This was not entirely the case, however, with regard to the African-American nonviolent civil rights movement. Merton believed that in this movement, under Martin Luther King Jr., the *kairos* moment was "met with a courageous and enlightened response."[364] In his view, "The nonviolent-Negro civil rights drive has been one of the most positive and successful expressions of Christian social action that has been seen anywhere in the twentieth century. It is certainly the greatest example of Christian faith in action in the social history of the United States."[365]

Certainly the heroic spirit of Christian faith manifested by African Americans in the Birmingham demonstrations or the March on Washington in 1963, as well as the prophetic response of white Protestants and Catholics across the U.S., decisively influenced the

---

362 Ibid., 156.

363 Raboteau, 157.

364 Merton, "Religion and Race in the United States," *Selected Essays*, 206.

365 Ibid.

passage of the Civil Rights Act.[366] At the same time, it is important to note that the white Christians supporting racial justice constituted a minority of U.S. Christians at the time. Merton was thus compelled to challenge U.S. Christians with the following words,

> If there is a *kairos*, and perhaps there still is, it is not a "time" in which once again we will convince the world that we are right, but perhaps rather a time in which the crisis of man will teach us to see a few sobering truths about our own Christian calling and our place in the world—a place no longer exalted and mighty, or perhaps even influential. . . .
>
> The American racial crisis which grows more serious every day offers the American Christian a chance to face reality about himself and recover his fidelity to Christian truth, not merely in institutional loyalties and doctrinal orthodoxies (in which no one has taken the trouble to accuse him of failing) but in recanting a more basic heresy: the loss of that Christian sense which sees every other man as Christ and treats him as Christ.[367]

Merton saw "the error of racism" as a "logical consequence of an essentialist style of thought" prevalent in Western culture, which objectifies others and reduces them to precise categories in order to control them. This entails "finding out what a man is and then nailing him to a definition so that there can be no change."[368] It was by scapegoating African Americans that whites managed to maintain their identity and power. According to Merton, "blaming the Negro... has become a strong emotional need for the white man," giving him "a stronger sense of identity, or rather it *protects* an identity which is seriously threatened with pathological dissolution. It is by blaming the Negro that the white man tries to hold himself

---

366 Ibid., 206. According to the Civil Rights Law, "the freedom of all citizens to enjoy the facilities of the country equally is due to what one might call a Christian as well as a humanitarian and liberal conscience in the United States."

367 Ibid.

368 Thomas Merton, *Dancing in the Water of Life: Seeking Peace in the Hermitage*, The Journals of Thomas Merton, Vol. 5, ed. Robert E. Daggy (New York, NY: Harper Collins Publishers, 1997), 200.

together."[369] Merton believed that the racial crisis in the United States was a "colonial crisis" within the country itself rather than on a distant continent. At the same time, "the slogan 'Black Power' implies not only the intent to use political means in order to gain what is granted the Negro by law and refused him in fact. It implies a consciousness of revolutionary solidarity with the colored in other parts of the world."[370]

The *kairos* moment offered an opportunity for unity and healing between whites and African Americans. White society had sinned grievously against African Americans through racial injustices and cruelties, but "the time has come when both white and Negro have been granted, by God, a unique and momentous opportunity to repair this injustice and to re-establish the violated moral and social order on a new plane."[371] Merton held that Martin Luther King and other civil rights leaders bore the weight of suffering not only to liberate black people but to save the souls of white people by revealing to them the depth of their sin.

Peace and Nuclear War

Merton was born during the First World War and lived through the Second World War, the Korean War, the Cuban Missile Crisis, and the Vietnam War. In an essay published in *The Catholic Worker* in October 1961, he wrote, "The present war crisis is something we have made entirely for and by ourselves. There is in reality not the slightest logical reason for war, and yet the whole world is plunging headlong into frightful destruction, and doing so *with the purpose of avoiding war and preserving peace!*" Merton saw this astrue war-madness, an illness of the mind and the spirit that is spreading with a furious and subtle contagion all over the world. He directed his concern especially towards the United States, of all the countries that are sick the one that is most 'grievously afflicted. He asserted, "this is a nation that claims to be fighting for religious truth along with

---

[369] Merton, *CGB*, 33.

[370] Merton, "Religion and Race in the United States," *TME*, 209.

[371] Merton, *Faith and Violence*, 67. See also Givey, 93.

freedom and other values of the spirit. Truly we have entered the 'post-Christian era' with a vengeance. Whether we are destroyed or whether we survive, the future is awful to contemplate."[372]

Merton denied the traditional Catholic teaching on "Just War Theory" with regard to the rules that govern the just conduct of war (*jus in bello*). These rules fall under two broad principles: *discrimination*, which seeks to determine the legitimate targets of war, and *proportionality*, which considers the morally acceptable degree of force that may be used to wage war. A third principle, that of *responsibility*, is sometimes included. This principle considers where the responsibility lies in the waging of war.[373]

Merton felt that nuclear weapons violated the distinction between combatant and noncombatants and also violated the principle of proportionality. "To my mind," he writes, "there was very little doubt about the immorality of the methods used in modern war. . . . Methods that descend to wholesale barbarism and ruthless, indiscriminate slaughter of noncombatants practically without defense are hard to see as anything else but mortal sins."[374] This conviction led Merton to consider the noncombatant objector status before he ultimately entered the monastery.

In an essay entitled "Peace: A Religious Responsibility," Merton criticizes the effect of nuclear war and the use of nuclear weapons. He states that the purpose of this essay is

> to stand back from the imminent risks of the Cold War crisis, seeking to judge the problem of nuclear war not in relation to what seems to be our own interests or even our own survival, but simply in the light of moral truth. A Christian ought to consider whether nuclear war is not in itself a moral evil so great that it

---

[372] Dekar, 136.

[373] *Internet Encyclopedia of Philosophy* (IEP), accessed January 18, 2018, http://www.iep.utm.edu/justwar/#H3.

[374] Thomas Merton, *The Seven Storey Mountain* (New York: Harcourt Brace, 1948), 312.

> *cannot* be justified even for the best of ends, even to defend the highest and most sacrosanct of values.[375]

He laments that "both in the East and in the West nuclear weapons are taken for granted. Nuclear war is now assumed to be a rational option or at least nuclear deterrence is accepted as a reasonable and workable way of 'preserving peace.'" However, nuclear war will "lead nowhere but to the suicide of nations and of cultures, indeed to the destruction of human society itself." He asserts that "America and Russia are playing the paranoid game of nuclear war deterrence, each one desperately hoping to preserve peace by threatening the other with bigger bombs and total annihilation."[376]

Merton's articles on war and peace brought him into conflict with the Cistercian censors, who had to provide their imprimatur before Merton submitted what he wrote for publication. The greatest trial Merton faced in this regard was the strong opposition from his Abbot General, Dom Gabriel Sortais, who advised Merton that he could write on peace but not on war. Sortais thus saw to it that Rome banned Merton's manuscript *Peace in the Post-Christian Era*. However, this information was kept from Merton by Dom James for several months, thus allowing some of Merton's articles on war and peace to be published in such journals as *Commonweal* and *The Catholic Worker*. Shortly thereafter, Merton was delighted to see Pope John XXIII's encyclical *Pacem in Terris* (1963), which condemned nuclear war and its consequences. Subsequently, "he wrote to the Abbot General [Sortais] with tongue in cheek that it was a good thing the pope didn't have to get *Pacem in Terris* passed by Trappist censorship. He commented that the pope had condemned the use of nuclear weapons much better than he himself could have done with his writings."[377] Merton's greatest contribution to the pursuit of peace, therefore, was the prophetic denunciation of the roots of war and violence, namely fear, greed, and misuse of technology.

---

375 Merton, "Peace," *Selected Essays,* 128.

376 Ibid., 128-129.

377 Ibid., vii-viii.

Confronting the Vietnam War

Merton strongly opposed the Vietnam War. In May 1964, he wrote to President Lyndon Johnson regarding his concern about the War. He said, "As a priest and a monk of the Catholic Church I would like to add my voice to the voices of all those who have pleaded for a peaceful settlement in Vietnam."[378] He denounced the war not only on humanitarian and moral grounds but also in the belief that the war can only strengthen the appeal of communism in Asia. He condemned the "delusionary" vision of Americans, and their inability to see the struggles of the people of Vietnam, calling them "Men with incredible technical skill and no sense of human realities in Asia—lost in abstractions, sentimentalities, myths, delusions, narcissism and the Great Mania fixation of America!"[379]

In *Faith and Violence,* Merton included a chapter entitled "Vietnam—An Overwhelming Atrocity," in which he expressed deep concern for the cruelties perpetrated against the people of Vietnam. Americans were destroying the "lives, villages, and the entire habitats" of the people in Southeast Asia."[380] He was deeply saddened by the victims of Napalm bombs, many of whom were young children, the elderly or infirm. He highlighted two contrasting perspectives on the war. According to an American Catholic bishop seeking to console President Johnson, the Vietnam War was "a sad and heavy obligation imposed by the mandate of love," but from a Vietnamese Buddhist nun came these words: "You Americans come to help the Vietnamese people, but have brought only death and destruction. Most of us Vietnamese hate from the bottom of our hearts the Americans who have brought the suffering of this war."[381] Merton denounced

---

[378] Merton, *HGL*, 439.

[379] Thomas Merton, *Learning to Love: Exploring Solitude and Freedom*, ed. Christine M. Bochen (New York: Harper Collins Publishers, 1997), 41.

[380] Jim Forest, *The Root of War is Fear: Thomas Merton's Advice to Peacemakers* (Maryknoll, New York: Orbis Books, 2016), 168.

[381] Merton, *Faith and Violence: Christian Teaching and Christian Practice* (Kindle Locations 1283), University of Notre Dame Press. Kindle Edition.

American perspectives on the war for being completely out of touch with the human reality:

> The tragic thing about Vietnam is that, after all, the "realism" of our program there is so unrealistic, so rooted in myth, so completely out of touch with the needs of the people whom we know only as statistics and to whom we never manage to listen, except where they fit in with our own psychopathic delusions. Our external violence in Vietnam is rooted in an inner violence which simply ignores the human reality of those we claim to be helping.[382]

In May 1966, Merton welcomed Thich Nhat Hanh, a Vietnamese Buddhist monk, prominent peace-maker, and proponent of socially-engaged Zen Buddhism, to his hermitage at Gethsemani. Merton described him as "a perfectly formed monk." Nhat Hanh taught his disciples, "Do not avoid suffering or close your eyes before suffering. Do not lose awareness of the existence of suffering in the life of the world. Find ways to be with those who are suffering, including personal contact, visits, images, and sounds. By such means, awaken yourself and others to the reality of suffering in the world." As a consequence of this teaching, many Vietnamese Buddhists peacefully resisted the war and had worked toward a 'third way' solution that sought a negotiated end to the civil war and the exodus of American soldiers. The horrors of the war caused Nhat Hanh to temporarily give up "many of the externals of the monastic life in order to act as a spokesman for the war's victims," though he would always remain a contemplative.[383]

After Nhat Hanh's visit, Merton wrote a short reflection in which he called Nhat Hanh his "brother": "*He is more my brother than many who are nearer to me in race and nationality, because he and I see things exactly the same way. He and I explore the war for exactly the same reasons … reasons of sanity, justice and love. We deplore the needless*

[382] Ibid., 92.

[383] Forest, *The Root of War is Fear,* 159-160.

destruction the ... ravaging of human life, the rape of the culture..."[384] In Nhat Hanh, Merton had encountered "a monk who carried his hermitage invisibly around him, a contemplative wandering the face of the earth, bearing his own silence amid the surrounding noise."[385] Nhat Hanh's visit began to prepare Merton for his pilgrimage to Asia in 1968.

5. Prophetic Contribution to the Church

Prophetic Voice at the Vatican Council

Pope John XXIII convoked the Second Vatican Council, which opened in October 1962 and ended in December 1965. Through the council, Pope John hoped to restore the simple and pure lines that the face of the Church of Jesus had at its birth. Merton appreciated the Pope's approach: "Really Pope John has been a great gift from God to all of us. What a superb Pope, and what a heart."[386] Though he was not physically present at the council, Merton actively participated in it through correspondence and the circulation of his writings. The Pope was delighted to receive Merton's letters expressing his concerns for the world, society and the church.

Merton prepared himself well to understand the council by reading Hans Kung's *The Council, Reform and Reunion*.[387] Merton appreciated this book because it was "noble, straight and courageous . . . The vigor and honesty of the message was tremendous."[388] Merton had great expectations for the council: "The Council! Such hope and such fears! But the Holy Spirit really is in command there, though He may not be at the Pentagon."[389] At the same time, he feared that

---

[384] Thomas Merton, "Thich Nhat Hanh Is My Brother," was first published in *Jubilee*, August 1966 (PEP, 260-262); cited in Forest, *The Root of War is Fear*, 162-163 (Italics in original).

[385] Forest, *The Root of War is Fear*, 164.

[386] Merton, *RJ*, 243.

[387] Hans Kung, *The Council, Reform and Reunion*, translated Cecily Hastings (New York: Sheed and Ward, 1962).

[388] Merton, *RJ*, 246.

[389] Thomas Merton, *Witness to Freedom: The Letters of Thomas Merton in Times of Crisis*, selected and edited by William Shannon (New York: Farrar, Straus,

"authoritative demands" and obligations would be imposed, "without freeing the heart to receive the Holy Spirit in abundance."[390] He was certain the council would be a disaster if it "simply reaffirmed disciplinary rules that had been in place for centuries." He most wanted "reform and renewal in the Church."[391] Merton anticipated that some of the concerns of the council's agenda would include major liturgical reforms, clarification of the role of the bishops, peace in the world, reforming the Roman curia.

However, Merton was most concerned about the issues of war, peace, deterrence, conscientious objection and nonviolence. At the end of the third session of the council, Bishop John Taylor of Stockholm extolled Merton and spoke affirmatively of his position on nuclear war: "*Thomas Merton, one of the most profound mystical theologians of our times, has written that total nuclear war would be a sin of mankind equal only to the crucifixion of Christ. Modern means of war threaten the very existence of man. Moreover, the Council has a sacred duty to respond with all its moral power to this threat of mankind's self destruction.*"[392] Merton influenced the Holy Father regarding the formation of the encyclical *Pacem in Terris*. He was delighted when Pope John published the encyclical on Holy Thursday, April 11, 1963. The encyclical argued that, it is impossible for war to be an instrument of justice in the context of nuclear armaments.

The document of the council that reflected on the problem of war and peace was initially entitled "Schema 13," and later became the Pastoral Constitution on the Church in the Modern World (*Gaudium et Spes*). In 1965, when the fourth session of the Council was to begin, Merton wrote an article entitled "Schema Thirteen: An Open Letter to the American Hierarchy," in which he enjoined the bishops to transcend their "national interests" and to follow higher

---

Giroux, 1994), 283.

[390] Thomas Merton, Turning Toward the World: the Pivotal Years. The Journals of Thomas Merton, Vol. 4, ed. Victor Kramer (New York, NY: Harper San Francisco, 1996), 503.

[391] Merton, *Witness to Freedom*, 283.

[392] Forest, *The Root of War is Fear,* 144 (Italics in original).

values: "The Christian is called, as always, to a decision for Christ, not to a decision for this or that kind of society. He is called to obey the Gospel of love, for all men, and not simply to devote himself to the interests of a nation, a party, a class, or a culture."[393] He challenged them to condemn the indiscriminate slaughter of combatants and noncombatants. Merton urged that "The common man, the poor man, the man who has no hope but in God, everywhere looks to the Church as a last hope of protection against the unprincipled machinations of militarists and power politicians."[394] Heeding Merton's words, the council took a stand on nuclear war, declaring that the arms race is an entirely treacherous trap for humanity.

Merton welcomed the shift advanced by the council concerning the Church's self-understanding and internal structures. With regard to the Dogmatic Constitution on the Church (*Lumen Gentium*), he wrote, "Instead of considering the Church primarily and principally as a hierarchical society and a strictly organized institution, [the Constitution] affirms that the Church is the community of the faithful, the Mystical Body of Christ, the people of God."[395] This shift stresses the primacy of the spiritual life and its fruitfulness over organizational rigidity and institutional power. This was not to deny that the church was an organized institution, but that its laws and structures exist for the sake of love and of life, and to safeguard the freedom of the Spirit within the framework of earthly society. Thus, the ultimate purpose of the church is the transformation and consecration of all life to God by the leaven of holiness. Merton was gratified that the council had ushered in a new and vital understanding of the church, one which reversed the hierarchical, juridical ecclesiology of the second millennium. In this new understanding, "a static concept of the Church as organization is replaced by a dynamic concept of the

---

393 Merton, *Witness to Freedom*, 88; cited in Forest, *The Root of War is Fear*, 144.

394 Merton, *Witness to Freedom*, 90.

395 Thomas Merton, *Contemplation in a World of Action* (New York: Doubleday, 1973), 117.

Church as a living body moved by the invisible and divine Spirit of Truth and Love imparted to her by the Risen Christ."[396]

Another of Merton's contributions to the council was to the renewal of the liturgy. Early on, he had written two essays on *Sacrosanctum Concilium,* the council's document on the liturgy: Liturgy and Christian Personalism, and Liturgical Renewal: The Open Approach. The first article reflects on the liturgy as the primary way in which the faithful may express in their lives and manifest to others the mystery of Christ and the real nature of the true Church. In the second article, Merton explores the shift from rubricism to the active involvement of people in the liturgy; communion under both the kinds; and a new spirit of openness between priest and people. Moreover, he foresaw "the need for a translation of the Scriptures that was meant for public proclamation, and the need for good music."[397]

Finally, Merton brought to light the importance of re-conceiving the church's relationship with other world religions, and of opening the possibilities for interreligious dialogue. Merton's influence was clearly evident in the Declaration on the Relationship of the Church to Non-Christian Religions (*Nostra Aetate*), promulgated in October 1965. This document represented a remarkable reversal in the church's self-understanding in relation to other faith traditions, recognizing that these traditions reflect a ray of that Truth which enlightens all men. Therefore, the church exhorts the faithful that "through dialogue and collaboration with the followers of other religions, carried out with prudence and love and in witness to the Christian faith and life, they recognize, preserve and promote the good things, spiritual and moral, as well as the socio-cultural values found among these [religions]."[398] Merton's close friendships with spiritual seekers

---

[396] Merton, *Contemplation in a World of Action* 117/135; see also Shannon, "Vatican Council, The Second," *TME,* 506.

[397] Shannon, "Vatican Council, The Second," *TME,* 506.

[398] Paul VI, *The Relation of the Church to Non-Christian Religions: Nostra Aetate,* (October 6, 1965), 2, accessed February 2, 2018, http://www.vatican.va/archive/hist_councils/ii_vatican_council/documents/vat-ii_decl_19651028_nostra-aetate_en.html.

of other traditions, notably Rabbi Abraham Heschel,[399] had opened his eyes to the beauty, wisdom, and truth found in these traditions. It is clear that Merton's invisible presence pervaded the council, contributing substantially to the renewal and reforms of Vatican.

Renewal of Monastic Formation

Merton entered the monastery in 1941, to seek God and do God's will. As he grew in union with God through prayer, solitude, and contemplation, he felt the call to renew the monastic life. His entire program of renewal was focused on seeking "God Alone," which he saw as the purpose of the monastic life, "not farming, not chanting the psalms, not building beautiful monasteries, not wearing a certain kind of costume, not fasting, not manual labor, not reading, not meditation, not vigils in the night, but only GOD." Paul Dekar explains that in this regard, Merton was differentiating the "means and the one reason for the monk's existence."[400]

During the twenty-seven years of his monastic life, Merton contributed to the renewal of the monastic order regarding monastic formation, prayer, contemplation and engagement with people in the world. He was not concerned with the "institution of monasticism," per se, but focused on the "vision expressed in classic monastic sources and on insights for contemporary monks" that could be applied to their lives.[401]

Merton's first endeavor to renew the Cistercian Order began on September 10, 1949, when he sent three proposals to the annual meeting of the representatives of the Cistercians gathered in France from all over the world. The first proposal was to strengthen the theological training at the monastery. He sought to make the Cistercian program for priestly studies in spiritual theology, focusing on the Cistercian Fathers, mystical theology, canon law, and other important subjects to prepare the leaders of the future. In order to provide an

---

399 Merton, *HGL*, 430-34. See also Shannon, "Vatican Council, the Second," in *TME*, 507.

400 Thomas Merton, *The Waters of Siloe* (New York: Harcourt Publishing Company, 1979), 335; cited in Dekar, 37.

401 Ibid., 34, 40.

optimal learning environment, Merton wished to have a separate building for the students. Second, he wanted to construct a small chapel for the monks to spend time in retreats and solitude. Third, he recommended having a retreat master for groups of retreatants. To educate the brothers, Merton updated the Gethsemani library with books on the Bible, liturgy, and early Christian writings, and sowed the seeds of passion for the word of God in their minds.[402] As a novice master, "Merton sought to make each individual aware of his human experience so that it might be a channel for self-knowledge and a way of opening to the life of the Spirit. He taught in a way whereby students and teacher explored what is meaningful, real, and true for oneself and in life."[403] He introduced a new educational approach that was experiential and participatory rather than catechetical. In order that monks and students at Gethsemani spend more time in contemplation, Merton expressed to the abbot General Gabriel Sortais that "an area be set aside for them in the woods." Surprisingly, Sortais granted Merton's request. Thus, "on Sundays and feast days, students and novices could withdraw for several hours to relax in a beautiful setting, read Scripture, and pray."[404]

Merton believed that the monastery should not be an enclave of eccentric or archaic human beings who have rebelled against the world. He endeavored to form the monks to face the challenges of the twentieth century—not only to embrace the Mystery of Christ, but also the modern world of science, technology, and revolution. Merton believed that the monks, after having discovered their true selves in freedom, needed to find new ways to build, on earth, the Kingdom of God. He held that the ultimate meaning and purpose of monastic formation is to "acquire a heart that knows God, not just a heart that loves God or communes with God but one that knows God."[405] He realized that the most significant way to grow deeper into the knowledge and mystery of God was to grow in prayer.

---

[402] Dekar, 35-38.

[403] Ibid.

[404] Ibid., 38.

[405] Ibid., 47.

Another important contribution Merton made to monastic renewal was the introduction of hermitages into Cistercian practice. Notably, he was the first Trappist to move into a hermitage. This grew out of Merton's longing for a greater degree of silence and solitude, for himself and for other monks. For him, the solitary life was "the crown of the monastic vocation."[406] Merton expressed his concern that

> the environs and atmosphere of the large monastery tend sometimes to become increasingly noisy and active and unfavorable for the development of a deep, silent, contemplative life. It is more and more necessary for those called to a more intense and simple life of prayer to be able to seek silence and solitude at a distance from the monastery. . . . there is a real need to construct a hermitage at some distance from the monastery, with facilities for both relative and complete solitude, to provide for temporary and permanent vocations to solitude, without severing the bonds of the monk with the community of his vocation and of his profession.[407]

According to his request to the abbot's council, in 1965, Merton was granted permission to live as a full-time hermit in the house that was built for ecumenical meetings and discussions. After ten years of service as a novice master, Merton had chosen a new path to the place of his new freedom. As Shannon observes "It was a new and crucial stage of that real journey in life that is interior, that involves growth and an ever-greater surrender to the creative action of love and grace in human hearts." On April 24, 1965, he wrote to Ernesto Cardenal, a former Catholic priest who studied in Kentucky with Merton that, "It is a wonderful life. Actually it has transformed me, and I am now at last convinced that I have found what I have always been looking for."[408]

---

406 Thomas Merton, *The Monastic Journey,* ed. Patrick Hart, Cistercian Studies Series, no. 133 (Kalamazoo, Michigan, 1992), 135.

407 Ibid., 135-136.

408 Shannon, *SL*, 250-251.

Conclusion

In this chapter, I have explored the prophetic challenges Merton posed to the church and the world. For Merton, both inner and outer explorations were rooted in an intense awareness of the reality of God's presence in the individual heart and in the heart of human history. As a visionary, Merton contributed greatly to public life in America, to the universal church and the world at large through his contemplative experiences, his commitment to peace and non-violence, and his incisive writings. He was both appreciated and strongly criticized by religious and political leaders of his time for daring to raise his voice against the injustices in the society and the church, and to do so as a Christian monk. The following chapter will consider how Thomas Merton, who read the signs of the times, and confronted the injustices of his own era, can motivate the consecrated people of India today to become contemplative prophets and to reach out to the people on the margins with love and compassion.

Chapter 5

The Relevance of Thomas Merton's Spirituality for the Consecrated Life in India

Thomas Merton followed Jesus Christ radically through the monastic vows of chastity, poverty, obedience, and stability, reading the signs of the times through the lens of a mystical-prophetic spirituality. In this way, he contributed enormously to the transformation of U.S. political discourse, monastic life, and the Church's identity and mission in the modern world. The path Merton chose in following Christ may serve as an example to the consecrated men and women of India to pursue forms of contemplation that are transformative both of spiritual life and the social structures which lie at the root of suffering and injustice in India today. From this deep contemplative grounding will come the courage and determination to read the signs of the times and to respond to them "in the light of the Gospel."[409]

To consider the relevance of Merton's contemplative-prophetic spirituality for Indian consecrated life, this chapter is divided as follows. The first part deals with the goals of consecrated life in India as they pertain to the transformation of the society through the influence of education and the compassionate response to the cries of the marginalized. Part two examines some key internal and external

---

[409] *Gaudium et Spes: Pastoral Constitution on the Church in the Modern World*, The Documents of Vatican II (Vatican City: Libreria Editrice Vaticana), 4. (Hereafter cited as *GS*).

challenges to consecrated life in India today. The internal challenges include the call to deepen the mystical and contemplative dimensions of spiritual life, the institutionalization of the Indian church, and the declining of religious vocations in the consecrated life. The external challenges consist of religious fundamentalism (*Hindutva*), socio-economic incongruence, discrimination against women, and the growing ecological crisis. The third part explores the relevance of Merton's contemplative-prophetic spirituality to the challenges of Indian consecrated life, some of which include the necessity of re-igniting the spirit of contemplation through re-imagining union with God, re-building communities of fraternal love, and renewing the understanding of the vows. And the elements of Merton's prophetic spirituality relevant to the Indian Church include being a voice for the voiceless though denunciation of the social structures which oppress them, revitalizing the process of formation, re-imagining the identity and role of women in the church, and shaping an ecological consciousness through encountering God in Creation.

1. The Goals of Consecrated Life in India as Gospel Witness

Throughout the history of Christianity, God has called dedicated men and women to follow Jesus Christ radically, to bear witness to His love and compassion in this world. Consecrated people have dedicated themselves to furthering the vision and mission of Jesus on earth by living as monks, hermits, priests, or women religious. Today, Indian consecrated men and women number more than a hundred thousand. They are a mighty force in the Indian Church, spreading the good news of God's kingdom in a multi-religious, multi linguistic, and multi-cultural nation.

The consecrated men and women of India bear witness to Jesus amidst the challenges of religious fundamentalism, persecution, and violence. They proclaim the Gospel "among peoples who do not know Jesus Christ and the Gospel."[410] As followers of Christ, they "set aside their abilities, time, talents, work, the sweetness and goodness of their

[410] Kurien Kunnumpuram, *Prophets of the Lord Friends of the Poor: Indian Christian Reflections on the Religious Life* (Bandra, Mumbai: St. Pauls, 2014), 48.

hearts, all for the service of others."[411] They share the pain and hope of the sick, suffering, poor, marginalized and oppressed brothers and sisters of society. In this way, their words, their messages, the way they comfort the sorrowing and wipe the tears of those in pain are God's gifts and ways of expressing divine love.

Social Transformation through Education

Consecrated men and women in India play a significant role in the transformation of society through the mission of education. *The Catholic Education Policy*, promulgated by the Catholic Bishops' Conference of India, affirms that "the Church's presence in the world of education is a prophetic choice," and therefore, "the Church sees education not merely as a means for the personality development of individuals but also as an essential tool for the transformation of society, to build a more egalitarian, inclusive and integrated India."[412] As an educator, Dr. Lydia Fernandes, AC, comments on the benefits of the Catholic educational system in India:

> Wherever a Catholic school or college has been established, people of all castes and communities have flocked to it, acclaiming its academic excellence, good discipline, personal care and attention given to the students, the inculcation of values, dedication of the staff, promotion of healthy staff-student relationship, excellence in extracurricular activities, in a word, the all-round formation of the students.[413]

A large number of primary schools, secondary schools, colleges, engineering and medical colleges run by the religious men and women have borne witness to the "presence of Christ and His values," through the service to the people of India.

---

[411] George Kaitholil, *Consecrated Life: Challenges and Opportunities* (Bandra, Mumbai: St. Pauls, 2014), 23.

[412] Paul Parathazham, *Christianity in India: Sociological Investigations* (Bangalore: Dharmaram Publications, 2013), 261.

[413] Lydia Fernandes, "The Religious Educator," in *Consecrated Life in the Third Millennium: Challenges and Prospects*, ed. Joe Eruppakkatt (Bandra, Mumbai: St. Pauls, 2004), 92.

Despite these ideals and the profusion of exemplary service, however, the main categories of people who receive the higher quality education in India are "boys, people of urban areas, and the middle and upper classes and castes."[414] The Catholic educational institutions of India largely fail to educate women, the poor, the lower castes, and the people who live in rural and tribal areas. Catholic education is subject to criticism, sometimes justifiably so, for "the elitism and westernization exhibited through the fads and fashions in dress, attitudes, mentality, behavior, language and social values." This has led to the charge by some that the Catholic institutions "de-Indianize the students."[415] Furthermore, the institutional values, reflected most notably in a campus culture which is "pro-rich and urbane," prevent students from the economically disadvantaged sectors from feeling welcome and comfortable. Sadly, the prevailing ethos of these institutions "tends to be self-directed, result-oriented and competitive, whereby students get trapped in the rat-race for achievement and self-glory."[416]

Fortunately, there are prophetic voices within the church who are challenging the Catholic educational system in India to reflect more fully the vision set forth (above) by the bishops. Indian theologian and sociologist Paul Parathazham notes that education is never neutral; "although it tends to legitimatize and reproduce the status quo, it has also a liberative potential that can lead to social transformation."[417] Sadly, in his estimation, Catholic education in India largely serves the prior function.

Drawing on the critical pedagogies of Paulo Friere[418] and Jesuit biblical theologian George Soares-Prabhu, Parathazham calls for a

---

[414] Ibid.

[415] Parathazham, 278.

[416] Fernandes, 92-93.

[417] Ibid.

[418] Parathazham, 275; Paulo Freire, was a Brazilian educator. His "pedagogy of literacy education involves not only reading the word, but also reading the world." This approach was centered on developing an attitude of "critical consciousness" in the minds and hearts of the students which would lead them "to question the nature of their historical and social situation—to read their world—

"liberative thrust" in education, one which treats students "not as passive receptacles for the teacher to deposit the content," but as fully engaged participants in their own learning process. The teacher thus serves as one who accompanies the students on a "critical search for answers to questions that are relevant to them."[419] This educational philosophy is best understood in terms of its capacity to promote freedom, self-determination, and creativity rather than the internalization of the prevailing structures of inequality and oppression. According to Soares-Prabhu, the pedagogy of Jesus, which was "non-elitist, transforming, prophetic, dialogical, and critical," was liberative in two senses:

> It liberated people by making them conscious of their worth as children of the one Father in heaven. . .And as prophetic and critical teaching, it liberated them from the manipulative myths which legitimized their oppressive and alienating society by pointing towards a new fraternal and non-exploitative "world" in which people could live together as brothers and sisters.[420]

Sores-Prabhu thus imposes on Catholic educators the solemn charge that "Any pedagogy that claims to be Christian must be liberative in this double sense."[421] In this educational approach, the students have the responsibility to determine "what problems are worth studying and what procedures of enquiry need to be employed." Thus, the ultimate purpose of education is not teaching as such, but

---

with the goal of acting as subjects in the creation of a democratic society." Freire, implies "a dialogic exchange between teachers and students, where both learn, both question, both reflect and both participate in meaning-making." In this process conscientization takes place in the students as well as the teachers. Leslie Bentley, "A Brief Biography of Paulo Freire," (December, 1999); accessed February 24, 2018, http://ptoweb.org/aboutpto/a-brief-biography-of-paulo-freire/.

[419] Ibid., 276.

[420] Ibid., 274-275; George Soares-Prabhu, "Jesus the Teacher: The Liberative Pedagogy of Jesus of Nazareth," in *Christian Perspective in Education*, ed. H. Morissette (Bangalore: Xavier Board of Education, 1985), 85.

[421] Parathazham, 275.

rather "to inspire the desire for learning. Once the student's mind is set on fire, it will find a way to provide its own fuel."[422]

Parathazham also calls for an ethos of cooperation, in which educators encourage the students to develop the qualities of service, compassion and cooperation rather than . . . competition, which breeds individualism and personal ambition. In this view, students should be taught to look upon their companions not as rivals to be defeated, but as brothers and sisters to be cared for. The talented and brighter students should be encouraged to share their talents and skills to enrich the lives of the weaker and marginalized students in order to build a just and egalitarian society. In sum, an authentic Catholic education will guide students to not only "pursue their own personal dreams for a better tomorrow, but also to commit themselves to the task of building the India of our dreams."[423]

Responding to the Cries of the Marginalized

The hope-filled words of *Gaudium et Spes* encourage consecrated men and women to share the sufferings of their brothers and sisters: "The joys and the hopes, the griefs and the anxieties of the people of this age, especially those who are poor or in any way afflicted, are the joys and hopes, the griefs and anxieties of the followers of Christ."[424] With regard to the mission of the consecrated people to respond to the cries of the marginalized, Kaitholil expands the categories of poverty to include multiple forms of oppression and misery: "The poor are not only those who have no house or clothes or food. All the sad, the oppressed, the sick, the destitute, those who are deprived of spiritual development and progress, the illiterate, those who are ignorant of religious, cultural and social matters, the backward classes, and such others are all among the poor."[425] The missionary activities of education, healing, social work, and the other services by which

---

[422] Ibid., 276-277.

[423] Ibid., 286.

[424] *Gaudium et Spes: Pastoral Constitution on the Church in the Modern World.* The Documents of Vatican II (Vatican City: Libreria Editrice Vaticana, December 7, 1965), 1. (Hereafter cited as *GS*).

[425] Kaitholil, 83.

consecrated people are continuing to lessen the pain and struggles of the poor, constitute their response to the cries of the oppressed.

The service to the poor by consecrated people has been affirmed by the Indian Government. As Dr. Verrier Elvin, who served as the adviser to the welfare of the scheduled tribes of India, remarks, "They have brought to India the spirit of adventure and dedication. Hundreds of them have left all comfort and convenience, gone to distant lands and lived there for years. They were the first in treating the lepers. They helped the poor and the lowly; they befriended the untouchables. They took the lead in working for the welfare of the scheduled tribes."[426] Moreover, their service to the poor is enabling the people of other faiths to discover the path to God through service. As K.P. Naik, former secretary to the Central Education Commission of India, comments, "It is from Christian religion that Hindu religion received the idea that the way to God is through service to humanity. Though we (Hindus) have our own ways of meditation, action and devotion, it is from contact with Christian religion that we received the awareness of the importance of service, that service to humans is an important way of finding God."[427] Through their dedicated service, consecrated men and women "embody the spirit of Jesus for the renewal of human society."[428]

Amidst the challenges, complexities and contradictions of Indian society, the consecrated people bear witness to the good news of Christ through their various ministries of medical, social, pastoral, and educational work, and their care for the marginalized members of the society. Although the consecrated are committed to bearing witness to Christ by their presence and service, there is still much to

---

[426] Ibid., 84.

[427] Ibid.

[428] *CRI* (*Conference of Religious in India*), National Assembly, *Yesu Kristu Jayanti 2000*, *Religious Life in a New Era*, (Delhi: CRI House, 2000), 37; (Hereafter cited as *CRI*).

be done by way of moving out to the peripheries, to find and heal the poor and vulnerable members of society.[429]

2. The Internal and External Challenges to the Consecrated Life in India

Today, India is in the midst of a technological, economic, and communication revolution. This revolution involves the acceleration of science, technology, globalization, economic liberalization, and various means of mass media communications, much of which has influenced Indian people adversely and affected their moral values and worldviews.[430] Jesuit theologian Kurien Kunnumpuram sums it up in this way: "A consumerist culture is slowly spreading through India. A new vision of the world is exerting a lot of influence on our people. A secular outlook on life and a passion for enjoying it are becoming widespread. Christian faith and a lifestyle that is based on it are fast disappearing from Christian families."[431] These challenges deeply affect the lives of consecrated men and women in India—spiritually, psychologically, morally, socially, politically, and economically.

Current president of the Indian Theological Association, Shalini Mulackal, remarks that it is perhaps no exaggeration "to say that religious life is in crisis" today. While affirming the many positive elements, she asserts that "we cannot deny the fact that there is an erosion of credibility in the way religious life is lived in India." To this she adds that an "absence of a vibrant spirituality can be sensed everywhere," and a good number of consecrated men and women are "cocooned in comfort zones of security." The impact of "individualism, consumerism and careerism" has significantly reduced the spirit of commitment and availability among religious.[432] Although there are

---

[429] I shall explore the prophetic denunciation of the root causes of the suffering and misery of the poor below.

[430] Kunnumpuram, 15.

[431] Ibid.

[432] Shalini Mulackal, "Consecrated Life Today: Trends and Challenges in Society and Church" Paper presented at the *CRI* (*Conference of Religious in India*) *National Consultation*, organized by Streevani (Pune, 24th and 25th January 2009), (Unpublished), 7; Streevani is an organization which came into being at Ishvani

many challenges in Indian society which affect the consecrated life in India, I will focus on a few key elements. Internally, we see the need for the renewal of an authentic contemplative spirituality, the adverse influence of institutionalization, and the decline of religious vocations. The external challenges include Hindu religious fundamentalism, economic and social incongruence, gender discrimination, and ecological crisis.

The Internal Challenges

Need for a Renewal of Contemplative Spirituality

One of the major challenges the consecrated men and women encounter in India today is the need to renew the contemplative spirituality that lies at the heart of the rich spiritual heritage of India. Kunnumpuram remarks that there are many devotions and pious practices in Indian consecrated life, "but not enough spirituality."[433] Vandana Mataji, a Catholic nun who initiated the Christian Ashram movement in India, expressed that the consecrated people in India do not possess the "spirit of contemplation" that would enable them to "enter into relationship with others and to grasp what reality is." In her words, "Religious give themselves entirely to works or services at the cost of their contemplative dimension." She adds that the consecrated life in India has become a "smooth and easy life, an uninterrupted enjoyment of the goods of providence, full meals, soft raiments, well-furnished houses. . .the feeling of security, [and] the consciousness of wealth and power."[434] These and many other factors "have choked the spirit of Indian religious today."[435]

In the face of the demands of institutional life, apostolic ministries, and administrative tasks, consecrated people often fail to

---

Kendra, Pune as a research wing to explore women's visions and missions through participative research on how they consider themselves, their various roles in the family, workplace, community and religion, accessed October 30, 2017, http://streevani.org/history.php.

433 Kunnumpuram, 17.

434 Mulackal, 7.

435 Ibid.See also Kaitholil, 164.

pursue the deeper dimensions of a contemplative spirituality. Today it is urgent that they embrace such qualities of the spiritual life as "simplicity, hospitality, silence, sense of the sacred, contemplation, [and] community," as these values "have not yet become the indigenous and habitual expressions of consecrated life for us in our country."[436] It is a painful reality that the consecrated men and women of India, who are called to be the spiritual guides of the people, have largely failed to embrace the most essential spiritual dimensions of consecrated life in order to bear witness to Christ amidst the multiple challenges facing the nation today.

In the year 2000, *The Conference of Religious in India* (CRI) organized an event focusing on the theme of "Religious Life in a New Era" in order to address the lack of clarity among religious themselves with regard to the "specific purpose of religious life and witness to the Church in today's world." There it was observed that when the Christian missionaries came from Europe to India, the picture they gave to the Indian society was one of "dedicated active workers, not of men and women of deep spiritual experience primarily devoted to growing in union with God, the inner Ground of their being, and helping others to the same experiential and practical awareness of his presence and action within them and in human society in the perspective of eternity."[437] The missionaries failed to transmit to the future generation a Christian spirituality rooted in the Indian culture, and this fact has diminished the spiritual vibrancy of the consecrated life of India. Kaitholil observes,

> There can be no authentic consecrated Christian life unless it is rooted in the Gospel and in the culture of the people. Christian consecrated life in India is strongly influenced by western models and styles. Even the religious habits, food habits, and community language appear very much foreign … India is known for its wealth of spiritual experiences. It developed a style of consecrated life centuries before Christianity. It is therefore

---

[436] Kaitholil, 166.

[437] Ibid., 6.

unfortunate that Christian consecrated life in India today has largely ignored the religious traditions of this country.[438]

Thus, today, without blaming the predecessors of the Indian mission, consecrated people have a solemn responsibility to rediscover the vital spiritual resources of India, which will equip them to grow as contemplative prophets and to reflect a spirituality relevant to the context of India.

Institutionalization of Consecrated Life

The Catholic Church in general, and in India in particular, is an institutionalized, hierarchical structure, and seen by many as "foreign" or "Western," an intrinsic part of colonial history. This is so because, as Indian ecclesiologist Kuncheria Pathil argues, the church has failed to inculturate itself into the rich multi-cultural and local religious contexts of the Indian reality. Rather, the historical churches in India are "mere 'extensions' or 'transplantations' from outside," and consequently, church structures and patterns of worship are likewise extrinsic, with "only minor adaptations . . . made to fit into [the Indian] context." With their center in Rome, the local churches largely adhere to western cultural and religious norms. Pathil explains that "many of the Church's huge impressive institutions were mostly funded by the West and it is alleged that many of the church's educational and health institutions cater exclusively to the needs of the rich and the super rich." In this context, liturgical expression is Roman, Syrian, or Antiochean, and church doctrines are formulated in Greco-Roman and Scholastic categories.[439] The Indian church, therefore, seems to be alienated from the Indian cultural, religious, and spiritual ethos.

The sages of India remind us that the core of every religion is spiritual and mystical experience. If any religion fails to convey the spiritual experience, it becomes an empty shell. Though the early Christian community originated as a spiritual movement, the

---

[438] Ibid., 166.

[439] Kuncheria Pathil, "Theological Reflections on the Church from India," in *Asian Horizons*, Vol. 6, no. 4 (December 2012): 689-690.

church of today has become far too "institutionalized, ritualistic and legalistic."[440]

The various religious orders were founded in the church to bear witness to Christ's presence in the world and to serve the needs of the marginalized members of society through the various ministries of education, health care, the socio-pastoral apostolate, and evangelization. As charismatic leaders, the founders of these orders transmitted their deep-rooted spirituality and zeal for the mission to their members.

Religious charisma is a potentially subversive force in society and therefore a threat to the status quo. Following Max Weber, Parathazham observes that every religion is founded on the charismatic qualities of a spiritual leader who has an intrinsic authority and has demanded obedience from a community of followers. Such authority is considered to come neither from tradition nor from law but from the personal charisma of the leader. This charismatic leader, therefore, "does not recognize the established order based on tradition and law."[441] As religion becomes established, however, the charismatic/prophetic dimensions are gradually eroded and replaced by an institutional authority.

Yet, in the Indian church, the institutional structures provide security and comfort to those in consecrated life, shielding them from the human powerlessness and poverty to which the Indian populations are subjected. It is this pervasive institutionalization that dulls the church's prophetic edge. As Mulackal explains,

> Excessive institutionalisation has sucked the spirit and vitality of religious life today. Increasingly, the security of the institution has removed the basic insecurity demanded by the Gospel. Though religious life is of its essence prophetic, prophecy has become easily institutionalised by achievement. Religious are no longer seen as the people on the cutting edge, but rather

---

[440] Ibid., 689-690.

[441] Parathazham, 37.

are viewed as people intimately connected with maintaining the institutions of society.[442]

In the face of such institutionalization, religious are largely removed from the sense of the real mission to which they were called—the furthering of the reign of God. Instead, they have become deeply immersed in the institutionalized forms of ministry originally undertaken to carry out this very mission. Gradually, the mission dimension of consecrated life has given way to professionalism, careerism and the pursuit of personal objectives. However, given that "the vast majorities are pushed to the periphery because of their socio-economic and political powerlessness, promotion and furthering of the reign of God necessarily involves taking the side of the oppressed and working with them for their integral liberation."[443]

Regrettably, this loss of charismatic and prophetic leadership in religious life has led to the failure to denounce and struggle against the structural evil embedded in social structures and institutional forms. Parathazham contends that the loss of the prophetic dimension of religious life is a serious disorder of "authentic religiosity."[444] With this loss comes a lack of self-transparency. Parathazham laments that "the culture of open and honest self-criticism appears to be alien to most organized religions today." Therefore, consecrated people are called to cultivate periodical evaluations of their institutions, to reflect on the degree to which they embody the prophetic dimensions of the Gospel message that lead to the transformation of society and culture. In India, though institutionalization is an inevitable reality, "its pitfalls and dangers can be minimized if believers remain vigilant and engage in sustained and honest self-criticism."[445] These challenges enjoin consecrated men and women to rethink the institutionalized forms of mission and ministry in the church of India today.

---

[442] Mulackal, 8.

[443] Ibid.

[444] Parathazham, 58-59.

[445] Ibid., 62.

Decline of Religious Vocations

Today, most religious communities in India are facing the challenge of declining vocations to consecrated life. In many other countries, they began facing this problem decades ago. As theologian Joe Mannath observes, "Ever since the mid-sixties, the number of religious in Europe and North America has been diminishing rapidly. Many left, and very few have since joined. This has begun to happen in India, beginning with urban areas, like Mumbai or Chennai, and then, the more educated zones like Goa, Mangalore, Kerala and urban areas of other states."[446]

According to Mannath, there are two main factors affecting the decline of religious vocations in India. The first is "smaller families." Decades ago, many vocations came from larger families and therefore there was no great sacrifice on the part of parents to send a son or daughter to consecrated life. Further, in some situations, it was easier "for a financially hard-pressed family to let them go rather than educate them." The second factor involves the "far superior opportunities" available to young people today "for study, for work, for travel, for earning high salaries, for making their decisions, for getting to know people and places," in comparison to past generations. Today, young people look for more creative and dynamic lifestyles.[447]

The failure of consecrated people to assume a contemplative-prophetic role has affected the church in India. However, as theologian John Sankarathil argues, the "vocation crisis" may be perceived as a "challenge rather than a tragedy," an "eye-opener and a call to every consecrated person and every Institute to re-examine their mission and vision and the particular charism of the founder in the modern world."[448] The decline of vocations to consecrated life

---

[446] Joe Mannath, *A Radical Love, a Path of Light: The Beauty and Burden of Religious Life* (Okhla, New Delhi: CRI House, 2013), 172.

[447] Ibid., 173.

[448] John Sankarathil, "Religious Charism: Relevance for the Third Millennium," *Indian Journal of Spirituality* 14 (April-June 2001), 215; see also in Sankarathil, "Consecrated Life in India: The Asset of a Model, or A Challenge to Remodel," in *Vidyajyoti Journal of Theological Reflections* (March 2007): 189.

invites the members of the various religious orders to "to evaluate and re-evaluate the liberating dimensions of various ministries that are traditionally carried out." Sankarathil elucidates the contours of a vibrant, prophetic spirituality for consecrated life in India today, one which integrates the elements of prayer and prophetic witness:

> Consecrated persons should possess a spirituality of profound commitment to God and concern for the poor and the less-privileged. They should shine forth as a beacon of hope in the lives of Christians by helping them to gain a better understanding of their faith commitment. They should stand out as a distinguishing expression of the prophetic vocation to counteract the power of evil and poverty and enable others to take their place both in the Church and in society. The appropriate starting point of this commitment is Jesus Christ and his values and action for justice and equality. But religious life should not be reduced to an action-oriented life. As a prophetic sign, the consecrated vocation to become persons of God is an invitation to be persons of prayer and charity.[449]

There is thus a fundamental relationship between vocation and mission. As Pope John Paul's document, *Vita Consecrata*, urges, "The mission of the consecrated life, as well as the vitality of institutes, undoubtedly depends on the faithful commitment with which consecrated persons respond to their vocation. But they have a future to the extent that still other men and women generously welcome the Lord's call."[450] God is speaking to consecrated men and women today through the signs of the times. The present issue is not whether the numbers are large or small, but whether consecrated people are "listening to what God is telling us today." Through the centuries, consecrated life has assumed many forms. Today, we are called to move beyond the outmoded—to "remain open to hear what God is telling us in the new, and to be challenged by what our

---

[449] Ibid., 190.

[450] Pope John Paul II, *Vita Consecrata: Post Synodal Apostolic Exhortation on the Consecrated Life and its Mission in the Church and in the World* (Washington, DC: United States Conference of Catholic Bishops, 1996), 64.

contemporaries, especially the young, are telling us today. In keeping in touch with today's men and women, and listening to their needs with love, we will find the new forms that will revitalize religious life." Mannath concludes prophetically, "Each change, each apparent death, is a new beginning."[451]

The External Challenges

Hindu Religious Fundamentalism

India is a country characterized by its multi-religious, multi-cultural, and multi-linguistic elements, as well as its philosophy of non-violence (*ahimsa*).[452] According to the 2017 UN Census, the population of India was 1.21 billion (17% of the world's population). Hindus comprise 80.5%, Muslims 13.4%, Catholics 2.3% (29,138,323 million), Sikhs 1.9%, others 1.8%, and unspecified 0.1%.[453] Among the Hindu population, a resurgence of vicious religious nationalism and fundamentalism known as *Hindutva* has resulted in severe forms of discrimination against other religious traditions, notably Christians and Muslims. Right-wing Hindu fundamentalist organizations such as the Rashtriya Swayamsevek Sangh (RSS), Vishwa Hindu Parishad (VHP), Bhajrang Dal, Shiva Sena, Hindu Jagran Manch, and the political party of the Bharatiya Janata Party (BJP), among others, segregate the minority groups and divide people according to "race, language, caste or religion."[454]

Theologian and sociologist Jacob Peenikaparambil, explains that, "Hindutva ideology is diametrically opposed to the values upheld by the Indian Constitution, particularly secular democracy." Its proponents aim to convert "India into a Hindu Rashtra, a theocratic state based on the tenants of Hindu religion, where the minorities will be treated as second class citizens, where there will be no freedom of the citizens to profess, practice and propagate the religion of

---

[451] Mannath, 175.

[452] Sankarathil, "Consecrated Life in India," 185.

[453] Matt Rosenberg, "India's Population," (March 17, 2017); accessed October 11, 2014, ttps://www.thoughtco.com/indias-population-overview-1435263.

[454] Kaitholil, 168.

their choice."[455] Therefore, "fundamentalism is enforcing narrow sectarian practices for strengthening religious orthodoxy as well as achieving power, particularly political power. In order to consolidate political power, extreme coercion involves violence."[456] The focus of the Hindutva campaign is "*Brahminic* ideology," which upholds the supremacy of the upper castes. For this reason, the fundamentalist groups get the major support of the upper castes in India. In its most virulent forms, Hindutva avows that "India is a land of one culture and one religion; and that is Hinduism. All the others must either adopt this culture, or quit the land."[457]

Over the years, the minority groups have faced appalling forms of brutality: the demolition of Babri Masjid in Ayodhya (1992); the burning and destroying of various churches, notably in Gujarath and Orissa; the vandalization of Christian churches; the murder of Christian priests and missionaries; and the rape of nuns, are some of the manifestations of Hindutva's organized "hate campaign."[458] Ironically, these "nationalists" are singularly unconcerned about the corruption and bureaucracy which "eat up the very sap of the nation," though they consider conversion to Christianity to be a crime against the culture of the nation.[459]

To respond to the problem of religious fundamentalism, consecrated people have a responsibility to educate the young generation of India to discover the beauty and richness of their own religious traditions as well as to affirm the goodness and truth of other

---

455 Jacob Peenikaparambil, *The Saffron Surge: Humanistic Response to Hindutva* (Indore: Universal Solidarity Movement of Value Education for Peace, 2016), 8.

456 Ibid., 134.

457 Joseph Lobo, *Encountering Jesus Christ in India: An Alternative Way of Doing Christology in a Cry-for Life Situation Based on the Writings of George M. Soares-Prabhu* (Bangalore: Asian Trading Corporation, 2005), 58; Joseph Lobo's reflections are based on the writings of George M. Saores-Prabhu.

458 Lobo, 56.

459 Soares-Prabhu, cited in Lobo, 56-58. The Babri Mosque issue is central to understanding the Hindu militant revivalism and militancy that has left thousands dead in India in the last 50 years.

religious traditions.[460] Pluralism must be seen as a gift of God, and its promotion "the only way for building peace and human solidarity." The dream of India becoming an authentically developed country will be actualized only when the nation "preserves its pluralistic democracy."[461] Soares-Prabhu observes that in recent decades, the theology of India has shifted its focus from the "conquering mission" of the past to issues of "inculturation, interreligious dialogue, religious pluralism, ecumenical dialogue, communal harmony and liberation of the oppressed groups."[462] Whether these approaches will serve as antidotes to the hate campaigns of the fundamentalists remains to be seen. Nevertheless, the present circumstances have led many people belonging to all religions to serious introspection.

Socio-Economic Incongruence

India has rich religious traditions, natural resources, and a unique cultural diversity; however, the nation faces serious challenges with regard to socio-economic incongruence. According to the UN report of 2014, India had one third of the world's 1.2 billion poorest people. It had the highest under-five mortality rate in the world in 2012, with 1.4 million children unable to celebrate their fifth birthday.[463] In the present context of India, 28.5% of the people live below the poverty line. This population includes the Tribals, Dalits, and farm workers of the villages who are mostly from the states of Bihar, Jharkhand, Orissa, Madhya Pradesh, Chhattisgarh, Uttar Pradesh and Uttarakhand.[464] What is worse, despite the stark economic disparity, the Indian State seems to be working more and more for the interests of the affluent. The poverty of India ostracizes the poor socially,

---

[460] Parathazham, 61.

[461] Peenikaparambil, 136.

[462] Lobo, 58.

[463] Nilanjana Bhowmick, "India is Home to More Poor People than Anywhere Else on Earth," accessed October 25, 2017, http://time.com/2999550/india-home-to-most-poor-people/.

[464] Ramandeep Kaur, "Poverty and its Causes in India," (June 9, 2013); accessed October 25, 2017, https://www.mapsofindia.com/my-india/society/poverty-in-india-and-its-causes.

economically, morally and religiously through the caste system, which "presupposes an essential inequality among human beings." As such, the caste system "stands in direct contradiction to the political value of equality of all before the law, on which Indian democracy stands."[465] Soares-Prabhu calls the caste system a "social catastrophe" because it divides Indian society, hinders economic growth, and causes brutal exploitation of millions of people.[466] Moreover, as unjust as the caste system is, there are people who are not even included in these four groups. These are the "untouchables"—the Dalits. Though the social evil of "untouchability" was banned on November 26, 1949, it still exists in some parts of India. "Poverty, caste, and religiosity" in India are interrelated and their mutual influence affects the people socially, economically, and ethically.

Within the Indian population, a very small minority enjoy economic and social privileges. This is reflected in the fact that 70% of the country's wealth is utilized by 10% of the population. "What is alarming," writes Soares-Prabhu, is that "the religious men and women in India, their vow of poverty notwithstanding, come well within this 'privileged' category!"[467] As Mannath remarks,

> Our settings offer us extraordinary financial security, with no worries about our food or shelter, medicine or education, travel or clothing. This itself makes us a privileged group compared to most human beings. In countries like India where deprivation is widespread, the typical religious enjoys upper middle class living standards and, as a rule, higher social status than most people.[468]

---

[465] Lobo, 51-52.

[466] George Soares-Prabhu, "From Alienation to Inculturation: Some Reflections on Doing Theology in India Today," Collected Writings of George Soares-Prabhu, Vol. 1, ed. Isaac Padinjarekuttu (Jnana-Deepa Vidyapeeth Theology Series, Pune: Gujarat Sahitya Prakash, 1999), 86; cited in Lobo *Encountering Jesus Chris tin India,* 53.

[467] Lobo, 46.

[468] Joe Mannath, *A Radical Love, a Path of Light: The Beauty and Burden of Religious Life* (Okhla, New Delhi: CRI House, 2013), 213.

In this light, the words of Karl Rahner with regard to the relative wealth enjoyed by most religious communities are fitting: "No one can be poor if he [she] belongs to a rich community."[469] In his apostolic exhortation *Evangelica Testificatio*, Pope Paul VI appeals to consecrated people to turn toward the poor:

> You hear rising up, more pressing than ever, from their personal distress and collective misery, "the cry of the poor". . . In a world experiencing the full flood of development, this persistence of poverty-stricken masses and individuals constitutes a pressing call for "a conversion of minds and attitudes," especially for you who follow Christ more closely in this earthly condition of self-emptying.[470]

The poor people of India desire to see the consecrated men and women poor like them so that the consecrated may understand the struggles of the poor. This poses a challenge to consecrated people to simplify their lives to witness Christ among the poor, to "dedicate to God all our spiritual labors to grow in holiness, all our intellectual efforts to acquire knowledge, all our work for evangelization, all our care to use things in the best possible way, all our efforts to earn enough for ourselves and for our apostolate and all our efforts to avoid waste, to preserve things and to handle them appropriately."[471] The consecrated people have a mission to unite their efforts with those of Christ, and thus participate in the redemptive work of God to continue God's mission in this world to serve our marginalized brothers and sisters.

Discrimination against Women in the Society and the Church

Today, women in Indian society are awakening to a new consciousness of their true identity. This collective awakening is occurring globally

---

[469] Karl Rahner, "Theology of Poverty," in *Theological Investigation,* VIII, 172, 201; cited in Kunnumpuram, 19.

[470] Paul VI, *Evangelica Testificatio,* Apostolic Exhortations on the renewal of the religious life according to the teaching of the second Vatican council Pope Paul VI (Rome 1997), 17.

[471] Kaitholil, 81.

and locally, transcending the boundaries of nation, race, color and creed. Women are becoming politicians, engineers, professionals, activists and artists. Increasingly, women are leading nongovernmental organizations (NGOs) and people's movements. They are discovering their strengths and power, and thus mounting a courageous challenge to the male domination which exists in Indian society.[472] This transformation, however, belongs largely to the privileged and educated women of India. The status and power of women in India varies depending on educational level, economic status, and religious tradition.

The 28th Plenary Assembly of the Catholic Bishops' Conference of India, which gathered in Jamshedpur from February 13-January 20, 2008, explored the theme of the "Empowerment of Women in the Church and Society." The religious leaders examined the social, economic, moral and religious status of women in India, especially those on the periphery. Women who belong to the minority groups and the backward castes and classes of Dalits and tribals, are victimized due to poverty, ill-health, lack of access to education, and appropriate knowledge. In various parts of India, "female feticide, infanticide, rape, molestation, kidnapping, abduction, battering, dowry deaths, murder, trafficking for sex and slavery" are evident even today. Women are often forced to migrate from their own lands and livelihoods to an insecure place where they are unable to find resources for survival. Women "suffer systemic and structural violence that enslaves them and dehumanizes them economically, socio-politically and religio-culturally."[473]

---

[472] Kochurani Abraham, "The Place and Role of Women in the Catholic Church," in *Towards The Full Flowering of the Human,* ed. Kurien Kuumpuram (Mumbai: St. Pauls, 2011).

[473] The Universal Church celebrated the 20th anniversary of the Apostolic Letter of Pope John Paul II, *Mulieris Dignitatem*, on the Dignity of Women. On this occasion 160 Bishops in India belongs to the 3 Individual Sui Juris Churches Syro-Malabar, Syro-Malankara and Latin, gathered at Xavier School of Management in Jamshedpur, from 13th to 20th February 2008, for the 28th Plenary Assembly of the Catholic Bishops' Conference of India. The theme for the conference was the "Empowerment of Women in the Church and Society."

In a paper presented at the Plenary Assembly, theologian Inigo Joachim, the former superior general of the congregation of St. Anne, Madhavram, asserted that the 94,000 consecrated women of India are a powerful force in the Indian Church. They contribute immensely to the social transformation of society through their various ministries such as "educational and health services, legal advice, community development projects, communication media, inter-religious movements and other innovative ways of social and pastoral ministries to the needy and the marginalized in every nook and corner of the remote areas and cities of our country." Though they contribute to the betterment of the social order as well as to the development of the church, they nevertheless continue to face the challenges of discrimination in Indian society. They are controlled under a "patriarchal and androcentric [mentality], with men in the dominant role and women in a position of subservience."[474] The CBCI General Assembly of 1992 stated, "With a sense of sorrow we must admit that the women feel discriminated against, even in the Church."[475] As John Paul II writes in a letter to women:

> Unfortunately, we are heirs to a history which has *conditioned* us to a remarkable extent. In every time and place, this conditioning has been an obstacle to the progress of women. Women's dignity has often been unacknowledged and their prerogatives misrepresented; they have often been relegated to the margins of society and even reduced to servitude. This has prevented women from truly being themselves and it has resulted in a spiritual impoverishment of humanity.[476]

---

[474] Inigo Joachim, "Empowering Women," Presented at Catholic Bishops Conference of India (*CBCI)* Meeting at Jamshedpur, Scriptural and Theological Foundations, accessed October 27, 2017, http://inigojoachim.com/empowering-women (A nun who belongs to the St. Anne religious community in India and who was the only woman religious representatives to the Asian synod in Rome).

[475] 28th Plenary Assembly of the Catholic Bishops' Conference of India, "Empowerment of Women in the Church and Society," (February 20, 2008); accessed October 17, 2017.

[476] Pope John Paul II, "Letter of Pope John Paul II to Women," (June 29, 1995), 3; accessed October 17, 2017, https://w2.vatican.va/content/john-paul-ii/

The situation of women in the Indian church is one of subordination, as expressed concretely in the annual Indian Theological Association gathering held at Bangalore on April 24-29, 2004:

> As in other religions, patriarchal patterns—present in the hierarchical structures—also exist in Christianity and subjugate women in the Church. The Church today is impoverished and incomplete because it follows only one mode of being church, the patriarchal mode. Women encounter several restrictive barriers in their efforts to be Church. The ordinances surrounding the ordained ministry in the Church have excluded them from both mainstream Christianity and active participation in the Church. Like other marginalized groups, women may be consulted but their voice is conspicuously absent in decision-making. They are invited to catechize but not permitted to proclaim the word—as ordained men can—and thus share their unique God experience.[477]

The church must dare to ask the tough questions. How, for instance, does our fear of the feminine face of God devalue God's beauty in women and girl children? In what ways does this devaluation appear in our families, parishes, schools, congregations and ecclesial structures? Pope Francis calls for "a more widespread and incisive female presence" in the Church. Here the pope indicates the desirability of seeing "many women involved in pastoral responsibilities, in the accompaniment of persons, families and groups, as well as in theological reflection."[478] The Church in India will flourish only when it recognizes the full potential of women's

---

en/letters/1995/documents/hf_jp-ii_let_29061995_women.html.

[477] The members of the Indian Theological Association (ITA), gathered together at the 27th Annual Meeting, held at Dharmaram Vidya Kshetram, Bangalore, 25-29 April 2004, reflected on a strongly felt need of our times: "Women's Concerns and Indian Theological Response," 13.

[478] Pope Francis, "Pope Francis: women must truly participate in Church and society," (February 7, 2015); accessed December 28, 2015, https://www.youtube.com/watch?v=c7mt_WnQnqM.

contribution to the Church and society, and the necessity of structural changes in the existing patriarchal systems.

The Ecological Crisis

India is a land of mountains, rivers, seas, valleys, forests, gardens and a unique bio-diversity. From the earliest times, the people of India lived in harmony with nature and with one another amidst great cultural and religious diversity, affirming the presence of the divine in the natural world. Today, the people of India are losing this sense of the sacredness of nature in the drive toward predatory development and economic profit. Ironically, as Indian moral theologian Clement Campos observes, "India is a strange mixture of the old and the new, a land of contradictions, where the majority of its people are expected each morning to beg pardon of the earth for stepping on it, while almost blissfully, its rivers are fouled up and its environment polluted."[479]

Jesuit theologian Samuel Rayan warns, "The earth system is being polluted and destroyed through wasteful, profligate and predatory practices by modern profit-oriented scientific-technological culture, be it industrial, agricultural, or communicational. The earth's standing, meaning, and history as the Home of Life are under threat of death."[480] The precise causes of ecological crisis are difficult to identify, as Kunnumpuram asserts, as it is a "complex phenomenon." However, he posits that greed and selfishness, both individual and collective, as well as a utilitarian attitude to the cosmos [are] at the root of this crisis.

In his encyclical *Laudato Si,* Pope Francis laments the abuse we have inflicted upon the earth, our common home, though she is the mother who sustains us, and our sister with whom we share our life:

---

[479] Clement Campos, "*Laudato Si*: An Indian Perspective," in *Theological Studies,* Vol. 78 (1) (March: 2017): 215.

[480] Samuel Rayan, "The Earth is the Lord's," in *Collected Writings of Samuel Ryan,* ed. Kurien Kunnumpuram, Vol. 1, (Delhi: ISPCK, 2013), 19; cited Kunnumpuram, 263.

> This sister now cries out to us because of the harm we have inflicted on her by our irresponsible use and abuse of the goods with which God has endowed her. We have come to see ourselves as her lords and masters, entitled to plunder her at will. The violence present in our hearts, wounded by sin, is also reflected in the symptoms of sickness evident in the soil, in the water, in the air and in all forms of life. This is why the earth herself, burdened and laid waste, is among the most abandoned and maltreated of our poor; she "groans in travail" (Rom 8:22). We have forgotten that we ourselves are dust of the earth (Gen 2:7); our very bodies are made up of her elements, we breathe her air and we receive life and refreshment from her waters.[481]

In India today, Pope Francis's words ring especially true. India's environmental crisis is dire. The rapid growth in India's population has put a severe strain on the earth's resources and fueled the quest for ever-greater development.[482] Droughts, rapidly decreasing water sources, and the absence of clean drinking water cause the people to struggle for survival. As the industries grow and multiply, the quantity of water required for their functioning leaves the people of the locality without water. The rapid drop in the water table has precipitated a severe crisis: "Considering that 85% of rural drinking water and 55% of urban water comes from underground sources, this seems to be a very urgent problem as literally hundreds of millions people could be left without water." India's large numbers of people rely for their livelihood on the rivers, which today are destroyed by the chemicals, sewage, and other toxic waste from agricultural and industrial sites. Furthermore, India's cities suffer from inadequate disposal of solid waste and severe air and noise pollution from the transportation systems. Deforestation, as well as soil pollution through the use of

---

[481] Francis I, *Laudato Si: The Encyclical of Pope Francis on the Environment with Commentary*, with Commentary by Sean McDonagh (Maryknoll, NY: Orbis Books, 2016), 2; Campos, "*Laudato Si*: An Indian Perspective," 213.

[482] "Christian Education and Ecological Concerns: Ecological Issues in the Indian Context" (November 11, 2014); accessed October 31, 2017, http://bluwinchisik.blogspot.com/2014/11/christian-education-and-ecological.html.

poisonous pesticides and fertilisers, greenhouse gas emissions, and chemical pollution have ruined the land, oftentimes irrevocably.[483]

As Christian educators, consecrated men and women have a mission amidst the ecological crisis of India to prophetically raise their voices against the grave injustices perpetrated against mother earth and the poor, who disproportionately bear the weight of the environmental crisis. Furthermore, they are called to conscientize the people through motivational programmes and environmental awareness to become the stewards of God's creation. As Christian spiritual leaders, consecrated men and women have a mission to guide the people of India by drawing lessons from scripture and the sacred texts of other religious traditions, as well as the magisterial documents of the Church.

Campos calls for a multi-religious approach to the environmental crisis in India, noting that in *Laudato Si*, Pope Francis cites a broad variety of sources, not only from his own tradition, but from several episcopal conferences (notably from the southern hemisphere), the Orthodox Patriarch Bartholomew, Sufi mysticism, the Rio Declaration on Environment and Development, and the Earth Charter. In *Laudato Si,* the pope expresses his "wish to address every person living on this planet," and to "to enter into dialogue with all people about our common home." Emphasizing the intrinsic link between the poor and the ecological crisis, the pope declares that "the majority of people living on our planet profess to be believers. This should spur religions to dialogue among themselves for the sake of protecting nature, defending the poor, and building networks of respect and fraternity," an endeavor which, as Campos notes, has long been underway in Asia.[484] This dialogue can serve as a crucially important locus of collaboration among people of all faiths in India and a shared ethical response to protect and care for our Mother Earth.[485] We turn now to consider how the prophetic-contemplative

[483] Ibid.

[484] Campos, 217; *LS*,3, 201.

[485] Campos, 217.

spirituality of Thomas Merton may be brought to bear on the external and internal challenges to consecrated life in India today.

3. The Relevance of Merton's Spirituality for the Consecrated Life in India

As a contemplative, Merton left a legacy which called people to be rooted in their own religious traditions, while reaching out to others in openness and prophetic dialogue. He was "well-grounded in his own Catholicism, and he felt he could share it without being endangered. He also thought Buddhism was [more developed] in the practice of meditation and that Catholics could learn something from that tradition."[486] His contemplative-prophetic vision, deep spirituality, witness against injustice, and embrace of interreligious dialogue and ecumenism, continue to "touch the hearts and lives of women and men of our age."[487] It is time to consider how Merton's legacy might become a source of wisdom and guidance for the consecrated men and women of India, calling them to new forms of contemplative spirituality and prophetic witness that reflect an accurate reading of the signs of the times. As biblical scholar Rekha Chennattu asserts, "we need a spirituality that is rooted in our spiritual traditions, a spirituality that is responsible for building up a more humane world, and a spirituality that is relevant for the twenty-first century."[488]

---

[486] Jim Graves, "The Complex Spirituality of Thomas Merton: The Trappist Monk was One of the Most Famous Catholic Writers of the 20th Century, but Some Question the Legacy he Left Behind," *Our Sunday Visitor*, OSV News Weekly, accessed December 16, 2017, https://www.osv.com/Article/TabId/493/ArtMID/13569/ArticleID/17544/The-complex-spirituality-of-Thomas-Merton.aspx.

[487] Daniel P. Horan, *The Franciscan Heart of Thomas Merton: A New Look at the Spiritual Inspiration of His Life, Thought, and Writing* (Notre Dame, IN: Ave Maria Press, 2014), 159.

[488] Rekha M. Chennattu, "To be Rooted and Relevant a Call for a Paradigm Shift in the Life of Women Religious." AMOR XV, Bangkok, Thailand (October 13-21, 2009): 47-6152.

Re-Igniting the Spirit of Contemplation

Merton's contemplation, which sprang from his deep rootedness in Christ and union with God, is the foundation of his spirituality. He shared this experience not only with fellow monastics and Christians, but also with the entire world. Drinking from the wells of such contemplation, the consecrated men and women of India may be strengthened to follow Christ more authentically amidst the contradictions and challenges of a multi-religious, multi-lingual and multi-cultural nation. As Kaitholil expresses, the people of India do not want the consecrated men and women to be "efficient administrators or competent professionals," but deeply spiritual men and women who "walk the talk." And he adds "without a committed pursuit of God in contemplation, all kinds of good activities lose all purpose and relevance."[489]

To experience authentic and fruitful contemplation, Indian consecrated people must be prepared to engage the concrete realities of this world, particularly those of the poor and marginalized, rather than retreating from them, and thus to see the world at large sacramentally. Regarding the need for engagement with the world in the contemplative life, Merton wrote,

> The contemplative is not just a person who sits under a tree with legs crossed, or one who edifies himself with the answer to ultimate and spiritual problems. He is one who seeks to know the meaning of life not only with his head but with his whole being, by living it in depth and in purity, and thus uniting himself to the very Source of Life . . . . The whole world and all the incidents of life tend to be sacraments—signs of God, signs of God's love working in the world.[490]

For Merton, therefore, contemplation is not an escape from the world and its suffering. It is to become part of the world in order to reveal the hidden face of Christ to suffering humanity. Rootedness in God therefore calls religious to a deeper integration "with

[489] Kaitholil, 173.

[490] Merton, *The Literary Essays of Thomas Merton*, 340.

everything—with one's body, with one's emotions, with nature, with others." In this way, consecrated people "find God in all things and all things in God."[491] Merton's vision of contemplative life presents a summons to more consecrated people of India to step outside their comfort zones into the peripheries.

Re-imagining the Union with Christ

In the context of Indian consecrated life, there is an urgent need to renew the interior life and to seek deeper union with Christ. According to Chennattu, "the world calls [religious] to develop a deeper spirituality, which liberates us from the slavery of our occupation and preoccupations and enables us to be attuned to the voice that transforms us constantly and makes us anew."[492] Such deeper forms of spirituality will prepare the consecrated people of India to engage the pressing social needs of the hour. With regard to certain trends among the religious of India today, Kaitholil comments,

> In the world at large there is a new search for spirituality, a deep hunger for interiority that will respond to the needs of the individual who is called to live in a more complex and conflict-ridden situation than before. This hunger is genuine and sincere and is one of the signs of our times. The sign is a deep felt need for something that would help individuals to cope with the situation in which they are called to live.[493]

Merton's incarnational vision could guide them in satisfying this hunger for deeper forms of spirituality. He writes, "as Christ unites in His one Person the two natures of God and of man, so too in making us His friends, He dwells in us, uniting us intimately to Himself." For Merton, this profound union with Christ is not a sentimental relationship, but "a mutual consent of minds and wills."[494]And this merging of one's being with Christ is the mystical union in which Christ Himself becomes the source and principle of divine life within

---

[491] Ibid.

[492] Chennattu, 52.

[493] Kaitholil, 162.

[494] Merton, *NS,* 158.

us. To grow in relationship with Christ through contemplation, consecrated people need to let go of their internal blocks:

> If we are only involved in our surface existence, in externals, and in the trivial concerns of our ego, we are untrue to Him and to ourselves. To reach a true awareness of Him as well as ourselves, we have to renounce our selfish and limited self and enter into a whole new kind of existence, discovering an inner center of motivation and love which makes us see ourselves and everything else in an entirely new light.[495]

It is a call to awaken to a new awareness of ourselves in Christ, created in Him, redeemed by Him, to be transformed and glorified in and with Him. This transformation is akin, in Blake's terms, to an opening of the "doors of perception," in which "all life takes on a completely new meaning; the real sense of our own existence, which is normally veiled and distorted by the routine distractions of an alienated life, is now revealed in a central intuition." This form of knowledge "sees everything transfigured 'in God,' coming from God and working for God's creative redemptive love."[496]

The hunger for deeper forms of spirituality in India today, as Kaitholil stresses, "cannot be satisfied with traditional acts of piety and external liturgical practices, but something that is deeper."[497] It is this deep spiritual union with Christ, in which all of life is "transfigured in God," that will satisfy this hunger in the lives of the consecrated people of India. Consecrated life will undergo renewal when Indian religious rediscover a rootedness in contemplation through silence, solitude, and prayer, expressions which are part of the rich spiritual and cultural heritage of India.[498] Similarly, Chennattu urges the consecrated people, "to spend quality time with oneself in

---

[495] Merton, *CWA*, 157.

[496] Ibid., 158.

[497] Kaitholil, 162.

[498] Kurien Kunnumpuram, ed., *In Spirit and Truth: Indian Christian Reflections on Spirituality and Worship*, Selected writings of Samuel Rayan, SJ, Vol. II (Bandra, Mumbai: St Pauls, 2012), 42-43.

the presence of God to hold the different aspects of consecrated life together." The consecrated people of India today

> are being called out of piety and ritualism into deep communion and communication with God, which results in a vibrant spirituality that is nurtured by the experience of the Paschal mystery in our daily life, made relevant in constant interaction with the challenges of present society and sustained by ongoing renewal (metanoia) in our way of life.[499]

Such a spirituality, which is deeply grounded in the Christ of the incarnation and immersed in the material realities of society, seeing in these realities sacraments of "God's love working in the world," will impart new meaning and relevance to religious life in India today. Thus rooted in the love of God, the consecrated people may become, in Merton's terms, "the strength of the world, because they are the tabernacles of God in the world."[500]

Rebuilding Communities of Love

Community life is one of the essential elements in the life of consecrated people. It is in the community that the members grow into maturity and find their true identities through giving and receiving love. A religious community which is united in the Lord stays together and shares their God-experiences with one another. Today, however, many communities are "rife with conflicts, misunderstanding and mistrust," writes Chennattu. When the members are not united with one another in the Lord, the interests of the individuals will conflict with those of the community.[501]

Offering an approach to love that was practical and prophetic, Merton called for the creation of new communities of love. His contemplative experience encouraged him to see the presence of God in other members of the community, which was expressed through mutual love and care. In *No Man is an Island,* he writes, "If I am to love my brother, I must somehow enter deep into the mystery of

---

[499] Chennattu, 52.

[500] Merton, *NS*, 288.

[501] Chennattu, 53.

God's love for him . . .The truth I must love in my brother is God Himself, living in him."[502] He emphasized that "Wherever there is human presence, we have to be present to it. And wherever there is a person, there has to be personal communication. There Christ can work. Where there is presence there is God."[503] He believed that wherever human beings are respected, loved and cared for, God abides among them.

To re-build communities of love, Merton invites consecrated people to love in a manner reflected in the Gospel of John: "'If you love me, you will keep my word. And my Father will love you and we will come to you and make our home with you.' Now, what is 'my word'? Christ's word is: *love one another*. Community." Therefore, he urges consecrated people to "Live in community, have a community of love, let God dwell right here among you. God is experientially present, and we are aware that God is with us. . . Praising God together, praising God individually. Seeking God together, seeking God individually."[504] In order for religious communities to be united, therefore, they need to pray and seek God together, while immersing themselves in deep contemplation as individuals.

With regard to building religious communities in India, Kunnumpuram suggests that "Relationship to God is the basis of a religious community. Commitment to God in personal faith and a deep and joyful acceptance of one's vocation are important elements of one's relationship with God."[505] Just as personal prayer deepens one's relationship with God, so does community prayer. Thus, a religious community that prays together—not merely reciting prayers but sharing God-experiences—stays together. Even if the members of the community live in different places, "if they are united in spirit and bound together by the bond of love and common vision, then it bears witness to an authentic and consecrated community living—

---

[502] Merton, *No Man is an Island,* 7.

[503] Thomas Merton, *The Springs of Contemplation* (Notre Dame, IN: Ave Maria Press, 1992), 35; (Hereafter cited as *SC*).

[504] Ibid., 51.

[505] Kunnumpuram, 190.

an alternative prophetic community." Through this love, Christian communities have a mission to make "God's invisible presence visible in the world."[506] Religious communities become authentic, according to Merton, when the members are able to respect, give space to, and allow each other to act and speak out in freedom.[507] In a manner similar to Merton, Chennattu calls communal life in India to assume this form: "We are being called out of individualism and personal perfection into community living and sharing of our resources and talents. We are called out of our secure and fixed community into an alternative prophetic community bound by love and lived in common mission."[508]

Renewing the Vision of Vows

The ultimate purpose of the three vows in consecrated life is to liberate a person to love and serve God and others unconditionally. Merton defines the religious profession as "the act by which a Christian formally embraces the religious state, renouncing his former way of life to follow Christ, uniting himself with a particular religious community, and finally consecrating his life to God by public vows."[509] In committing oneself to Christ through the vows, the consecrated person seeks to arrive at a "stable state of perfection" by placing oneself under a "*permanent threefold obligation.*"[510] Such obligation aims to counter the "triple concupiscence" of the desire for riches, the passions of the flesh, and the inordinate love of our own free will, by countering them with the vows of poverty, chastity, and obedience, respectively. At the same time, Merton notes that the passions are given by God to help the human person to serve God. Therefore, the purpose of the vows is not to extinguish the normal

---

[506] Chennattu, 53.

[507] Merton, *SC*, 53.

[508] Chennattu, 53.

[509] Thomas Merton, *The Life of the Vows: Initiation into the Monastic Tradition*, ed. Patrick F.O' Connell, Preface Augustine Roberts, Monastic Wisdom Series: no. 30 (Collegeville, Minnesota: Liturgical Press, 2012), 183. (Hereafter cited as *LV*).

[510] Ibid., 159. (Italics in original).

human passions and desires but "to bring them under the guidance of the Holy Spirit so that we are able to love God with our whole heart as well as with all our mind and all our strength." Therefore, the greatest motive driving the vows is the "*desire to give ourselves* wholeheartedly to God."[511] Thus, the vows enable consecrated men and women to grow in intimate relationship with the person of Christ through the surrender of one's whole being to God.

Merton emphasized that the following of Christ entails participation in his life. In sharing his life, we live in this world as he lived: in poverty, obedience, obscurity, labor, and self-sacrifice. This union makes the vowed life fruitful and dynamic. Furthermore, the imitation of Christ has profound implications for communal life in that the religious community is a *society of love*, bound by the *charity of Christ*. In this union, the members seek to help one another attain eternal life in Christ and share in the supernatural goods and benefits given by the Holy Spirit. Merton held that if the vowed life does not help consecrated men and women to "live in sincere fraternal union," the vows are not fulfilling their purpose.[512]

Chennattu asserts that the purpose of the vows in consecrated life is to build "right relationship with God, with fellow human beings and with the entire universe." They are "ultimately the manifestation of our profound openness to God, of our liberating love for our fellow human beings, and of our radical freedom in using material wealth." Therefore, through the vow of obedience, one makes a wholehearted commitment to the person of Christ and to his mission. Chastity takes on new significance as the capacity to love others with a liberated mind and to work for the wellbeing of all people. The vow of poverty signifies the inner freedom to let go of attachments to material wealth in the midst of a consumeristic society, and to be more dependent on God and others.[513] Like Merton and Chennattu, Soares-Prabhu underscores the significance of the communal dimension of the vows, stressing the positive rather than the merely restrictive elements:

---

511 Ibid., 183.

512 Ibid., 156-157, 160.

513 Chennattu, 54-55.

> Religious poverty is not just an individual's renunciation of possessions but the sharing that creates a community of sharing. Celibacy is not just the individual renunciation of marriage and family, but the unrestricted love which fashions a community capable of loving. Obedience is not just the renunciation of one's self-will, but the commitment to God's will that enables a community to make common cause for the Kingdom.[514]

The mission of the consecrated people of India today through the vowed life is to grow as loving, sharing, and caring persons in their communities and to bear witness to Jesus as contemplative-prophets. For Merton, the lifelong commitment one makes on the day of profession must be carried out effectively by giving one's entire life to God and others.[515]

4. Renewing the Stimulation of Prophetic Actions

Merton's prophetic vision was the result of his "quest for the Divine and his intense life of contemplation and solitude." He believed that the "one who practices contemplation, engages in the social action that flows from it."[516] Precisely as a cloistered monk, he contributed greatly to public life in America, to the social mission of the universal church, and to worldwide efforts at peacemaking. Today, Merton's contemplative-prophetic spirituality holds the potential to motivate the consecrated people of India to read critically and respond effectively to the signs of the times through prophetic witness and transformative action.

---

[514] George M. Soares-Prabhu, "Prophetic Dimension of Religious Life," in *Biblical Spirituality of Liberative Action,* Collected Writings of George Soares-Prabhu, ed. Scaria Kuthiralkkattel, Vol. 3 (Pune: Jnana-Deepa Vidyapeeth, 2003), 219; cited in Chennattu, 54-55.

[515] Merton, *LV*, 178.

[516] David W. Givey, *The Social thought of Thomas Merton: The Way of Nonviolence and Peace for the Future* (Winona, MN: Anselm Academic, 2009), 109.

Renewal in the Indian Church

Merton's genuine love and concern for renewal in consecrated life is clearly seen in his prophetic approach to monastic life and apostolic religious orders. This is reflected in a series of conferences on monastic renewal he gave to novices and members of the monastery in 1963 and 1965.[517] Patrick O'Connell comments, "Responding to the call of the Second Vatican Council for religious orders to recover the charisms of their founders, Merton repeatedly calls for a genuine renewal and recovery of an authentic monastic spirit rather than merely a reform of structures and observances."[518]

Merton asserted that in order for true renewal to take place, religious orders must be ready to risk their security as they raise prophetic voices against the "triumphalism, bureaucracy, and inertia" of ecclesial and monastic structures.[519] But risk their security they must: "It may be the price of sacrificing our security, *sacrificing the psychological stability we have built on foundations that we do not dare to examine.* We have to examine those foundations even though it will mean unrest, even though it will mean loss of peace, even though it will mean disturbance and anguish, even though it may mean the radical shaking of structures."[520]

In the renewal of the church, both internally and in its mission to the world, religious have a singular role to play. In her reflections on the creative and prophetic dimensions of the church's mission, Chennattu draws on German political theologian Johannes Metz, who speaks of the "innovative and corrective function" of religious life. Metz writes, "Against the dangerous accommodations and

---

[517] These 1963 and 1965 conferences are available on CD: Thomas Merton, Vatican II: The Scared Liturgy and Religious Life (Rockville MD: Now You Know Media, 2012); cited in Bonnie Thurston, "'An Absolute Duty to Rebel': Thomas Merton, Religious Women and the Challenges of Vatican II," (March 2013); accessed February 23, 2018. http://merton.org/ITMS/Seasonal/39/39-2Thurston.pdf.

[518] Merton, *LV*, lvi.

[519] Elena Malits, *The Solitary Explorer: Thomas Merton's Transforming Journey* (San Francisco: Harper and Row Publishers, 1980), 66.

[520] Merton, *CWA*, 221.

questionable compromises that the Church as a large-scale institution can always incline to, they [religious] press for the uncompromising nature of the Gospel."[521]

Merton's stinging critique of static and ineffectual ecclesial and religious structures calls the Church in India to awaken from its apathy, both with regard to its rigid, centralized bureaucracy and the adequacy of its care for the poor and marginalized. With regard to the church's internal structures, Pathil asserts that "the Catholic Church is still too much a centralized institution that all the major decisions are taken at the Centre without sufficient participation, consultation, and communication. The principles of collegiality and co-responsibility still remain merely at the theological level, and are not yet translated into praxis." In this configuration, the hierarchy still dominates and the laity has virtually no role to play at the level of decision making. A "concern for unity and uniformity" pre-empts the values of plurality and diversity, and "crushes originality, creativity, and participation."[522] Regarding the option for the poor, though to a large extent the church is involved in the life of the people (primarily in the form of charitable works), it needs a deep conversion in order to take on and transform the suffering and struggles of the millions of people who are crucified today, especially women, girl children, and the lower castes and classes.

Moreover, Merton's prophetic openness to ecumenism and dialogue with other traditions, and his forward-looking vision of the church, could motivate the three independent churches of India—the Syro-Malabar, Syro-Malankara, and the Latin rites—to examine their mode of relationship with one another. Pathil remarks,

> Communion in the Catholic Church implies that the different Individual Churches have to share their heritage and values [with] each other with openness and learn from each other and move towards a convergence. Identity of the Indian Churches has to be continuously created and re-created in mutual relationship and not in opposition. Identity consists not in clinging to the

[521] Chennattu, 56.

[522] Pathil, 700-701.

> past, but moving forward to the future in the power of the Spirit.[523]

These churches in India need to work in collaboration with one another to build bridges of unity, peace and integrity through dialogue and reconciliation, among themselves and with other religious faiths, and to challenge and transform the institutionalized, centralized church structures in order to bear witness to Christ more effectively. In the words of the 1986 statement of the Indian Theological Association (ITA) entitled "The Church in India in Search of a New Identity,"

> We dream of an Indian Church that is authentically local, autonomous and participative, committed to the promotion of the Kingdom. Such a Church will be a community of hope, guided by the Spirit, exercising its prophetic function, fully convinced that it is in a pilgrim state, ever involved in dialogue with people of other faiths and ideologies, and with a special attention to the needs of the oppressed and marginalized.[524]

Indian society, which is dominated by Hindu fundamentalism and religious fanaticism, may well be conscientized by the consecrated people through the spirit of contemplation, dialogue, openness, respect, and reconciliation, to build a just society. In this society, all the religions may live tolerantly with one another in the spirit of Merton, who was open to accepting, learning from, and respecting the uniqueness of each culture and religious tradition.

Revitalizing Religious Formation

Religious formation in consecrated life requires constant renewal in order for members to grow as integrated persons through contemplation and prophetic witness. Filled with concern for the vitality of religious life, Merton sought to renew monastic formation according to the directives of Vatican II. As a formator, Merton revitalized the formation program in his Cistercian order. His vision

---

[523] Ibid., 705.

[524] Ibid., 706.

for renewal is a rich resource for the consecrated people of India to reform the formation programs for initial and ongoing formation.

To lay a strong, integrative foundation for the formation process and enable the members of the order to respond to the signs of the times, Merton emphasized the theological, social, spiritual, and psychological dimensions of spiritual life, and a solid, contemplative, mystical spirituality. In the words of Paul Dekar, Merton considered Gethsemani "a school of charity in which monks are to prefer nothing to the love of Jesus Christ. Monks learned love in living, not from books."[525] Merton encouraged the members of the community to spend more time in retreats, in solitude, and in silence, as he himself always sought to do. In these times of prayer, Merton simply entered into the presence of God and stayed quiet, letting the silence sink in. Sometimes, the only noise was the sound of a tractor on the farm. Today, in India, in order to revitalize the initial and ongoing formation of consecrated life, members need to spend focused time in contemplation, prayer, silence, and solitude.

Merton realized that the young men entering the monastery were from a broken society and thus deeply affected by consumerism, family conflict, alcoholism, and other social evils. As a formator, Merton felt the need to support and understand these young men in the manner of a "good spiritual father."[526] He emphasized in the formation process the importance of self-identity and the search to discover one's true self. He wrote, "My task is only to be what I am, a man seeking God in silence and solitude, with deep respect for the demands and realities of his own vocation, and fully aware that others too are seeking the truth in their own way."[527] Merton believed that self-integration would lead one to discover one's true self in God.

Similarly, young men and women entering consecrated life in India carry with them the complex social, economic, spiritual, cultural, and emotional problems of Indian society. The formators are already making efforts to introduce integral formation programs

---

[525] Dekar, 36.

[526] Ibid., 48, 173.

[527] Merton, *CWA,* 245, cited in Givey, 109.

to their new members to help them face the challenges of the consecrated life and to read the signs of the times. These programs include spiritual, intellectual, social, communal, affective, and psychological dimensions, as well as attention to the mind-body connection. Though much is being done, formators need to focus more on the contemplative-prophetic dimensions of religious life, as did Merton.

Merton accompanied those in formation according to the authentic monastic spirit, which emphasized the human and transcendental values of "personal integrity, inner peace, authenticity, identity, inner depth, spiritual joy, the capacity to love, the capacity to enjoy God's creation."[528] He wrote,

> Our first task is to be fully human and to enable the youth of our time to find themselves and develop as men and sons of God. There is no need for a community of religious robots without minds, without hearts, without ideas and without faces. It is this mindless alienation that characterizes "the world" and life in the world. Monastic spirituality today must be a personalistic and Christian humanism that seeks and saves man's intimate truth, his personal identity, in order to consecrate it entirely to God.[529]

In the formation process, Merton emphasized the need to cultivate sensitivity, compassion, and attention to the needs of others. He believed that the ultimate purpose of formation is to enable members to grow in deep union with God. In its essence, monastic formation is "not contemplation, not action, not works, not rest, not this or that particular thing, but God in everything, God in anything, God in His will, God in other men, God present in his own soul."[530]

Living a God-centered life is the focus of the integral formation of the consecrated people of India today. Genuine religious formation empowers the members to live their charism in radically new ways in the contemporary context. A sound formation program leads

---

[528] Merton, *CWA*, 82.

[529] Ibid., 83.

[530] Thomas Merton, *Waters of Siloe* (New York: Harcourt Brace, 1949), 335; see also Dekar, 37.

members of the various religious orders to grow in openness and dialogue:

> We are called to transcend the boundary of our individual institute or congregation; we are called to deeper networking among religious as well as between religious and laity, and to collaborate with all people of good will in other religious traditions (like Hindus, Muslims, Buddhists, etc.,). This networking is an imperative today to create a civilization of freedom with responsibility, to build up a society of compassionate justice, and thus realizing the reign of God here and now.[531]

Consecrated people need to cultivate openness, dialogue and collaboration with other religious orders and people of other faith traditions, so that our religious formation programs may be fully equipped to read the signs of the time in India today. In the manner of Merton, those in religious life are called to grow in deeper silence, solitude, and contemplative-prophetic spirituality. They are called to find the presence of God in all things, to discover the true self, to read critically the signs of the times and to become a voice for the voiceless in the current Indian society.[532]

Social Justice to Empower the Powerless

Though he was a cloistered monk, Merton sought to awaken the church from its apathy, and with the help of other spiritual seekers and activists to work for peace and social justice. He asserted that, "identification with the poor and alienated members of society was

---

[531] Chennattu, 58.

[532] Merton's prayer life consisted largely of simply "walking with God," in every moment of the day, finding God's presence everywhere, in all things: "in the everydayness of life, in the body, in nature, and in the people we encounter." For him, all occasions were opportunities for prayer: "preparing a meal, working in a garden, reading a book, taking a walk in the woods, playing with children—all these can be undertaken with a sense of divine presence." Thomas Merton, *An Invitation to the Contemplative Life*, ed. Wayne Simsic (Maryland: The Word Among Us Press, 2006), 65. As we become increasingly sensitized to the sacramental presence of the divine in all things, we are correspondingly awakened to our own identity and our great need for continuing conversion.

the duty of monks and flowed quite naturally from living out the Gospel message. Since monks are simply a community of believers who live the Gospel in a certain radical way, he felt deeply that they should above all espouse movements of peace and justice."[533]

Merton's contribution as a prophet of social justice can encourage Indian consecrated men and women to become more daring and prophetic in the church's mission. Consecrated people need "to renew the preferential option for the poor and the marginalized and [their] zeal to establish justice."[534] Today, in India, this means working for systemic change, an approach to development based on the people's rights, and for sustainable development. We need to make the shift from developmental-and-charity model approach to that of transformative model.

According to Kaitholil, the consecrated people of India are often afraid to risk their lives and security for the sake of the people on the periphery; instead, "most of us withdraw from the scene when we are faced with opposition from the powerful . . . Even if there are individuals who are ready, as a rule they do not get the needed support and encouragement from their institutes."[535] As the ultimate consequence of challenging and disturbing the economic and political status quo, one might even lose his or her life. Rani Maria, a Franciscan Clarist nun, was killed on February 25, 1995, as she worked for the empowerment of the poor tribals who were exploited by the money lenders at Bijnor in Udayanagar. Another religious, Valsa John Malamel, a member of the Sisters of Charity of Jesus and Mary, fought for the rights of the tribal people who were displaced by the mining mafia in Jharkhand State. She was brutally killed by 50 people who broke into her house on the night of November 15, 2011.[536] Similarly, today, the consecrated people of India are called to become courageous witnesses of Christ by standing in solidarity

---

[533] Givey, xiv.

[534] Chennattu, 56.

[535] Kaitholil, 159.

[536] Ibid., 191-192.

with the poor and powerless, and working for the transformation of the structures that oppress them.

Empowering Women's Leadership in the Church

Women played a significant role in shaping Merton's life. At various times, they offered him "perspective, inspiration, counsel, support, concern, challenge, and affection."[537] Though Merton's writings are limited with regard to women, he did encourage "women religious to interpret and implement the challenges of Vatican II," notably those set forth in the document *Perfectae Caritatis* (Decree on the Appropriate Renewal of Religious Life), issued October 28, 1965.[538] This document called for "a continuous return to the sources of all Christian life and to the original inspiration behind a given community," and "an adjustment of the community to the changed conditions of the times."[539] Merton encouraged religious women to be responsible for making their own decisions concerning these changes. His interest in the spiritual growth of women religious led Merton to organize a retreat for contemplative nuns at Gethsemani in 1967, in which he emphasized the importance of women's leadership in the Church and in the society.

Merton asserted that "women's vocations demanded a new maturity within a patriarchal system." He encouraged them to be confident of their call, and to believe in themselves and their convictions. He urged women religious to be independent and self-determined, and to "give courage to the creative and imaginative new members who need a compassionate community."[540] Most importantly, he challenged contemplative nuns to "rebel" against the "feminine mystique" imposed upon them by the male hierarchy, by which women are both idealized and humiliated. By such a mystique, Merton indicates

---

[537] Bochen, "Women," *TME*, 540-541.

[538] Thurston, Bonnie. "'An Absolute Duty to Rebel': Thomas Merton, Religious Women and the Challenges of Vatican II," 17 (March 2013); accessed February 23, 2018. http://merton.org/ITMS/Seasonal/39/39-2Thurston.pdf.

[539] Ibid.

[540] Merton, *SC*, 10-11.

> an idealization of supposed special feminine qualities which are put up on a pedestal and made much of. It's also tied in with a cloistered, contemplative mystique. The woman is said to be essentially such and such, like "passive" and "mysterious." But *everybody* is mysterious and sometimes passive. These things are not specialties of women. To make a mystique out of things like this is nonsense.[541]

This mystique serves as an instrument of women's oppression. In order for women religious to liberate themselves, they must reject this image—"this view that you can't make your own decisions because you are passive and mysterious and veiled and different."[542] Against this mystique, Merton urged religious women to stand up for their rights, for the good of the Church, so that the church and society might benefit from their leadership and prophetic witness.

Merton's words can speak cogently to Indian women, both lay and religious, who remain largely subordinate to men in the patriarchal society and the institutional church. Today, in India, consecrated women and men are called to work for gender equality in the church and in the society. To address gender issues, men and women are called to relate to one another in creative reflections, dialogue, reconciliation, and respect.[543] Chennattu encourages consecrated women to work for "new models of Christian leadership which are more participatory, creative, enabling and empowering."[544]

The church in India needs to recognize the crucial importance of women's leadership roles, at all levels. As Joachim expresses, religious women should be "included in the diocesan and local level Councils and in the decision making process."[545] Furthermore,

> We have to popularize inclusive language in liturgy, in the prayer of the Church, catechesis, homilies and should judiciously use

---

[541] Ibid., 125.

[542] Ibid., 126.

[543] Ibid., 134-135.

[544] Chennattu, 58.

[545] Inigo Joachim, "Empowering Women as Evangelizers," *Asian Journal of Vocation and Formation*, Vol. XXXIX, no. 1 (Pune: January-June 2014), 35-36.

> more feminist and liberative passages: Deborah, Judith, Naomi and other women from the old and New Testament. It should be announced from the pulpit that discrimination and violence against women is sinful. Parishes should involve women in the ministry of the proclamation of the Good News. Women should be included as co-workers and co-leaders by recognizing their leadership competence and intellectual and creative potentialities.[546]

In the Indian church, the voices of women leaders need to reverberate in order to build a participatory church. In order to empower women as leaders in the church, Merton urged to change the masculine form of a hierarchical structure, "the whole idea of priesthood has to be changed," adding, "we need to develop a whole new style of worship in which there is no need for one hierarchical person to have a big central place, a form of worship in which everyone is involved."[547]

Today, the Indian church has a mission to build a participatory church so that religious as well as lay women have the freedom to live as true children of God. For Merton, only through the empowered leadership of women in the church and in the society can gender justice be possible. As Chennattu asserts, today there is a need for women to grow in "greater union with God, authenticity, freedom, commitment and integration. It is up to us to imbibe the passion of the prophets and of Jesus in our lives to become women on fire to meet the new challenges of the emerging society."[548]

Refueling to Confront the Social Evils in the Interreligious Context

India is a land of rich spiritual heritage. Spirit filled charismatic leaders of various religious traditions have contributed immeasurably for the growth and renewal of the nation. Influenced by the religious fundamentalism, communalism, caste system, gender inequalities

---

[546] Ibid.

[547] Merton, *SC*, 134-135.

[548] Chennattu, 60.

and various other social evils, the nation breaks down its rich spiritual heritages. Today 'Novel India' could be built again based on religious harmony, acceptance, respect, dialogue and compassion to the people of different faith. These interreligious values were concretely emphasized by Thomas Merton through his contemplative spirituality, openness and acceptance to the people of different cultures, and religions. William Shannon observes that "Wherever Merton looked in the various fields of religious thought and experience, he sought areas of common affirmation rather than points of disagreement."[549] Christoffer H. Grundmann the professor of religion and the healing arts, reflects:

> Merton opposed any form of violence in resolving conflict, including taking an outspoken stance against violence during the racially charged civil rights movement of 1960s. At the height of the Vietnam War in 1968, fully aware of the political crisis, he published an article proposing interreligious dialogue as a spiritual discipline and declared the Vietnamese Buddhist monk Thich Nhat Hanh to be his 'brother.'[550]

Rooted and grounded in the Lord through the contemplative spirituality Merton was filled with love for the spiritual traditions of East and West. "Merton pleads for dialogue as the way to communicate genuine faith 'intelligently.'"[551] This was expressed concretely in his candidness to the other religious traditions and other religions—Islam, Hinduism, Buddhism and all the rest. Merton's love, acceptance and high esteem to Gandhian nonviolent spirituality is well expressed in his writings and reflections. His close relationship with the Tibetan spiritual leader Dalai Lama, the Japanese Zen master D.T. Suzuki, Vietnamese Buddhist monk Thich Nhat Hanh, the Jewish Rabbi Abraham Heschel all speak of Merton's benevolent approach to the people of other religious traditions. Merton believed that "One must

---

[549] SL, 266.

[550] Thomas Merton, "Apologies to an Unbeliever," Christoffer H. Grundmann, *Interreligious Dialogue: An Anthology of Voices Bridging Cultural and Religious Divides* (Winona, MN: Anselm Academic, 2015), 85.

[551] Ibid.

be well grounded in, and faithful to, one's own tradition,"[552] before one engages to know the richness of the other religious traditions. Enlightened by the openness of Merton the consecrated men and women of India are called to be rooted in their own faith of the Christian traditions to refuel to confront the social evils in the interreligious context.

Today, the consecrated people of India have a mission to work for the establishment of God's reign by working for peace, and justice, through openness, dialogue and freedom in relation to the people of various religious backgrounds. They are called to be an agent of reconciliation and conversation between people and nation to build peace, and harmony justice like Thomas Merton. Through the various ministries of education, social, medical and pastoral the religious men and women are called to witness Christ daringly in this pluralistic country. Today there is a growing awareness among the consecrated people of India to incorporate themselves with this reality of pluralism in their ministries. Considering the interreligious dialogue a writer A. Suresh reflects: "The serenity and compassion taught in Buddhism, the total renunciation and detachment preached by Jainism, the desire for right social order and the courageous life of Sikhism and the life of holiness and purity stressed in Zoroastrianism simply reflect the essential teachings of Christianity."[553] Therefore, in communion with other religions and discovering their goodness, the people of Christian faith are called to live their life meaningfully and joyfully as the followers of Christ.

The consecrated people have a great task to encourage the Christian brothers and sisters to support the people of other faith in their pilgrim journey, towards the ultimate goal of human existence. These characteristics of "openness to religious differences, sense of solidarity with other faith communities as co-pilgrims and the readiness to acknowledge God's saving presence in the midst of all believers

---

[552] Ibid.

[553] A. Suresh, "Interfaith Dialogue in India," in Journal of Dharma: Dharmaram Journal of Religions and Philosophies, Vol. 25, Issue Number:1 (January-March2000): 7-17.

that should prompt the Christians in India to have dialogue with the people of other religious traditions." Dialogue, enables everyone to create an atmosphere of openness to empower the powerless, "sharing of material and spiritual resources with the people who are in great struggle for justice and liberation." Therefore, Interreligious Dialogue transforms "simple sharing of faith experience to social action for just society. Against this background Interreligious Dialogue becomes an indispensable need of the hour in India."[554]

Developing a hateful attitude towards the people of other religions through fundamentalism and communalism needs to be confronted by the consecrated people in this tolerant country. Regarding this concern the Church in India is called to play a vital role for the promotion of religious pluralism and communal harmony in the nation. Consecrated people are called to guide the Christians to confront every form of violence and discrimination among people based on status, race or creed (NA. 5). May the spirit of Christ and Interreligious values of Thomas Merton enable the church in India, together with the people of other faith to work for the religious harmony amidst the religious diversities, to build unity and respect among all people irrespective of caste, color, language, culture, etc. and above all to cultivate a magnanimous heart towards everyone and to read the signs of the times in addressing the social problems.[555] Today, in this twenty first century this is the mission of the church in India to transform a 'Novel India' in alliance and dialogue with the people of all faith and religions, and to be a sign which reveals the reign of God established by Jesus Christ.

Recreating an Ecological Consciousness

In the twenty-first century, India is disfigured by human selfishness, ecological problems of pollution, poverty, overpopulation, and natural and human-made calamities. The sacred land of India is groaning to be protected, respected and cared for in the manner of the early saints and mystics, who lived in harmony with nature and

---

[554] Ibid.

[555] Ibid.

therein encountered God's presence. As Chennattu comments, " In the context of global warming and environmental distress that bring anxiety over the future of our planet, commitment to God's mission includes reconciliation in the midst of violence and divisions, establishment of justice and peace, and working for sustainable development that protects and preserves our beloved planet for future generations."[556] Merton's "keen awareness of nature and his growing sense of justice, are illustrated in his journals, letters, and public writings."[557] His admiration and love for the natural world awakened in him an emerging ecological consciousness in the 1960s. In his journal, on December 11, 1962, he expressed the desire to read Rachel Carson's explosive and groundbreaking book, *Silent Spring*, with its revelations of the toxic effects of "indiscriminate pesticide use on bird populations."[558] He expressed his concern for "*both* birds and people." He wrote: "we are in the world and part of it and we are destroying everything because we are destroying ourselves, spiritually, morally and in every way. It is all part of the same sickness, and it all hangs together."[559]

Merton was one of the first writers to take Carson's concern for the environment seriously, and he responded with an affirming letter in which he expressed to her, "though you are treating of just one aspect, and a rather detailed aspect, of our technological civilization, you are, perhaps without altogether realizing, contributing a most valuable and essential piece of evidence for the diagnosis of the ills of our civilization."[560] Speaking from a strictly religious perspective, he writes, "man is at once a part of nature and he transcends it. In maintaining this delicate balance, he must make use of nature wisely,

---

[556] Ibid., 58.

[557] Monica Weis, *The Environmental Vision of Thomas Merton* (Lexington, KY: The University Press of Kentucky, 2011), 129.

[558] O'Connell, "Ecology," in *TME*, 126.

[559] Thomas Merton, *Turning Toward the World: The Pivotal Years.* The Journals of Thomas Merton, Vol. 4, ed. Victor Kramer (San Francisco: Harper San Francisco, 1996), 274.

[560] Merton, *Witness to Freedom,* 70.

and understand his position, ultimately relating both himself and visible nature to the invisible . . . to the Creator . . . to the source and exemplar of all beings and all life." Tragically, "man has lost his 'sight' and is blundering around aimlessly in the midst of the wonderful works of God. It is in thinking that he sees, in gaining power and technical know-how, that he has lost his wisdom and his cosmic perspective." Merton notes that human beings have lost an integral approach to the self, and consequently, they are unable to relate to the creation of God. In preparing for the future, however, we must consider all of creation, bringing "the rest of the living along with us." He asserts that "we must not try to prepare the millennium by immolating our living earth, by careless and stupid exploitation for short term commercial, military, or technological ends which will be paid for by irreparable loss in living species and natural resources."[561] Similar words are echoed by Pope Francis: "any harm done to the environment . . . is harm done to humanity . . . because every creature, particularly a living creature, has an intrinsic value, in its existence, its life, its beauty and its interdependence with other creatures."[562] Every living being in this world is interrelated, and if one is wounded the others are affected.

Merton grew in love for the natural world, particularly towards the end of his life. In his prayer, Merton "found his being merging with the sacred and rhythmic dance of all creation."[563] His contemplative prayer expresses his love for the creation of God: "Today, Father, this blue sky lauds you. The delicate green and orange flowers of the tulip poplar tree praise you. The distant blue hills praise you, together with the sweet-smelling air that is full of brilliant light. . . I too, Father praise you, with all these my brothers, and they give voice to my own heart and to my own silence."[564]

[561] Ibid., 71, 74.

[562] Pope Francis, *Caring for Creation: Inspiring Words from Pope Francis*, ed. Alicia Von Stamwitz (Cincinnati, Ohio: Franciscan Media, 2016), 41.

[563] Thomas Merton, *An Invitation to the Contemplative Life*, ed. Wayne Simsic (Frederick, MD: The Word Among us Press, 2006), 97.

[564] Merton, *CGB*, 117.

Today, the consecrated men and women of India have a vital role to play in conscientizing the people of India to redeem mother earth from the ravages of global warming, rapid deforestation, atmospheric pollution, industrial poisoning of air and water, toxic wastes, and lack of clean drinking water. Mother earth is groaning to be liberated from "human selfishness, both individual and collective, as well as a utilitarian attitude to the cosmos."[565] The consecrated people are called to make a difference in renewing the face of the earth, to foster a sacramental vision of the beautiful web of life that sustains us all. May the words of Merton ring in the hearts of the consecrated people of India, to believe that God has created the world "as a temple, a paradise, into which God Himself would descend to dwell familiarly with the spirits He had placed there to tend it for Him."[566]

Conclusion

Thomas Merton faced resolutely the challenges of his own time. His contemplative-prophetic spirituality can encourage the consecrated men and women of India today to become mystical prophets and peacemakers, to reach out to broken humanity and to mother earth with love and compassion, and to struggle against the forces of injustice and oppression in Indian society. As the disciples of Jesus, the consecrated people are called to be instruments of love, dialogue, peace, justice, and reconciliation. Merton invites the consecrated people of today to cultivate the contemplative dimension amid the whirlwind of many urgent and pressing responsibilities and challenges, to become prophets who are willing to go out to the peripheries to reveal the compassionate face of Jesus. In the spirit of Merton, may these dimensions of prophetic mysticism, which are the genuine gifts of the Holy Spirit, nurture a transformative vision for the consecrated life in India.

---

[565] Kurien, 263-264.

[566] Merton, *NS*, 290.

EPILOGUE

In this book *The Relevance of Thomas Merton's Spirituality for the Consecrated Life in India*, I have explored the contemplative-prophetic spirituality of Thomas Merton and its significance for the consecrated life in India. I have argued that although consecrated life is a vital presence in Indian society, consecrated men and women of today often experience challenges of relevance and identity in their vocations. These concerns have their basis in the fundamental need for a renewal of religious life itself, one which embraces a Christ-centered spirituality and nurtures the prophetic charism that marks apostolic religious life.

Merton sought a deep union with God in contemplation that is inextricably bound to a prophetic mission. As a mystic and visionary, Merton contributed greatly to public life in America, to the universal church, and the world at large through his contemplative experiences, his commitment to peace and non-violence, and his incisive writings. In the words of John Dear, Merton's message was at once "deeply spiritual" and "profoundly political."[567] Given that Indian religious life upholds the values of contemplation, prophecy, and community, I have therefore sought to demonstrate the deep affinity between the ideals of Indian consecrated life and Thomas Merton's contemplative-prophetic spirituality.

In the midst of a society enamored of status, power, and temporary pleasure, the consecrated people of India are called to a

---

[567] John Dear, *The Sound of Listening: A Retreat Journal from Thomas Merton's Heritage* (New York: Continuum Publishing Company, 1999), 10.

spirituality rooted in the prophetic and mystical dimensions of Jesus. As a monastic, Merton confronted the contradictions and social evils of his time. He thus challenges the consecrated men and women of India to deepen their spirituality as contemplative prophets and to reach out to those on the peripheries with love and compassion. This calls not only for works of charity, but for the prophetic denunciation of the structures of injustice in Indian society. Consecrated people are called to remain alert and to embrace a "mysticism of open eyes" (in the words of Johannes Metz), to stand in solidarity with the defenseless against those who oppress them, and to critically read the signs of the times in order to determine the causes of their suffering.

For Merton, contemplation is not an escape from the world and its suffering. It is to become part of the world in order to reveal the hidden face of Christ to suffering humanity. Merton's vision of contemplative life summons the consecrated people of India to step outside their comfort zones into the peripheries.

Merton's concern for a genuine renewal of religious life based in the reforms of Vatican II sounds a call to the religious congregations and the institutional church in India. He asserted that for true renewal to take place, religious orders must be ready to risk raising prophetic voices against the "triumphalism, bureaucracy, and inertia" of ecclesial and religious structures and to examine the adequacy of their care for the poor and marginalized.[568]

Addressing the challenges and status of consecrated life in India today, Jessy Merlyn emphasizes that "the religious are called to rediscover the prophetic and mystical dimension and creative fidelity to their vocation," and to retrieve "their original charism without identifying too much with institutions and organizations."[569] The Spirit is calling the followers of Jesus to become prophetic mystics in the context of India today, to bring Jesus back into their personal

[568] Elena Malits, *The Solitary Explorer: Thomas Merton's Transforming Journey* (San Francisco: Harper and Row Publishers, 1980), 6; see the full discussion in Chapter five of this study, 39.

[569] Jessy Merlyn, "Religious Discuss Challenges of Consecrated Life," (February 5, 2013); accessed December 16, 2015, http://www.ucanindia.in/news/religious-discuss-challenges-of-consecrated-life/20208/daily.

lives, homes, communities, institutions, churches, society, country, and the world through their deep faith, hope, love and compassion.[570]

I have proposed that Merton's prophetic-contemplative spirituality might become a source of wisdom and guidance for the consecrated men and women of India, calling them to new forms of contemplative spirituality and prophetic witness that reflect an accurate reading of the signs of the times. Through the study of the spirituality of Thomas Merton, the consecrated people, notably the Ursulines of Mary Immaculate, may draw inspiration to become God's voice to the people, to denounce the injustices of society.

The Ursulines are called to live in deep union with Christ Crucified in the manner of our foundress, Blessed Brigida Morello, for whom "the whole history of the consecrated life can be considered a living expression of Jesus' words: 'as you did it to one of the least of these my brethren, you did it to me.'"[571] In the words of the congregation's new document, "Charism, Spirituality, and Identity of the Ursulines of Mary Immaculate," Blessed Brigida's "love for solitude served to be a source from which flowed the invitation to an active apostolic life: 'Go out and care for souls.' Her deep spiritual insight from [this] vision helped her to realize that her original desire for the contemplative life was perfectly compatible with the active ministry "to give glory to God."[572]

Nourished by a deep contemplative life, we are called, therefore, according to our charism, "to become relevant to the 'signs of the times,'" listening to the voice of God and entering into the life of the people, raising our voices against the evils of society. We need to become a voice for the voiceless in new ways by standing for justice and truth, and by supporting the broken and wounded on the margins, particularly women and children, and our grieving Mother Earth.

---

570 Patricia Santos, "Reinforcing a Renewed Prophetic Ministry: Remembering the Heroic Biblical Women," *Asian Journal of Religious Studies* 58, No. 5 (September 2013): 14.

571 Mt 25:45.

572 Adel Thomas, Anu George, *Charism, Spirituality and Identity of the Ursulines of Mary Immaculate* (Rome, Italy: Orsoline di Maria Immacolata, 2018), 12.

In the words of our present superior general, Elvira Mattappally, UMI, we Ursulines are called to "live our Charism, Spirituality and Identity [by] taking a realistic look at the new situations in which our consecrated life is called to challenge and incarnate itself and become more and relevant for the world of today."[573]

Today, we need to be prompt in welcoming the homeless, the refugees, and the downtrodden of our society. As Ursulines, we are challenged to leave behind our security, comfort-seeking mindset, fear of criticism, and lack of inner strength and courage to withstand conflict, and place great trust in God. In intimate relationship with Christ Crucified, we need to be in touch with our inner selves, and experience true freedom to serve God's crucified people. Like Merton, the Ursulines need to spend focused time with the Lord in contemplation amidst our pressing responsibilities of the mission.

Today, the charism of the Ursulines calls us "to renew our vision and mission of a Christ-centered spirituality, to love with the crucified, love those whom [we] encounter and serve in the suffering members of the society."[574] For this form of spirituality, we must, like Merton, be willing to be rooted in the reality of our time and place, to keep our eyes open to the injustice and idolatry around us, and to be willing to speak the word of God that calls people to justice and right relationship with God and neighbor. From Merton's example, we learn that God does not call only those who have purged themselves from all weaknesses and who have achieved a high degree of perfection. God does not extend God's call only to the brave, to those who never have doubts or problems; rather, God entrusts God's message to people who struggle as Merton did.

Thomas Merton and Blessed Brigida call us to a "mysticism of open eyes," obliging us not to run away from the painful realities of our people but to become deeply immersed in their suffering. As followers of Jesus, we are not called to live as islands; we have a

573 Elvira Mattappally, *Charism, Spirituality and Identity of the Ursulines of Mary Immaculate*, forward, 3.

574 Constitutions of the Ursulines of Mary Immaculate of Piacenza (Rome: 2005), 21.

mission to bring the crucified people down from the cross. In the spirit of Merton and Blessed Brigida, may the fruits of contemplative-prophetic mysticism, which are the gifts of the Holy Spirit, become a transformative paradigm for the Church in India today as we struggle against the forces of injustice and oppression in Indian society, and, as disciples of Jesus, strive to become instruments of love, dialogue, peace, justice, and reconciliation.

BIBLIOGRAPHY

I. Church Documents

Francis I. *Laudato Si: The Encyclical of Pope Francis on the Environment with Commentary*. With Commentary by Sean McDonagh. Maryknoll, NY: Orbis Books, 2016.

________.*Evangelii Gaudium*: *Apostolic Exhortation*. Washington, DC: United States Conference of Catholic Bishops, 2013. Accessed February 5, 2018. http://www.worldcat.org/title/joy-of-the-gospel-evangelii-gaudium-apostolic- exhortation/oclc/865733415.

________. *To All Consecrated People*. Apostolic Letter on the Occasion of "The Year of Consecrated Life." Vatican City: Libreria Editrice Vaticana, 2015. Accessed November 10, 201. https://w2.vatican.va/content/francesco/en/apost_letters/documents/papa-` francesco_lettera-ap_20141121_lettera-consacrati.html.

Gaudium et Spes:Pastoral Constitution on the Church in the Modern World. The Documents of Vatican II. Vatican City: Libreria Editrice Vaticana, December 7, 1965. Accessed February 6, 2018. http://www.vatican.va/archive/hist_councils/ii_vatican_council/documents/vat-ii_cons_19651207_gaudium-et-spes_en.html.

John Paul II. *Vita Consecrata: Post Synodal Apostolic Exhortation on the Consecrated Life and its Mission in the Church and in the World.* Washington, DC: United States Conference of Catholic Bishops, 1996.

Lumen Gentium: Dogmatic Constitution on the Church. The Documents of Vatican II. Edited by Walter Abbot. New York: Guild Press, 1966.

Nostra Aetate: Declaration on the Relation of the Church to Non-Christian Religions. Proclaimed by his Holiness Pope Paul VI on October 28, 1965. Accessed February 6, 2018. http://www.vatican.va/archive/hist_councils/ii_vatican_council/documents/vat- ii_decl_19651028_nostra-aetate_en.html.

Paul VI. *Evangelica Testificatio*, Apostolic Exhortations on the renewal of the religious life according to the teaching of the second Vatican council Pope Paul VI. June 29, 1971. Accessed March 20, 2018. http://w2.vatican.va/content/paul-i/en/apost_exhortations/documents/hf_p-`vi_exh_19710629_evangelica-testificatio.html

Perfectae Caritatis: Adaptation and Renewal of Religious Life. Vatican City: Libreria Editrice Vaticana October 28, 1965.

Sacrosanctum Concilium: Constitution on the Sacred Liturgy. Promulgated by his Holiness Pope Paul VI on December 4, 1963. Accessed February 10, 2018. http://www.vatican.va/archive/hist_councils/ii_vatican_council/documents/vat- ii_const_19631204_sacrosanctum-concilium_en.html.

II. Primary Sources

Merton, Thomas. A Vow of Conversation. Edited by Naomi Stone. New York: Farrar, Straus and Giroux, 1988.

________. *An Introduction to Christian Mysticism: Initiation into the Monastic Tradition.* Edited by Patrick F. O'Connell. Kalamazoo, MI: Cistercian Publications, 2008.

________. *An Invitation to the Contemplative Life.* Edited by Wayne Simsic. Frederick, MD: The Word Among us Press, 2006.

________. *Asian Journal of Thomas Merton.* Edited by Naomi Burton, Brother Patrick Hart and James Laughlin, Consulting editor Amiya Chakravarty. New York: New Directions Book, 1973.

________. *Basic Principles of Monastic Spirituality*. Bardstown, KY.: Abbey of Our Lady of Gethsemani, 1957.

________.*Come to the Mountain: New Ways and Living Traditions in the Monastic Life*. Snowmass, Colorado: St. Benedict's Monastery, 1964.

________. *Conjectures of a Guilty Bystander*. Garden City, NY: Doubleday and Company, Inc., 1966.

________. *Contemplation in a World of Action*. New York: Doubleday, 1973.

________. *Contemplative Prayer.* Garden City, NY: Doubleday and Company, Inc., 1971.

________. *Dancing in the Water of Life: Seeking Peace in the Hermitage*. Edited by Robert E. Daggy. The Journals of Thomas Merton, Vol. 5. New York: HarperCollins Publishers, 1997.

________. *Dialogues with Silence: Prayers and Drawings*. Edited by Jonathan Montaldo. New York: HarperCollins Publishers, 2001.

________. *Disputed Questions*. New York: Harcourt Brace Jovanovich, 1960.

________.*Entering Silence: Becoming a Monk and Writer*. The Journals of Thomas Merton. Vol. 2. Edited by Jonathan Montaldo. New York: HarperCollins Publishers, 1996.

________. *Faith and Violence.* Notre Dame, IN: University of Notre Dame Press, 1968.

________. *Gandhi on Non-Violence*. New York: New Directions Publishing Corporation, 1965.

________. *Honorable Reader.* Edited by Robert E. Daggy, Forward by Harry James Cargas. New York: The Crossroad Publishing Company, 1981.

________. *Learning to Love: Exploring Solitude and Freedom*. Edited by Christine M. Bochen. The Journals of Thomas Merton, vol. 6. New York: HarperCollins Publishers, 1997.

________. *Letters from Tom: A Selections of Letters from Father Thomas Merton, Monk of Gethsemani, to W.H. Ferry, 1961-1968*. Edited by W. H. Ferry. Scarsdale, NY: Fort Hill Press, 1968.

________. *Love and Living*. Edited by Naomi Burton Stone and Patrick Hart. New York: Farrar, Straus and Giroux, 1979.

________.*Merton's Paradise Journey: Writings on Contemplation*. Edited by Shannon, H.William. Cincinnati, OH: St. Anthony Messenger Press, 2000.

________. *My Argument with the Gestapo*. New York: New Directions, 1968.

________. *New Seeds of Contemplation*. New York: New Directions, 1961.

________. *No Man is an Island*. New York: Dell, 1957.

________. *Raids on the Unspeakable*. New York: New Directions, 1966.

________.*Run to the Mountain: The Story of a Vocation*. The Journals of Thomas Merton. Edited by Patrick Hart, vol. I. New York: HarperCollins Publishers, 1995.

________.*Search for Solitude*. Edited by Lawrence S. Cunningham. The Journals of Thomas Merton, vol. 3. San Francisco: Harper San Francisco, 1996.

________. *Seeds of Contemplation*. New York: Dell, 1960.

________. *The Ascent to Truth*. New York: Harcourt, Brace and Company, 1951.

________. *The Asian Journal*. Edited by Naomi Burton, Patrick Hart and James Laughlin. New York: New Directions, 1973.

________. *The Collected Poems of Thomas Merton*. New York: New Directions, 1977.

________. *The Hidden Ground of Love: The Letters of Thomas Merton on Religious Experience and Social Concerns*. Edited by William H. Shannon. New York: Farrar, Straus and Giroux, 1985.

________. *The Inner Experience: Notes on Contemplation.* Edited by William H. Shannon. San Francisco: Harper San Francisco, 2003.

________. *The Intimate Merton: His Life from His Journals.* Edited by Patrick Hart and Jonathan Montaldo. New York: HarperCollins Publishers, 1995.

________. *The Life of the Vows: Initiation into the Monastic Tradition.* Edited by Patrick F. O'Connell. Monastic Wisdom Series: no. 30. Collegeville, MN: Liturgical Press, 2012.

________. *The Literary Essays of Thomas Merton.* Edited by Patrick Hart. New York: New Directions, 1981.

________. *The Monastic Journey.* Edited by Patrick Hart. Cistercian Studies Series, no. 133. Kalamazoo, MI: Cistercian Publications, 1992.

________. *The New Man.* London: Burns and Oates, 1962.

________. *The Other Side of the Mountain: The End of the Journey.* Edited by Patrick Hart. The Journals of Thomas Merton, vol. 7. New York: HarperCollins Publishers, 1998.

________. *The Power and Meaning of Love.* London: Sheldon Press, 1976.

________. *The Road to Joy: Letters to New and Old Friends.* Edited by Robert E. Daggy. New York: Farrar, Straus and Giroux, 1990.

________. *The School of Charity: The Letters of Thomas Merton on Religious Renewal and Spiritual Direction.* Edited by Patrick Hart. New York: Farrar, Straus and Giroux, 1990.

________. *The Secular Journal of Thomas Merton.* New York: Farrar, Straus and Cudahy, 1959.

________. *The Seven Storey Mountain.* New York: Harcourt Brace, 1948.

________. *The Sign of Jonas.* New York: Harcourt, Brace and Company, 1953.

________. *The Springs of Contemplation.* Notre Dame, IN: Ave Maria Press, 1992.

________. *Thomas Merton in Alaska. Prelude to the Asian Journal: The Alaskan Conferences, Journals and Letters.* New York: New Directions, 1989.

________. *Thomas Merton: Selected Essays.* Edited by Patrick, F. O'Connel. Maryknoll, NY: Orbis Books, 2013.

________. *Thomas Merton: Pilgrim in Process.* Edited by Donald Grayston and Michael W. Higgins. Toronto: Griffin House, 1983.

________. *Thoughts in Solitude.* New York: Farrar, Straus and Giroux, 1958.

________. *Turning Toward the World: The Pivotal Years.* Edited by Victor Kramer. The Journals of Thomas Merton, Vol. 4. San Francisco: Harper San Francisco, 1996.

________. *Witness to Freedom: The Letters of Thomas Merton in Times of Crisis.* Edited by William Shannon. New York: Farrar, Straus, Giroux, 1994.

III. Books

Adams, J. Daniel. *Thomas Merton's Shared Contemplation: A Protestant Perspective.* Kalamazoo, MI: Cistercian Publications, 1979.

Apel, William. *Signs of Peace: The Interfaith Letters of Thomas Merton.* Maryknoll, NY: Orbis Books, 2006.

Arcement, Ephrem. *In the School of the Prophets: The Formation of Thomas Merton's Prophetic Spirituality.* Collegeville, MN: Liturgical Press, 2015.

Atkinson, C. Morgan and Montaldo Jonathan, edited. *Soul Searching: The Journey of Thomas Merton.* Collegeville, MN: Liturgical Press, 2008.

Baker, Thomas James. *Thomas Merton: Social Critic.* Lexington, KY: The University Press of Kentucky, 1971.

Bamberger, Eudes John. *Thomas Merton: Prophet of Renewal.* Monastic Wisdom Series, no. 4. Kalamazoo, MI: Cistercian Publications, 2005.

Blake, William. *Selected Poems of William Blake.* Oxford: Oxford University Press, 1927.

Bochen, M. Christine. *Thomas Merton: Essential Writings.* Maryknoll, NY: Orbis Books, 2000.

Bouyer, Louis. *An Essay on the History of the Word and Understanding Mysticism.* New York: Image Books, 1980.

Cashen, Anthony Richard. *Solitude in the Thought of Thomas Merton.* Cistercian Studies Series: Kalamazoo, MI: Cistercian Publications, 1981.

Cimperman, Maria. *Social Analysis for the 21st Century: How Faith Becomes Action.* Bangalore: Theological Publications, 2016.

Conference of Religious in India, National Assembly: Yesu Kristu Jayanti 2000, Religious Life in a New Era. Delhi: CRI House, 2000.

Cooper, D. David. *Thomas Merton's Art of Denial: The Evolution of a Radical Humanist.* Athens and London: The University of Georgia Press, 1989.

Cunningham, S. Lawrence. *Thomas Merton and Monastic Vision.* Grand Rapids, MI: William B. Eerdmans Publishing Company, 1999.

________, edited. *Thomas Merton: Spiritual Master.* Mahwah, NJ: Paulist Press, 1992.

Dalai Lama, 14th. *Freedom in Exile: The Autobiography of Dalai Lama.* New York: Harper San Francisco, 1990.

Day, Dorothy. *The Long Loneliness.* New York: Harper and Brothers, 1997.

Dear, John. *The Sound of Listening: A Retreat Journal from Thomas Merton's Heritage.* New York: Continuum, 1999.

________. *Thomas Merton, Peacemaker: Meditations on Merton, Peacemaking, and the Spiritual Life*. Maryknoll, NY: Orbis Books, 2015.

Dekar, R. Paul. *Thomas Merton. Twentieth-Century Wisdom for Twenty-First- Century Living*. Eugene, OR: Cascade Books, 2011.

Dreyer, A. Elizabeth and Burrows, S. Mark, edited. *Minding the Sprit: The Study of Christian Spirituality.* Baltimore and London: The John Hopkins University Press, 2005.

Eagan, D. Harvey. *An Anthology of Christian Mysticism*. 2nd edition. Collegeville, MN: The Liturgical Press, 1991.

________. *Christian Mysticism: The Future of a Tradition*. New York: Pueblo Publishing Company, 1984.

Eruppakkat, Joe, edited. *Consecrated Life in the Third Millennium.* Mumbai: St. Pauls, 2004.

Feldmeier, Peter. *Christian Spirituality: Lived Expressions in the Life of the Church*. Winona, MN: Anselm Academic, 2015.

Finley, James. *Merton's Palace of Nowhere*. Notre Dame, IN: Ave Maria Press, 1978.

Forest, Jim. *Living with Wisdom: A Life of Thomas Merton*. Maryknoll, NY: Orbis Books, 1991.

________. *The Root of War is Fear: Thomas Merton's Advice to Peacemakers*. Maryknoll, NY: Orbis Books, 2016.

Francis I. *Caring for Creation: Inspiring Words from Pope Francis.* Edited by Alicia Von Stamwitz. Cincinnati, OH: Franciscan Media, 2016.

Freeman, Laurence. *Journey to the Heart: Christian Contemplation through the Centuries: An Illustrated Guide*. Edited by Kim Nataraj. Maryknoll, NY: Orbis Books, 2012.

Furlong, Monica. *Merton: A Biography*. San Francisco: Harper and Row Publishers, 1980.

Givey, W. David. *The Social thought of Thomas Merton: The Way of Nonviolence and Peace for the Future*. Winona, MN: Anselm Academic, 2009.

Grayston, Donald. *The Camaldoli Correspondence: Thomas Merton and the Noonday Demon*. Eugene, OR: Cascade Books, 2015.

________. *Thomas Merton the Development of a Spiritual Theologian*. Toronto Studies in Theology, Vol. 20. New York and Toronto: The Edwin Mellen Press, 1985.

Griffin, Howard John. *Follow the Ecstasy: Thomas Merton the Hermitage Years 1965-1968*. Fort Worth, TX: Latitudes Press, 1983.

Harpur, James. *Love Burning in the Soul: The Story of the Christian Mystics, from Saint Paul to Thomas Merton*. Boston: New Seeds, 2005.

Hart, Patrick, edited. *Survival or Prophecy? The Correspondence of Jean Leclercq and Thomas Merton,* Monastic Wisdom Series, no. 17. New York: Farrar, Straus, and Giroux, 2002.

________. *Thomas Merton Monk: a Monastic Tribute. To the Memory of Thomas Merton, 1915-1968*. New York: Sheed and Ward, Inc., 1974.

________. *The Message of Thomas Merton: The Memory of Thomas Merton*. The Cistercian Studies Series, no. 42. Kalamazoo, MI: Cistercian Publications, 1981.

________, edited. *The Legacy of Thomas Merton.* Cistercian Fathers Series, no. 92. Kalamazoo, MI: Cistercian Publications, 1986.

Heschel, J. Abraham. *The Prophets*. New York and Evanston: Harper and Row Publishers, 1962.

Higgins, W. Michael. *The Unquiet Monk. Thomas Merton's Questing Faith*. New York: Orbis Books, 2015.

________. *Thomas Merton: Faithful Visionary*. Collegeville, MN: Liturgical Press, 2014.

Horan, P. Daniel. *The Franciscan Heart of Thomas Merton: A New Look at the Spiritual Inspiration of His Life, Thought, and Writing*. Notre Dame, IN: Ave Maria Press, 2014.

Inchausti, Robert. *Thomas Merton's American Prophecy.* New York: State University of New York Press, 1998.

Jose, Fabian. *Renewed Vision for Consecrated Life: Mystics, Prophets and Jesus Christ.* Christian Heritage Rediscoverd-27. Jnana-Deepa Vidyapeeth, Pune, India: Christian World Imprints, 2016.

Kaitholil, George. *Consecrated life: Challenges and Opportunities.* Bandra, Mumbai: St. Pauls, 2014.

Kannath, Sheila. *A Journey into Mysticism.* Palakkad, India: Mercy College, 1993.

King, M. Thomas. *Merton: Mystic at the Center of America.* The Way of the Christian Mystics 14. Collegeville, MI: The Liturgical Press, 1992.

King, Ursula. *Christian Mystics: Their Lives and Legacies throughout the Ages.* Mahwah, NJ: Hidden Spring, 2001.

Kountz, Peter. *Thomas Merton as Writer and Monk: A Cultural Study, 1915-1951.* Brooklyn, NY: Carlson Publishing Inc., 1991.

Kramer, A. Victor. *Thomas Merton: Monk and Artist.* Cistercian Studies Series, no. 122. Kalamazoo, MI: Cistercian Publications, 1984.

Kunnumpuram, Kurien. *Prophets of the Lord, Friends of the Poor: Indian Christian Reflections on the Religious Life.* Mumbai: St. Pauls, 2014.

Labrie, Ross. *Thomas Merton and the Inclusive Imagination.* Columbia, MO: University of Missouri Press, 2001.

Lipsey, Roger. *Make Peace Before the Sun Goes Down: The Long Encounter of Thomas Merton and His Abbot, James Fox.* Boston and London: Shambala, 2015.

________. *Angelic Mistakes: The Art of Thomas Merton.* Boston and London: New Seeds, 2006.

Lobo, Joseph. *Encountering Jesus Christ in India: An Alternative Way of Doing Christology in a Cry-for-Life Situation Based on the Writings of George M. Soares-Prabhu.* Bangalore, India: Asian Trading Corporation, 2005.

Malits, Elena. *The Solitary Explorer: Thomas Merton's Transforming Journey*. San Francisco: Harper and Row Publishers, 1980.

Mannath, Joe. *A Radical Love, a Path of Light: The Beauty and Burden of Religious Life*. Okhla, New Delhi: CRI House, 2013.

Menezes, de Rui. *Voices from Beyond: Theology of the Prophetical Book*. Mumbai: St Pauls, 2003.

Metz, Baptist Johann. *A Passion for God: The Mystical-Political Dimension of Christianity*. Edited by J. Matthew Ashley. New York: Paulist Press, 1998.

Miranda, Porfirio Jose. *Marx and the Bible: A Philosophy of the Critique of Oppression*. Translated John Eagles. Maryknoll, NY: Orbis Books, 1974.

Mott, Michael. *The Seven Mountains of Thomas Merton*. Boston: Houghton Mifflin, 1984.

Nouwen, J. M. Henri. *Encounters with Merton: Spiritual Reflections*. New York: The Crossroad Publishing Company, 1981.

Padovano, T. Antony. *The Human Journey: Thomas Merton Symbol of a Century*. Garden City, NY: Doubleday and Company, Inc., 1982.

Parathazham, Paul. *Christianity in India: Sociological Investigations*. Bangalore, India: Dharmaram Publications, 2013.

Peenikaparambil, Jacob. *The Saffron Surge: Humanistic Response to Hindutva*. Indore, India: Universal Solidarity Movement of Value Education for Peace, 2016.

Pennington, M. Basil. *Thomas Merton Brother Monk: The Quest for True Freedom*. New York: Harper and Row Publishers, 1987.

________, edited. *Toward an Integrated Humanity: Thomas Merton's Journey*. Cistercian Series Studies, no. 133. Kalamazoo, MI: Cistercian Publications, 1988.

Perrin, B. David. *Studying Christian Spirituality*. New York and London: Routledge, Taylor and Francis Group, 2007.

Pramuk, Christopher. *At Play in Creation: Merton's Awakening to the Feminine Divine.* Collegeville, MN: Liturgical Press, 2015.

________. *Sophia: The Hidden Christ of Thomas Merton.* Collegeville, MN: Liturgical Press, 2009.

Puriyadom, Teresa. *Holistic Spirituality in Formation for Consecrated Life: A Study in the Light of Adrian Van Kaam's Thought.* Bangalore, India: Claretian Publications, 2010.

Raboteau, J. Albert. *American Prophets: Seven Religious Radicals and Their Struggle for Social and Political Justice.* Princeton and Oxford: Princeton University Press, 2016.

Rayan, Samuel. *Collected Writings of Samuel Rayan.* Edited by Kurien Kunnumpuram, Vol. 1. Delhi: ISPCK, 2013.

Rice, Edward. *The Man in the Sycamore Tree: The Good Times and Hard Life of Thomas Merton.* Garden City, NY: Doubleday & Company, Inc. 1970.

Ruffing, K. Janet. *Mysticism and Social Transformation.* Forward by Robert J. Egan. Syracuse, NY: Syracuse University Press, 2001.

________. Christine M. Bochen and Patrick F. O'Connell. Edited by *The Thomas Merton Encyclopedia.* Maryknoll, NY: Orbis Books, 2002.

________. *Silent Lamp: The Thomas Merton Story.* New York, NY: Crossroad Publishing Company, 1992.

________. *Thomas Merton's Dark Path.* New York: Farrar, Straus and Giroux, 1987.

Shaw, Mark. *Beneath the Mask of Holiness: Thomas Merton and the Forbidden Love Affair that Set Him Free.* New York: Palgrave Macmillan, 2009.

Sheldrake, Philip. *Spirituality: A Brief History*, 2nd edition. Chichester, UK: Wiley- Blackwell, 2013.

Slade, Herbert. *Exploration into Contemplative Prayer.* London: Darton, Longman and Todd, 1975.

Somerville, M. James. *The Mystical Sense of the Gospels: A Handbook for the Contemplatives.* New York: The Crossroad Publishing Company, 1997.

Taylor, C. Brian. *Becoming Christ: Transformation through Contemplation.* Cambridge, MA: Cowley Publications, 2002.

Teasdale, Wayne. *Essays in Mysticism: Explorations into Contemplative Experience.* Lake Worth, FL: Sunday Publications, Inc., 1982.

Twomey, Gerald, edited. *Thomas Merton: Prophet in the Belley of a Paradox.* New York: Paulist Press, 1978.

Underhill, Evelyn. *The School of Charity and the Mystery of Sacrifice.* New York: Green and Co., 1965.

Washington, M. James, edited. *A Testament of Hope: The Essential Writings and Speeches of Martin Luther King, Jr.* San Francisco: HarperCollins, 1991.

Waldron, G. Robert. *Thomas Merton in Search of His Soul: A Jungian Perspective.* Notre Dame, IN: Ave Maria Press, 1994.

Weis, Monica. *The Environmental Vision of Thomas Merton.* Lexington, KY: The University Press of Kentucky, 2011.

Wilkes, Paul. *Merton by Those Who Knew Him Best.* New York: Harper and Row, Publishers, Inc., 1984.

Wild, A. Robert, edited. *Compassionate Fire: The Letters of Thomas Merton and Catherine de Hueck Doherty.* Notre Dame, IN: Ave Maria Press, 2009.

Zuercher, Suzanne. *The Ground of Love and Truth: Reflections on Thomas Merton's Relationship with the Woman Known as "M."* Chicago: In Extenso Press, 2014.

IV. Articles in Edited Books and Journals

Abraham, Kochurani. "The Place and Role of Women in the Catholic Church." In *Towards the Full Flowering of the Human.* Edited by Kurien Kunnumpuram. Mumbai, India: St. Pauls, 2011, 50-60.

Brown, M. Jason. "Thomas Merton, Wildness and the Sacramental Power of Place." *The Merton Annual,* vol. 29 (2016): 86-87.

Fernandes, Lydia. "The Religious Educator." *Consecrated Life in the Third Millennium: Challenges and Prospects*. Edited by Joe Eruppakkatt. Bandra, Mumbai: St. Pauls (2004), 91-99.

Francis I. "Address of the Holy Father to a Joint Session of the United States Congress September 24, 2015." *The Merton Annual* 28 (2015): 22-23.

Joachim, Inigo. "Empowering Women as Evangelizers." *Asian Journal of Vocation and Formation*, Vol. XXXIX, No. 1 (January-June 2014): 10-24.

________. "Spirituality for the Religious of Our Time." In *Consecrated Life in the Third Millennium: Challenges and Prospects*. Edited by Joe Eruppakkatt. Mumbai, Bandra: St. Pauls (2004), 9-17.

Kadaplackal, Abraham. "Witnesses of the Primacy of God." *New Leader*, Vol. 128, No. 1 (January 2015): 15-20.

Lescher, H. Bruce. "Thomas Merton (1915-68) New Seeds of Contemplation." In *Christian Spirituality: The Classics.* Edited by Arthur Holder. London and New York: Routledge, 2010, 353-364.

McGregory, N. Micheal. "The Persistence of Harlem in the Life and Legacy of Thomas Merton." *The Merton Annual*, Studies in Culture, Spirituality, and Social Concerns, Vol. 29, (2016): 90-98.

Menezes, de Rui. "Prophet." In *A Concise Encyclopedia of Christianity in India*. Pune, Mumbai: Jnana–Deepa Vidyapeeth and St. Paul's Publications, 2014, 676-686.

Merton, Thomas. "St. Bonaventure Journal." Unpublished Manuscript, New York: St. Bonaventure University Library, 1959.

________. "Poetry and Contemplation: A Reappraisal." In *Thomas Merton: Selected Essays.* Edited by Patrick F. O'Connell. Maryknoll, NY: Orbis Books, 2013, 23-38.

________. "Peace: A Religious Responsibility." In *Thomas Merton Selected Essays.* Edited by Patrick F. O'Connell. Maryknoll, NY: Orbis Books, 2013, 126-149.

________. "Perry Street Journal." Unpublished manuscript. St. Bonaventure, NY: St. Bonaventure University Library (1940): 274-275.

________. "Thich Nhat Hanh Is My Brother." *Jubilee* (August 1966): 260-262.

________. "Blake and New Theology." *The Literary Essays of Thomas Merton.* Edited by Brother Patrick Hart. New York: New Directions, 1960, 3-22.

________. "Gandhi and the One-Eyed Giant." *Gandhi on Non-Violence.* New York: New Directions Publishing Corporation, 1965, 1-20.

Monteiro, Evelyn, "The Call of Women Religious to Mystical Contemplation." In *Asian Journal for Religious,* Vol. 53, no. 2 (March 2008): 7-22.

________."The Call of Women Religious to Live Prophetically." In *Asian Journal for Religious.* Pune: Jnana-Deepa Vidyapeeth (May 2008): 24-30.

Pathil, Kuncheria. "Theological Reflections on the Church from India." In *Asian Horizons,* Vol. 6, no. 4 (December 2012): 677-706.

Pramuk, Christopher. "Theodicy and the Feminine Divine: Thomas Merton's 'Hagia Sophia.'" In Dialogue with Western Theology." *Theological Studies* Vol. 77 (1), (2016): 48–76.

Principe, Walter. "Toward Defining Spirituality." *Sciences Religieuses/ Studies in Religion* 12 (Spring 1983): 123-141.

Rakoczy, Susan. "The Dynamic of Discernment in the Life of Thomas Merton." *The Merton Annual,* Vol. 41, No. 4 (Winter 2016): 17-28.

Rayan, Samuel. "The Earth is the Lord's." *Collected Writings of Samuel Ryan.* Edited by Kurien Kunnumpuram, Vol. 1. Delhi: ISPCK, 2013, 19-25.

Sankarathil, John. "Religious Charism: Relevance for the Third Millennium." *Indian Journal of Spirituality* 14 (April-June 2001): 215-232.

________. "Consecrated Life in India: The Asset of a Model, or A Challenge to Remodel." In *Vidyajyoti Journal of Theological Reflections* (March 2007): 185-194.

Soares-Prabhu, George. "From Alienation to Inculturation: Some Reflections on Doing Theology in India Today," in *Collected Writings of George Soares-Prabhu.* Edited by Isaac Padinjarekuttu, Vol. 1. Jnana-Deepa Vidyapeeth Theology Series, Pune: Gujarat Sahitya Prakash, 1999, 86-95.

________. "Jesus the Teacher: The Liberative Pedagogy of Jesus of Nazareth." In *Christian Perspective in Education.* Edited by H. Morissette. Bangalore, India: Xavier Board of Education, 1985, 85-10.

Santos, Patricia. "Reinforcing a renewed prophetic Ministry: Remembering the Heroic Biblical Women." In *Asian Journal of Religious Studies,* vol. 58, no. 5 (September 2013): 14 -20.

Schneiders, M. Sandra. "The Study of Christian Spirituality: Contours and Dynamics of a Discipline." In *Minding the Sprit: The Study of Christian Spirituality.* Edited by Elizabeth A. Dreyer and Mark S. Burrows. Baltimore and London: The John Hopkins University Press, 2005, 4-22.

________. "A Hermeneutical Approach to the Study of Christian Spirituality." In *Minding the Spirit: The Study of Christian Spirituality.* Edited by Elizabeth A. Dreyer & Mark S. Burrows. Baltimore and London: The Johns Hopkins University Press, 2005, 48-60.

________. "Christian Spirituality: Definition, Methods and Types," In *The New Westminster Dictionary of Christian Spirituality.*

Edited by Philip Sheldrake. Louisville, KY: Westminster John Knox, 2005, 1-6.

Spencer, Thomas. "'I must Pray to Him for Aid Now': Thomas Merton's and Dorothy Day's Diaries." In *The Thomas Merton Seasonal*, Vol. 41, No. 1 (Spring 2016): 7- 8.

Suresh, A. "Interfaith Dialogue in India." In *Journal of Dharma: Dharmaram Journal of Religions and Philosophies*, Vol. 25, Issue Number: 1 (January-March 2000): 7-17.

Thomas Merton, "Apologies to an Unbeliever," Christoffer H. Grundmann, *Interreligious Dialogue: An Anthology of Voices Bridging Cultural and Religious Divides*. Winona, MN: Anselm Academic, 2015, 85-87.

Vineeth, V.F. "Mysticism." In *A Concise Encyclopedia of Christianity in India*. Edited by Errol D' Lima and Anthony De Silva. Pune, Mumbai: Jnana – Deepa Vidyapeeth and St. Paul's Publications, 2014, 610-620.

V. Electronic Resources

Aquinas, Thomas. *Summa Theologica*, II-II, Qu. 180, Art. 1. December 12, 2009. Accessed May 26, 2017.https://literaturesave.files.wordpress.com/2009/12/s- thomas-aquinas-summa-theologica-part-ii-ii-secunda-secundae1.pdf.

Augustine of Hippo. Sermons on Selected Lessons of the New Testament, sermon on the words of the gospel, Mt 10: 28, "be not afraid of them that kill the body." Delivered on a Festival of Martyrs." Accessed December 5, 2015. http://kingsgarden.org/English/Organizations/LCC.GB/LCIS/Scriptures/Fathers/D octors/ Augustine of Hippo/Sermons/Sermon15.html.

Bentley, Leslie. "A Brief Biography of Paulo Freire." December, 1999. Accessed February 24, 2018. http://ptoweb.org/aboutpto/a-brief-biography-of-paulo-` freire/.

Bhowmick, Nilanjana. "India is Home to More Poor People than Anywhere Else on Earth," July 17, 2014. Accessed October 25,

2017. http://time.com/2999550/india-home-to-most-poor-people/.

Christian Education and Ecological Concerns: Ecological Issues in the Indian Context." November 11, 2014. Accessed October 31, 2017. http://bluwinchisik.blogspot.com/2014/11/christian-education-and-` ecological.html.

Fernandes, Ivan. "Religious Life in Crisis, Say Superiors," October 30, 2012. Accessed February 2, 2017.www.ucanews.com/news/religious-life-in-crisis-say-` superiors/63684.

Forest, Jim. "Thomas Merton's Advice for Peace Makers," May 2, 2006. Accessed May 14, 2016. http://www.jimandnancyforest.com/2006/05/02/mertons-advice/.

Francis I, "Message of Pope Francis for the first World Day of the Poor." November 17, 2017. Accessed November 17, 2017. http://kingscourtparish.ie/2017/11/message- of-pope-francis-for-the-first-world- day-of-the-poor/.

________. "Pope Francis' important message on the 'vocations crisis' at the end of the Year of Consecrated Life." February 2, 2016. Accessed October 22, 2017. http://www.catholic.org/vocations/story.php?id=67005.

________. "Without Prophecy, Only Clericalism." Vatican Radio, December 16, 2013. Accessed December 5, 2015. http://www.news.va/en/news/pope-francis-without- prophecy- only-clericalism.

________. "Pope Francis: women must truly participate in Church and society," February 7, 2015. Accessed December 28, 2015, https://www.youtube.com/watch?v=c7mt_WnQnqM.

Joachim, Inigo. "Empowering Women." Presented at CBCI Meeting at Jamshedpur, Scriptural and Theological Foundations, February 13-20, 2008. Accessed January 4, 2018. http://inigojoachim.com/empowering-women.

John Paul II. "Letter of Pope John Paul II to Women." June 29, 1995, 3. Accessed October 17, 2017. https://w2.vatican.va/

content/john-paul- ii/en/letters/1995/documents/hf_jp-` ii_let_29061995.

Kleinhenz, Christopher. *"Movement and Meaning in the Divine Comedy: Toward an Understanding of Dante's Processional Poetics."* Bernardo Lecture Series, A Global Academic Publishing Book, No. 14. January 2005. Accessed July 22, 2017. http://www.sunypress.edu/p-5395-movement-and-meaning-in-the-`div.aspx.

Matt, Rosenberg. "India's Population: India Likely to Surpass China in Population by 2030," March 17, 2017. Accessed October 11, 2014. https://www.thoughtco.com/indias-population-overview-1435263.

Pramuk, Christopher. "Thomas Merton and the Future of Faith," April 23, 2016. Accessed December 17, 2017. http://marginalia, lareviewofbooks.org/thomas- merton-future-faith-christopher-pramuk/ Thomas Merton and the Future of ` Faith.

Priya, Rashmi. "The Max Weber's Theory of Social Action." Accessed February 24, 2018. http://www.yourarticlelibrary.com/sociology/the-max-webers-theory-of- social-` action/43752.

Ramandeep, Kaur. "Poverty and its Causes in India." June 9, 2013. Accessed October 25, 2017. https://www.mapsofindia.com/my-india/society/poverty-in-india-` and-its-causes.

Rosenberg, Matt. "India's Population." March 17, 2017. Accessed October 11, 2014, ttps://www.thoughtco.com/indias-population-overview-1435263.

Royal, Robert. "The Several-storied Thomas Merton." February 1, 1997. Accessed January 6, 2018. http://content.bangtech.com/thinking/thomasmerton.htm.

Thomas Merton Poetry Foundation. Accessed December 1, 2018. http://www.poetryfoundation.org/bio/thomas-james- Merton.

________. "Excerpt from Concerning the Collection in the Bellarmine Library." November 10, 1963, Accessed January 15, 2018. ` http://www.merton.org/collection.aspx.

Thurston, Bonnie. "'An Absolute Duty to Rebel': Thomas Merton, Religious Women and the Challenges of Vatican II," March 2013. Accessed February 23, 2018. http://merton.org/ITMS/Seasonal/39/39-2Thurston.pdf.

VI. Papers Presented at a Meeting or Conference

Chennattu, M. Rekha. "To be Rooted and Relevant a Call for a Paradigm Shift in the Life of Women Religious." AMOR XV, Bangkok, Thailand (October 13-21, 2009): 47- 61.

Garcia, Ciro. "Mysticism and Prophecy: A style of life and New Areopagus." *Plenary Assembly of UISG* (Rome: May 2010): 1-13.

Mulackal, Shalini. "Consecrated Life Today: Trends and Challenges in Society and Church." *CRI National Consultation.* Streevani, Pune, India (January 24-25, 2009): 1-7.

Serrao, Francis. "Integration of Mission and Pastoral Aspects in Ministry." Talk given for the Celebration of the VI Provincial Chapter of the Congregation of Ursulines of Mary Immaculate at Bangalore (November 2014): 1-5.

The Catholic Bishops' Conference. "Empowerment of Women in the Church and Society." 28th Plenary Assembly of the Catholic Bishops' Conference of India. February 20, 2008, 1-5.

VII. Thesis or Dissertation

Shay, Susan. *Other Voices: The Transforming Voice of Women and the Sacred Feminine in the Life of Thomas Merton.* 1958-1968. MA (Thesis). Graduate Theological Union, Berkeley, California, 2012.

The Thomas Merton Center at Bellarmine University. "Theses and Dissertations Specifically about Thomas Merton." Accessed October 26, 2017. http://merton.org/Research/Theses/.

Vazhakoottathil, John Antony Theodore. *Thomas Merton's Mystical Quest for the Union with God.* Dissertationen Theologische Reihe, Band 63. Zugal: EOS Verlag Erzabtei St. Ottilien, 1993.

INDEX